THE MAKING OF PARIS

THE MAKING OF PARIS

*The Story of How Paris Evolved from a Fishing
Village into the World's Most Beautiful City*

RUSSELL KELLEY

LYONS
PRESS

Guilford, Connecticut

An imprint of The Rowman & Littlefield Publishing Group, Inc.
4501 Forbes Blvd., Ste. 200
Lanham, MD 20706
www.rowman.com

Distributed by NATIONAL BOOK NETWORK

British Library Cataloguing in Publication Information available

Library of Congress Cataloging-in-Publication Data

Names: Kelley, Russell, 1949– author.
Title: The making of Paris : the story of how Paris evolved from a fishing
  village into the world's most beautiful city / Russell Kelley.
Other titles: Story of how Paris evolved from a fishing village into the
  World's most beautiful city
Description: Guilford, Connecticut : Lyons Press, [2021] | Includes
  bibliographical references and index. | Summary: "The story of how Paris
  has evolved over two thousand years from a fishing village into the
  world's most beautiful city"—Provided by publisher.
Identifiers: LCCN 2020039345 (print) | LCCN 2020039346 (ebook) | ISBN
  9781493049103 (cloth ; alk. paper) | ISBN 9781493050543 (electronic)
Subjects: LCSH: Paris (France)—Buildings, structures, etc.—History. |
  Paris (France)—History. | Historic buildings—France—Paris. |
  Monuments—France—Paris—History. |
  Architecture—France—Paris—History.
Classification: LCC DC771 .K45 2021 (print) | LCC DC771 (ebook) | DDC
  944/.361—dc23
LC record available at https://lccn.loc.gov/2020039345
LC ebook record available at https://lccn.loc.gov/2020039346

CONTENTS

CONTENTS

PREFACE

When my wife and I first moved to Paris in 1987, our favorite pastime was to walk the streets and admire the splendid monuments, perspectives, and panoramas. After a while I wanted to understand how the city had evolved over time. I started to read about the history of Paris and the evolution of its urban landscape, and to explore the different neighborhoods of the city. Any friends who came to town would be subjected to walking tours of the city, which one hapless visitor memorably described as "relentless." Being a linear thinker, I always tried to organize the walks so that they would show the sites in chronological order to better understand how the story of Paris unfolded. This book came out of those walks and the desire to comprehend how Paris became the world's most beautiful city.

The intent of this book is to give an overview of how the city of Paris developed over the ages. It is written for the reader who is familiar with the layout of Paris and its individual monuments but wishes to better understand the narrative of the evolution of the city. This is not a history of Paris, but I do try to hit the highlights in order to put the building works into their historical context. Accordingly, each chapter begins with a brief summary of the history of the relevant period, followed by a description of the major building works undertaken during the period. The focus is on monumental architecture in the historic center of Paris, but the scope broadens after 1800, and especially after the Annexation of 1860, to include a wider range of buildings and projects, especially on the periphery of the expanding city. In general, the dates when projects started and finished are included to show the ambition of the builders (Notre-Dame took 182 years to complete!): They were not necessarily building for themselves, but for future generations.

In my research I often came across conflicting dates for the beginning and/or end of building works, and varying numbers for the population of Paris at different times. To keep it simple, I picked the dates and populations that seemed most reasonable under the circumstances, without listing the alternatives.

Bonne lecture!

Russell Kelley
Paris

Note on the Images

Most of the more than 120 images included in this book are historical and in the public domain.

The maps mostly come from the Norman B. Leventhal Map & Education Center of the Boston Public Library and the Kyoto University Library—especially the images from the extraordinarily detailed Plan de Turgot, which was published in 1739 with a bird's-eye view of the streets and buildings of Paris in 1734.

Many of the famous buildings and monuments of the Middle Ages and Renaissance are represented by engravings or paintings—sometimes contemporary, sometimes later—and by reconstitutions by Théodore Joseph Hubert Hoffbauer (1839–1922), a German-born architect and painter in France, that were published in *Paris à travers les âges: Aspects successifs des monuments et quartiers historiques de Paris depuis le XIIIe siècle jusqu'à nos jours* (Paris: Fermin-Didot et Cie, 1882). The Paris of Henri IV was contemporaneously portrayed in the engravings of the drawings of architect Claude de Chastillon (1559–1616), and the Paris of Louis XIV in those of artist Adam Pérelle (1640–1695). The Paris of Louis XV was vividly represented in the oil paintings of Nicolas Jean-Baptiste Raguenet (1715–1793). These engravings, paintings, and so much more can be found on the website of Paris Musées: parismuseescollections.paris.fr.

There is a treasure trove of photographs of nineteenth-century Paris by Charles Marville (1813–1879), Gustave Le Gray (1820–1884), and many other early photographers, to be found on the websites of, among other sources, Gallica/Bibliothèque Nationale de France (gallica.bnf.fr) (especially from the albums *Vues de Paris et de ses environs*, with photographs by Charles-Henri Plaut [1819–?] taken between 1865 and 1870, and *Paris et ses environs*, with photographs from the Collection Georges Sirot [1898–1977] taken between 1890 and 1900), the Ville de Paris (especially from the book *Paris vu en ballon* [1909]), and the wonderful website Vergue (vergue.com).

I have attempted to insert prints, illustrations, photographs, maps, and other images to illustrate roughly the period in which they were made or represent, but sometimes I have inserted them in a different historical period because they seemed to me to be the best representation of the subject matter; the dates of the images are mentioned to avoid any confusion.

The credits for the images are set out after the bibliography.

Note on Style

In general, French words, titles of books, names of restaurants, etc. appear in italics, but not proper names and common street and place names. Uncommon names and expressions are italicized at least the first time they appear. Certain French terms are italicized each time they are used, especially when they might be confused with English words that have different meanings (e.g., *place* and place).

While the French generally do not capitalize *rue* (as in *la rue de Seine*), *boulevard, avenue, place, quai,* etc., I have done so throughout this book to draw attention to the street, boulevard, etc. under discussion.

The three years that appear after the names of kings refer to the year of their birth, the first year of their reign, and the year they died and their reign ended. A fourth year is added for the year of the death of the three kings and two emperors who outlived their reigns. Including the years of their birth allows the reader to see at a glance just how young many of them were when they acceded to the throne.

English translations of certain key French words and phrases are given, and French and English names for the same site are used interchangeably. I generally refer to the kings using their names in French. Measurements are given in feet/yards/meters, miles/kilometers, and acres/hectares.

INTRODUCTION

Paris is best seen on foot. It is, after all, Parisians who perfected the art of *la flânerie*—strolling as a way to explore the city.

While there is plenty to be seen inside Paris's roughly 130 museums, two hundred churches, one thousand art galleries, and many bookshops, the focus of this book is on Paris as seen from the street by the *flâneur*, in order to understand the evolution of the urban landscape of Paris through the buildings, monuments, and other structures from its long and eventful past, and especially those that are still standing today.

Paris is a small, large city: Its 2.3 million inhabitants live *intra muros*, inside the *Boulevard Périphérique*, which is 22 miles/35 kilometers long and encircles the city. Paris is approximately 9 miles/16 kilometers from

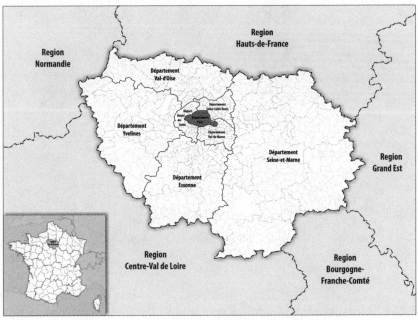

Figure 1. The Paris *département* within the Île de France *région*. AUTHOR TSCHUBBY.

east to west, and 6 miles/9.5 kilometers from north to south, giving the city a surface area of around 40.5 square miles/106 square kilometers. (By comparison, the surface area of Greater London is 607 square miles/1,572 square kilometers.) One can walk from one end of Paris to the other in two hours, and most of the best of Paris is within 1 mile/1.6 kilometers in any direction from the Louvre, which is the geographical epicenter of Paris today.

Paris is in the center of the *Île-de-France* (Isle of France) region, which historically was the personal domain of the king of France, so-called because it was a virtual "island" surrounded by the rivers Seine, Oise, Aisne, Ourcq, and Marne. The thirty-four provinces established under the *Ancien Régime* of the Bourbon dynasty, including the

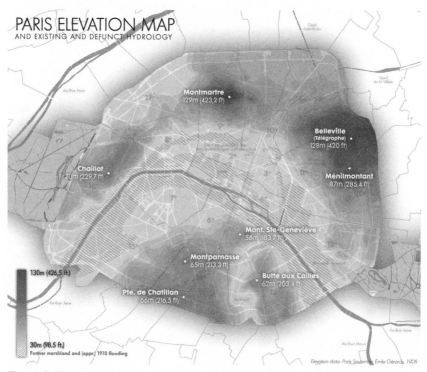

Figure 2. The striped sections of this map indicate the low-lying areas of Paris, including the Marais, which flooded last in 1910. AUTHOR J. M. SCHOMBURG (2012).

Île-de-France, were abolished during the Revolution and replaced with eighty-three new administrative units called *départements*. There are now ninety-six *départements* in *France métropolitaine* and five *départements d'outre-mer* (overseas *départements*). In 1976, a new Île-de-France region was constituted with Paris as its center, not entirely corresponding to the historical Île-de-France province. Since January 2016, there are thirteen administrative regions in France (down from twenty-seven). The Île-de-France region remained unchanged. Today, there are twelve million people living in the Île-de-France, who are known as *Franciliens*.

Paris is bracketed by the Bois de Boulogne forest to the west and the Bois de Vincennes forest to the east, with the river Seine winding 8 miles/13 kilometers through the middle of the city. The Seine, France's second longest river after the Loire, originates in Burgundy and flows for 483 miles/777 kilometers in a northwesterly direction, passing through

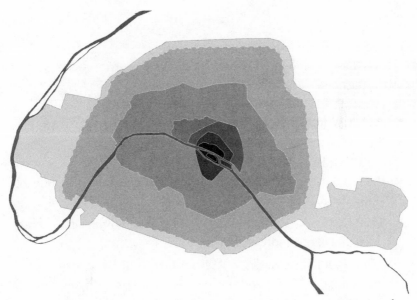

Figure 3. Map showing the 7 walls of Paris from the Roman wall around the Île de la Cité to the Thiers Wall (now the Boulevard Périphérique). The light-colored shapes to the left and right of the circle are the Bois de Boulogne and the Bois de Vincennes, respectively, that are within the city limits. AUTHOR PARIS 16.

Troyes, Paris, and Rouen, before emptying into the English Channel between Le Havre and Honfleur. Thousands of years ago, the bed of the Seine in Paris was much wider, covering much of today's Right Bank between the Place de l'Alma to the west and the Port de l'Arsenal to the east. As its channel narrowed over the millennia, it left behind wetland known as the *marais* (marsh). Although this land was drained by the Middle Ages, it is prone to flooding even to this day.

Paris started on the largest island in the Seine and later spread out on the banks of the river—the Right Bank (*Rive Droite*) and the Left Bank (*Rive Gauche*), when facing downriver. It made more sense to have Right and Left Banks than to have North and South Banks, as in London, for example, because of the looping course of the Seine. The *Île de la Cité* (Isle of the City—the center of medieval Paris, just like the City of London was the center of medieval London) was originally the center of government and the Church; the Right Bank, the center of commerce; and the Left Bank, the university and the Latin Quarter.

How did Paris become Paris?

Paris has expanded in ever-widening concentric circles, like the growth rings of a tree, with 7 city walls (*enceintes*):

- AD 308–360: The Gallo-Roman wall, around the Île de la Cité.
- The "Wall of the Eleventh Century," a wooden palisade enclosing the Right Bank *bourgs* of Saint-Gervais and Saint-Merri, around the present-day Hôtel de Ville. Its eastern boundary was probably along the Rue des Barres.
- 1190–1215: The Philippe-Auguste Wall, around the city on both the Right Bank and Left Bank.
- 1365–1420: The Charles V Wall, on the Right Bank only, including the Marais and the Temple Enclosure (*l'Enclos des Templiers*).
- 1633–1636: The Louis XIII Wall (also known as *les Fossés jaunes*, or Yellow Moat), extending the western part of the Charles V Wall to

enclose the Jardin des Tuileries up the Rue Royale to la Madeleine (together with the Charles V Wall, now where the *Grands Boulevards* are located).

- 1785–1791: The Farmers-General Wall (sometimes known as the Tax Wall), where a second ring of boulevards beyond the Grands Boulevards is now located.
- 1841–1844: The Thiers Wall (also known as the *Enceinte Fortifiée*, *les Fortifications*, or *les Fortifs*).

The *Rue Militaire*, which was improved to become the *Boulevards des Maréchaux* (Boulevards of the Marshals) after the Annexation of 1860, and *la Petite Ceinture* (Little Belt) railway line were constructed just inside *les Fortifs*. The *Boulevard Périphérique* ring road around Paris was built on the no-man's-land outside the Thiers Wall between 1958 and 1973.

While the territory of Paris expanded nearly equally in all directions from the Île de la Cité, in fact the center of gravity of the city first jogged east to the Marais in the fourteenth century, when Charles V made the Hôtel Saint-Pol his principal residence and often stayed at the Donjon du Château de Vincennes to the east of the city, and remained there through the reign of Henri IV. Ever since the middle of the seventeenth century, however, the most important expansion has been to the west. This was in part because Louis XIV had moved to Versailles, which is 12 miles/20 kilometers southwest of Paris, and in part because the prevailing wind was from the west and Parisians wanted to be upwind from the smoke and stench of the industrial section of the city, which in Paris was historically located to the east, in and around the *faubourg* Saint-Antoine.

The ten kings and emperors who had the greatest impact on the making of Paris, in part because of their long reigns, were:

- Philippe II Auguste/Philip II Augustus (reigned 1180–1223—forty-three years).
- Louis IX/Saint Louis (1226–1270—forty-four years).
- Philippe IV le Bel/Philip IV the Fair (1285–1314—twenty-nine years).

- Charles V le Sage/the Wise (1364–1380—sixteen years).
- François Ier/Francis I (1515–1547—thirty-two years).
- Henri IV/Henry IV (1589–1610—twenty-one years)—especially following Henri's entry into Paris in 1594, after four years of civil war with the Catholic League.
- Louis XIII (1610–1643—thirty-three years).
- Louis XIV (1643–1715—seventy-two years)—especially the years after his coronation at Reims in 1654 and before the court moved to Versailles in 1682.
- Napoléon Ier (1799–1804 as first consul, 1804–1814 as emperor—15 years)—especially the five years of peace between 1800 and 1805.
- Napoléon III (1848–1852 as president of the Second Republic and then as first consul, 1852–1870 as emperor—twenty-two years), aided by Georges-Eugène Haussmann, Prefect of the Seine (1853–1870—seventeen years).

To this list must be added two postwar presidents: Georges Pompidou, the great modernizer of Paris, and François Mitterrand, who carried out

THE *HISTOIRE DE PARIS* PLAQUES

In 1992, Mayor Jacques Chirac installed 767 plaques throughout the city with historical information about monuments and other places or events of interest. They were designed by Philippe Starck in the shape of an oar, in reference to the city's coat of arms since 1358, which depicts a sailing vessel—the symbol of the powerful medieval *corporation des nautes* (boatmen's guild). Due to their distinctive shape, the plaques are sometimes referred to as the "Starck Shovels (*pelles*)" or the "Starck Lollipops (*sucettes*)."

The text on the plaques is all in French, but a series of English-language guidebooks called "Paris by Plaque" translates the plaques and suggests walks to visit them.

numerous "pharaonic" works in Paris during his fourteen years in office, many in commemoration of the bicentennial of the French Revolution in 1989.

The most dramatic changes to the urban landscape of the historic center of Paris occurred in the seventeenth century during the reigns of Henri IV, Louis XIII, and Louis XIV, and in the nineteenth century during the First Empire of Napoléon Ier, the reign of Louis-Philippe, and especially during the Second Empire of Napoléon III.

Street names were first engraved on street corners in 1729; they were printed on enamel plaques starting in 1835. The street names in Paris always tell a story. In the oldest sections of Paris, the names often refer to the occupations of their original inhabitants (Rue des Ciseaux [scissor-makers], Rue des Boulangers [bakers], Rue de la Verrerie [glassmakers], Quai des Orfèvres [goldsmiths]), or to the destinations the streets led to (Rue Saint-Antoine, Rue Saint-Denis, Rue du Temple, Rue Montmartre, Rue de Seine, Rue de Vaugirard, etc.). Later, streets were named after distinguished citizens (Quai Voltaire, Rue Richelieu, Rue Bonaparte, Avenue Victor Hugo). After Napoléon Ier, many streets were named after battles won by the *Grande Armée* and the generals (*maréchaux*) who fought in them (Rue de Rivoli, Pont de l'Alma, Pont d'Austerlitz, les Boulevards des Maréchaux), as well as one victory by the Free French Army in North Africa during World War II (Pont de Bir-Hakeim). Helpfully, many plaques of street names explain after whom or what the streets are named.

There are so many people and places to name streets after that many Paris streets and boulevards have the confusing habit of changing names every few hundred yards/meters. This is the case for the names of the quais along the Seine and around the Île de la Cité and the Île Saint-Louis. By way of example, the Île Saint-Louis is surrounded by the Quai d'Orléans, the Quai de Béthune, the Quai d'Anjou, and the Quai de Bourbon. The name *Grands Boulevards* refers to a continuous series of boulevards with eleven different names that follow the trace of the old Charles V and Louis XIII walls. Haussmann's Boulevard de Sébastopol suddenly becomes Boulevard de Strasbourg when it crosses the Boulevard Saint-Denis (one of the Grands Boulevards), where the Charles V Wall once stood. There is a second ring of boulevards outside the former

THE STREETS OF PARIS

In his *Atlas Historique des Rues de Paris* (Parigramme, 2016), Pierre Pinon divides the streets of Paris into three categories:

Rues de faubourgs, which are the oldest streets, that originally led from the city to the villages outside. Examples include the Rue du Faubourg Saint-Antoine, which led to the village of Saint Antoine to the east of Paris, or the Rue Saint-Denis, which led to the town and church of the same name to the north.

Rues de lotissements, which were built when subdividing property. They were laid out in great numbers starting in the seventeenth century (for example, all the streets on the Île Saint-Louis) and account for 70 percent of the streets in Paris today.

Les percées (openings), meaning a new street, avenue, or boulevard that penetrates a built-up urban area to connect two points. Examples built by Haussmann, who was famous for his many *percées*, include the Boulevard de Sébastopol, Rue de Rennes, Boulevard Saint-Michel, and Boulevard Saint-Germain. The Avenue des Champs-Élysées, however, is not a *percée* because it was built on open land to the west of the city.

According to the city government, there are 6,486 streets in Paris. The longest street is the Rue de Vaugirard, 6e and 15e (2.7 miles/4.3 kilometers long). The shortest is the Rue des Degrés, 2e (19 feet/5.75 meters long). The widest is the Avenue Foch (394 feet/120 meters wide).

Pierre Pinon has determined when each street was built since 1450 (before then there are no reliable records). According to his calculations, the number of new streets of all types built during the different historical periods is as follows:

1450: 490 streets in Paris
1450–1550: 60 new streets added
1550–1650: 117 new streets added
1650–1720: 91 new streets added
1720–1820: 289 new streets added
1820–1850: 370 new streets added
1850–1870: 736 new streets added, including 70 percées
1870–1914: 1,047 new streets added
1914–2016: 933 new streets added

Construction of new streets peaked during the Second Empire and the Belle Époque, largely because of Haussmann's *Grands Travaux*, the Annexation of 1860 which doubled the surface area of Paris, and the aggressive subdivision of the newly acquired land.

Pierre Pinon's total number of streets is two-thirds of the total given by the City of Paris since he counts as one street any street that has different names at different points.

Farmers General Wall, originally called the *Boulevards Extérieurs*. On the Right Bank most are named after the villages previously located just outside them (Boulevards des Batignolles, de la Chapelle, de la Villette, de Belleville, de Charonne, and de Bercy). The *Boulevards des Maréchaux*, which encircle the periphery of Paris, just inside the Boulevard Périphérique, are made up of a series of continuous boulevards originally named after nineteen marshals who served under Napoléon Iᵉʳ.

Finally, many street names have changed over the years, in particular to honor distinguished individuals.

Napoléon Iᵉʳ imposed order wherever he went. It was Napoléon Iᵉʳ who decreed in 1805 that all buildings must be identified by a street number (before then, important buildings had names). For streets perpendicular or at an angle to the Seine, street numbers were to start at the end of the street nearer the Seine; for streets parallel to the Seine, they were to start at the upstream end of the street. In both cases, even numbers were on the right side and odd numbers were on the left. The current porcelain enamel plaques with white numbers on a blue background were imposed by Rambuteau, the prefect of the Seine Department, in 1847.

Ever since Paris reached its present size in 1860, incorporating the surrounding *faubourgs* into the city, Paris has been divided into twenty *arrondissements* (districts), organized in the shape of a snail, with the first arrondissement centering on the Louvre, and each arrondissement is officially divided into four *quartiers*. While certain *quartiers* are commonly referred to by Parisians, such as the Odéon and Saint-Germain-des-Prés neighborhoods in the 6th arrondissement, most Parisians think of locations in Paris in terms of arrondissements. (Ironically, the *Quartier*

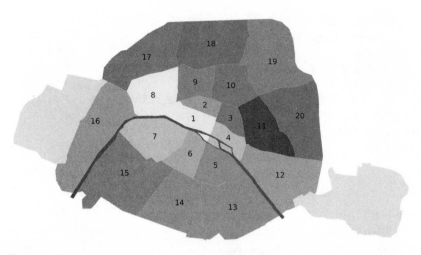

Figure 4. Map showing the twenty arrondissements of Paris and their population density in 2012 (the darker, the denser). The 1st and 8th arrondissements, where businesses predominate, are the least densely populated. AUTHOR PARIS 16.

Latin [Latin Quarter], which is mostly in the 5th arrondissement around the Sorbonne, is not an official *quartier*.) Accordingly, street addresses in this book include the relevant arrondissement—for example, the 4th arrondissement (*le 4ème arrondissement*) is abbreviated as "4ᵉ."

Faubourg means suburb, or "outside town/burg," so when the Rue Saint-Honoré becomes the Rue du Faubourg Saint-Honoré, one has passed beyond what used to be the city wall built by Charles V in the fourteenth century into what used to be the suburbs of Paris.

Similarly, *des Prés* and *des Champs* both mean "of the fields." The Abbeys of Saint-Germain-des-Prés and Saint-Martin-des-Champs were so named because they used to be in the middle of fields, well outside the city walls of Philippe-Auguste.

Because Paris was for most of its history surrounded by walls, it has always been densely populated, with multi-story buildings lining narrow streets. With fifty-five thousand inhabitants per square mile/twenty-one thousand inhabitants per square kilometer, Paris is the most densely populated city in Europe today, and is twice as densely populated as New York City and four times more densely populated than London. Except for the fortunate few who lived in *maisons individuelles*, Parisians have always lived in multi-family dwellings—and since the end of the eighteenth century in what we now call apartment buildings (the English word being derived from the French *appartement*).

PART I

THE FIRST THOUSAND YEARS

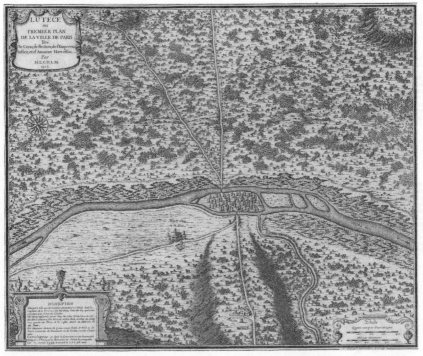

Figure 5. Lutetia, or the First Plan of the City of Paris during Gallic times. This is the first of eight maps of Paris at different times in its history created by Nicolas de La Mare (1639–1723) and engraved by Nicolas de Fer in 1705 that were published in the *Atlas des anciens plans de Paris*. It shows the island in the Seine inhabited by the Parisii before the conquest of Gaul by Julius Caesar in 52 BC. The Right Bank is at the top, with marshy land alongside the river. The Left Bank at the bottom is dominated by a hill, later named the Montagne Sainte-Geneviève after the patron saint of Paris.

Chapter i

Gallo-Roman Period (52 BC–AD 486)

The history of Paris began on an island in the Seine over two thousand years ago, and the first thousand years were marked by successive invasions by Romans, Huns, Franks, and Vikings.

During the third century BC, a Celtic tribe called the Parisii lived in the region of present-day Belgium, which was then part of Gaul. The Senones, one of the oldest tribes then living in Gaul, established around today's city of Sens in Burgundy, allowed the Parisii to settle in the northern part of their territory on an island in the Seine that would later be known as the *Île de la Cité.* **As recounted by Julius Caesar in his *Commentaries on the Gallic War*, the Romans invaded Gaul in 58 BC and defeated the Gauls led by Vercingétorix at the Battle of Alésia in 52 BC. That same year the Parisii were defeated by General Titus Libenius near the present-day Champ de Mars. The Romans established the city they called Lutetia (*Lutèce*) on the Île de la Cité and the hill on the Left Bank, and remained there for more than five hundred years until their defeat by the Franks in AD 486.

Under the Romans, the island was connected to the right and left banks of the river by wooden bridges known as the *Grand Pont* (Big Bridge) and *Petit Pont* (Little Bridge), respectively.

On the island, the Romans built a temple on the site of present-day Notre Dame Cathedral, in front of which were baths and a port for the

---

* In fact, Paris remained under the religious jurisdiction of the archbishop of Sens until the reign of Louis XIII.

** Some archaeologists think the Parisii lived near present-day Nanterre—7.5 miles/12 kilometers west of the Île de la Cité, behind La Défense—and never inhabited the island.

delivery of goods, as well as the Pillar of the Boatmen (*Pilier des Nautes*), which is the oldest monument in Paris (AD 14–37) and is on display at the Musée de Cluny–Musée National du Moyen Âge (Cluny Museum–National Museum of the Middle Ages, which opened in 1844); vestiges can be seen in the *Crypte Archéologique* below the Parvis Notre-Dame. The ruins in the crypt are 13 feet/4 meters below the surface of the *parvis* (square) today, which indicates how much higher the island has been built over the past two thousand years—among other reasons, to avoid the catastrophic floods that occurred regularly throughout the history of Paris.

The Romans built a new city on the Left Bank, since it was high and dry, whereas the Right Bank was a marsh (*marais*). They constructed a Forum at the top of what is now the Montagne Sainte-Geneviève (near where the Panthéon now stands), then known as Mount Lucotitius, and three large baths, including *les Thermes du Nord* (the largest, also called *les Thermes de Julien*), which are now part of the Musée de Cluny, the *Thermes de l'Est* located at the current Collège de France, and baths that were

Figure 6. The Arena of Lutetia, 1813. PHOTOGRAPHER UNKNOWN.

located in the Forum but no trace of which exists today. To supply the baths with water, in the first century AD the Romans built the Aqueduct of Arcueil, which transported water 16 miles/26 kilometers from Wissous (near Orly Airport). About the same time, they also built an amphitheater (*Arènes de Lutèce*) capable of holding seventeen thousand spectators (entrance at 49 Rue Monge, 5ᵉ). Given the capacity of the amphitheater, the population of Paris at the time of its construction may have been around thirty thousand.*

On the marshy Right Bank, the Romans built a temple to Mars on top of what is now called Montmartre.

Most visible today of the Roman constructions is the *cardo maximus*—the principal north-south road in the center of Roman cities: the Rue Saint-Jacques on the Left Bank (which in the Middle Ages became part of the pilgrims' route to Saint Jacques de Compostelle, or Santiago de Compostela, in northwestern Spain), which continues north across the Petit Pont onto the Île de la Cité, then across the Grand Pont (now the Pont Notre-Dame) to the Rue Saint-Martin on the Right Bank, which led to the monastery Saint-Martin-in-the-Fields. (The Rue Saint-Denis was a second *cardo* on the Right Bank.) The principal east-west road on the Left Bank—the *decumanus*—was around today's Rue Cujas, just below the Panthéon. The Forum was constructed at the intersection of the *cardo* and the *decumanus*. The principal east-west road on the Right Bank was along what is now the Rue (formerly Cours) Saint-Antoine, which led from the Grand Pont across the marshes to Melun.

According to the *Historia Francorum* written in the sixth century by Grégoire, the bishop of Tours, the pope sent Denis to Lutetia in AD 250 to convert its inhabitants to Christianity. The future Saint Denis became the first bishop of Paris, but in 261, at age ninety, he was beheaded by the Romans on what is now Montmartre (Mountain of Martyrs). Legend has it that he walked from there to the site of the present-day Saint-Denis

---

* By comparison, the population of Lyon, the capital of Roman Gaul, was between fifty thousand and two hundred thousand. (After the fall of the Western Roman Empire, Lyon became the capital of the Kingdom of the Burgundians, an East Germanic tribe.) Around the same time, the population of Rome is estimated to have peaked at around one million people—a number no other city in Europe would reach until London did so in 1800.

Basilica, 6 miles/10 kilometers north of Paris, holding his severed head in his hands, where he died.*

When barbarians (Vandals, Alamans, Franks, Avars, and Huns) began to invade Gaul, the Romans built a wall between 308 and 360 around the Île de la Cité, where the Gallo-Romans took refuge when under attack. An outline of the Gallo-Roman wall can be seen at 6 Rue de la Colombe, which indicates how much wider the present-day Île de la Cité has become, largely due to the construction of the high embankment around the island, starting at the end of the sixteenth century and continuing into the nineteenth century.

In 360, Lutetia was renamed Paris after the Parisii tribe who first inhabited the island in the Seine.

In 451, after pillaging Metz and Reims in the eastern part of Gaul, Attila the Hun and his hordes threatened Paris. The future Sainte Geneviève (419–512), patron saint of Paris, persuaded Parisians not to abandon the city, promising that they would be delivered from the Hun. In the end, Attila bypassed Paris and headed further upriver to Orléans and Burgundy, where he was finally defeated by the Roman and Visigothic armies at the Battle of Châlons.

In 464, the Merovingian king of the Franks, Childeric, besieged Paris, which was once again successfully defended by Geneviève.

In 476, the Western Roman Empire fell when the Germanic chieftain Odacer deposed the last emperor, Romulus Augustus.

In 486, Childeric's son, Clovis, defeated the Roman armies and became ruler of Gaul north of the Loire River, ending Paris's 538-year-long Gallo-Roman period.

———

As a result of Haussmann's excavations in the second half of the nineteenth century and the digging of underground parking garages in the second half of the twentieth century, the following Roman ruins were discovered and can be visited today:

---

* Constantine stopped Roman persecution of Christians in AD 313.

- Archaeological Crypt (beneath the Parvis Notre-Dame, inaugurated in 1980).
- Thermes de Cluny (at the Musée de Cluny, 6 Place Paul-Painlevé, 5ᵉ).
- Arènes de Lutèce (entrance at 49 Rue Monge, 5ᵉ).
- Outline of the Gallo-Roman wall built around the Île de la Cité in the fourth century AD (6 Rue de la Colombe).

Moreover, key elements of the layout of Lutetia remain today:

- An important secular center is still at the western end of the Île de la Cité, where the Conciergerie and the Palais de Justice are located.
- The religious center is still at the eastern end of the Île de la Cité, where Notre-Dame is located.
- The site of the rectangular Forum, the center of the new Roman city, at the top of the hill on the Left Bank now known as the Montagne Sainte-Geneviève, was near the location of the Place du Panthéon, with its many important buildings.
- The Rue Saint-Jacques is still a major north-south *cardo* on the Left Bank, even if the *cardo maximus* is now Haussmann's Boulevard Saint-Michel.

Chapter 2

Early Middle Ages (Fifth–Tenth Century)

The early Middle Ages (formerly known as the Dark Ages) began with the fall of the Western Roman Empire in 476.

THE FRANKS (476–987)

The Franks were a confederation of Germanic tribes who occupied the Lower and Middle Rhine in the third century. The Frankish tribes were united under the Merovingians, descendants of the Salian Franks, one of the principal Frankish tribes, who conquered most of Gaul in the sixth century. The Merovingians were succeeded in the eighth century by the Carolingians, whose empire evolved into the states of France and the Holy Roman Empire.

The Merovingians (476–751)

The Merovingian dynasty, known as "the long-haired kings," are considered to be the "first race" of the kings of France.

The name Merovingian derives from Merovech, who was the father of Childeric I, who ruled a tribe of Salian Franks between 457 and 481 from his capital at Tournai, in what is now southwestern Belgium.

Childeric was succeeded by his son Clovis I (circa 466–511). Clovis was the first king of the Franks to unite all of the Frankish tribes under one ruler in 486, establishing a hereditary monarchy. Clovis went on to defeat the Gallo-Romans in 486. In 496, Clovis defeated the Alemanni, another confederation of Germanic tribes, at the Battle of Tolbiac and Alsace became part of the Frankish kingdom known as Francia.

In 496, Clovis converted to Christianity—according to Grégoire de Tours, to fulfill his vow to convert to his wife Clotilde's religion if he won the Battle of Tolbiac. His kingdom was the first since the fall of the Western Roman Empire to declare allegiance to the pope, marking the beginning of the close relationship between France and the Roman Catholic Church, which earned France the sobriquet "*la fille ainée de l'église*" ("the eldest daughter of the Church").

In 506, Clovis founded the Abbaye Sainte-Geneviève on what is now called the Montagne Sainte-Geneviève on the Left Bank. The Tour Clovis, which was the clock tower of the abbey, was part of a church built in the eleventh century; it is now within the walls of the Lycée Henri IV, behind the Panthéon, but the top of the tower can be seen from the street. The original base of the tower is Romanesque; the two upper floors were rebuilt during the fifteenth century in the Gothic style.

In 508, Clovis established his capital in Paris, where he resided in the Palais de la Cité. He died in 511 and was interred at the church of the Abbey of Saint Genevieve; his remains were moved to the Saint Denis Basilica in the eighteenth century.* Geneviève died the following year, at eighty-nine years of age.

Clovis is considered to be the founder of the Merovingian dynasty that ruled the Franks for the next two centuries, and "the first king of what would become France." When Clovis died, his kingdom was divided between his four sons: Theuderic, Chlodomer, Childebert, and Clotaire, creating four kingdoms ruled from Reims, Orléans, Paris, and Soissons, respectively, and resulting in power struggles that continued intermittently until the end of the Merovingian dynasty in 751.

Building Works

In 502, Clovis and his queen Clotilde founded an abbey dedicated to the apostles Peter and Paul on the former site of the Roman Forum at the top of today's Montagne Sainte-Geneviève. The abbey was later renamed the Abbaye Sainte-Geneviève in honor of the patron saint of Paris. In 508, Clovis constructed the abbey church.

---

* A "cathedral" is the principal church of a diocese, while "basilica" is the name given by the pope to certain churches as a special distinction.

Between 511 and 558, Childebert (496/511–558) built Saint Stephen's Cathedral (*la Cathédrale Saint-Étienne*), the largest church in Frankish Gaul, just in front of the present location of Notre Dame Cathedral. Today, the outline of Saint Stephen's Cathedral, its nave and side aisles, is traced in small granite paving stones embedded in the square in front of Notre-Dame.

In 542, Childebert and his wife Ultrogothe founded the Church of Saint-Germain-l'Auxerrois, named after the fifth-century bishop of Auxerre, as opposed to the bishop of Paris at the time.

Between 543 and 558, Childebert also built Saint Vincent's Church in the fields outside Paris, which was consecrated by Germain, the bishop of Paris (later Saint Germain), and served as the necropolis for Childebert and later Merovingian kings. A monastery was constructed nearby and its abbots were given administrative control over the surrounding area. Until the late seventeenth century, the abbey owned most of the land on the Left Bank west of today's Boulevard Saint-Michel.

In 651, Saint Landry, the bishop of Paris, founded the first hospital in Paris—the Hôtel-Dieu (House of God)—next to Saint Stephen's Cathedral. The latest version of the hospital, built in the nineteenth century, stands near the original site today.

The Carolingians (751–987)

The Carolingian dynasty ruled Western Europe between 751 and 887, and France until 987. The name is derived from the large number of kings named Charles (Carolus, in Latin), most notably Charlemagne (Charles the Great).

The forebears of the Carolingian dynasty came to power as hereditary mayors of the palace of Austrasia, one of three kingdoms in Francia (along with Neustria and Burgundy) created at the end of the sixth century. The most famous of the mayors was Charles Martel (Charles the Hammer, circa 688/715–741), who defeated the Saracens (Arab Muslims) at the Battle of Tours in 732. His son Pépin le Bref (Pepin the Short, circa 714/751–768) was the first of the Carolingians to become king.

Under Pépin's son Charlemagne (742/768–814), the Frank kingdom became first the Frank Empire and then the Holy Roman Empire in 800. Charlemagne was called the "Father of Europe" because he united most of Western Europe for the first time since the fall of the Western Roman Empire in 476. Charlemagne made Aix-la-Chapelle (Aachen, now in Germany) his capital, however, and Paris was relegated to being the capital of the western Frank kingdom of Francia, ruled by the count of Paris (*Comte de Paris*). As a result, Francians increasingly looked to the local governors, rather than to Charlemagne's successors, for leadership.

There is an imposing equestrian statue of Charlemagne in the square in front of Notre-Dame, but Charlemagne only made one trip to Paris in 775, to dedicate the Saint-Denis church.

The Vikings

The Vikings sailed up the Seine and attacked Paris four times over forty years during the ninth century: in 845, 856, 861, and 885.* The first three

Figure 7. Nineteenth-century drawing of the Viking Siege of Paris in 885.

---

* The Vikings raided monasteries, ports, and cities along the coast and far up the rivers of France throughout the ninth century.

times Parisians abandoned the riverbanks and retreated to the island and the Vikings laid waste to the city and its surrounding monasteries. Finally, the Parisians repaired the old Roman Wall around the island, and Charles the Bald (Charles le Chauve), grandson of Charlemagne and the king of West Francia (840–877) and later Holy Roman emperor (875–877), demolished the first Grand Pont leading north to the Rue Saint-Martin, built a new bridge to the Right Bank near today's Pont au Change, and erected two forts, the *Grand Châtelet* and the *Petit Châtelet*, to protect the new bridge and the Petit Pont, the only two bridges leading to the Île de la Cité. When King Sigfried sailed up the Seine in November 885 with forty thousand Danes in seven hundred longships,* he met resistance for the first time and put Paris under siege. Paris was defended by Eudes (Odo), the count of Paris. After twelve months, Eudes paid the Vikings a ransom to go around Paris, upriver to the Duchy of Burgundy.

NORMANDY

In 911, the Vikings were bought off definitively when King Charles III of West Francia (879/898–922/929) signed the Treaty of Saint-Clair-sur-Epte with Rollo the Ganger (the "walker" because Rollo was so huge no horse could carry him), leader of the Vikings, who were also known as "Norsemen" or "Northmen." The treaty permitted the Northmen to settle in Neustria, which became the Duchy of Normandy, in return for their protection of Charles's kingdom from any new invasion by other Vikings.

Normandy occupies the area around the mouth of the Seine, which the Vikings had sailed up to raid Paris. Rouen, the capital of the Duchy of Normandy, is on the Seine.

In 1066, thirty-eight-year-old William (Guillaume) "the Bastard," duke of Normandy, defeated Harold II at the Battle of Hastings and was crowned king of England. Harold was the last Anglo-Saxon king of England.

---

* Numbers no doubt exaggerated by the French chronicler Saint Abbo in his account of "The Siege of Paris by the Danes" (circa 1000).

In 1087, William, now "the Conqueror," died at Mantes (30 miles/50 kilometers west of Paris) when attacking France—which was the start of more than seven hundred years of hostilities between England and France that only ended with the cooperation between the two countries known as the "*entente cordiale*" in 1904.

The Duchy of Normandy remained part of the Anglo-Norman realm until 1204, when Philippe II Auguste of France conquered Normandy, which became part of the royal domain.

CONCLUSION

So after more than five hundred years of Roman rule, followed by almost exactly five hundred years of Frankish rule, Paris had come full circle and was once again confined to the original 25 acres/10 hectares of the Île de la Cité. The population had fallen from a peak of perhaps eighty thousand during the Gallo-Roman era to around twenty thousand at the end of the millennium, after the barbarian and Viking invasions. Today nothing remains of Paris's first thousand years except the Roman ruins and the religious institutions founded by the first Merovingian kings.

Part II

The Second Thousand Years— Modern France

CHAPTER 3

The Capetians (987–1328)

In 987, Hugues/Hugh Capet (941/987–996), count of Paris, was elected king of West Francia. As he was the first French—not Frankish—king, many historians consider his election to mark the birth of modern France. The royal domain itself consisted of the Île de France and the Orléanais (the area around the city of Orléans in the Loire Valley); the *apanages* (lands given to the sons of past kings that reverted to the throne if the

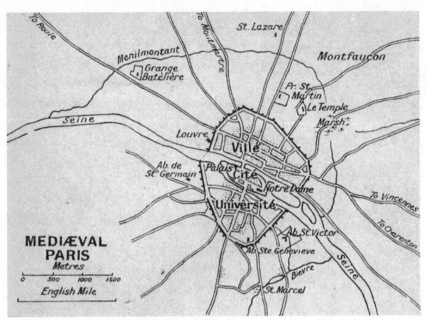

Figure 8. Map of medieval Paris surrounded by the Philippe-Auguste Wall (1912).

incumbent died without issue); and large provincial fiefdoms such as Guyenne and Flanders, which, while formally part of the kingdom, were effectively independent. The king was politically the *suzerain*, or feudal overlord, to all the nobles in the kingdom, but in reality had little power over vassals who had inherited their estates.

Hugues and his direct descendants (the Capetians) reigned from 987 until 1328, which included the sixty-year period from 1156 to 1214 when King Henry II and Eleanor of Aquitaine and their sons created and ruled the Angevin Empire that covered half of what is now France. It was the Capetians who shaped Paris.

The three kings who most marked Paris during the Capetian dynasty, with a total of 116 years on the throne between them, were:

- Philippe II Auguste/Philip II Augustus (1165/1180–1223—forty-three years).
- Louis IX/Saint Louis (1214/1226–1270—forty-four years).
- Philippe IV le Bel/ Philip IV the Fair (1268/1285–1314—twenty-nine years).

By 1300, the population of Paris was 228,000, versus forty thousand in London. The population of France was twenty-two million, versus two million in England. Paris was the largest city, in the largest country, in Europe.

From the thirteenth century, Paris was governed by a city council led by the provost of the merchants (*prévôt des marchands*). Members of the council were elected by merchants who were members of a guild (*corporation*). By the thirteenth century, there were more than one hundred guilds in Paris; by the fourteenth century, there were 350 guilds and the wealthy bourgeoisie who made up their membership had increasing influence on both the governance and the urban development of Paris.

The provost of the merchants had his office in the Grand Châtelet and was responsible for maintaining law and order in Paris and its surrounding *prévôté* (county). The first provost was Étienne Boileau. The most famous provost was Étienne Marcel, who served as provost of the merchants from

1354 until his assassination in 1358, following his attempt to seize power from the Dauphin, the future Charles V. An equestrian statue of Étienne Marcel stands on the south side of the Hôtel de Ville and a street on the border between the 1st and 2nd arrondissements is named after him. The last provost was shot after the storming of the Bastille on July 14, 1789; the first mayor of Paris was elected the following day.

Beginning around 1000, Parisians once again moved off the island, and this time they occupied the flat Right Bank, which had drained, as well as the steep Left Bank. Around 1200, the city was surrounded by a defensive wall and it developed the structure that continues in large part to this day: Secular power remained on the island, known as the *Cité*. Commerce took over the Right Bank, across from the Île de la Cité, known as the *Ville*. The new university moved to the Left Bank, known as the *Université*. And everywhere, there was the Church.

THE PHILIPPE-AUGUSTE WALL—*VILLE CLOSE*

To protect Paris from the Norman and English threat when he was in the Holy Land fighting in the Third Crusade, between 1190 and 1215 Philippe-Auguste built a wall around the 620 acres/250 hectares of the

Figure 9. The Louvre Fortress of Philippe-Auguste, before 1362. RECONSTITUTION BY T. J. H. HOFFBAUER.

city,* creating a *ville close* (walled city) that provided the security which permitted the number of Parisians to increase, also increasing the population density of the city.** He surrounded the wall—the *enceinte Philippe-Auguste*—with a moat on the Right Bank that was filled with water from the Seine. He constructed the Louvre Fortress on the Right Bank of the Seine just outside the wall and across the moat, to protect the western gate to the city.

The wall was 3.2 miles/5.2 kilometers long (about the same length on each bank), with 25 gates and 71 towers spaced every 200–260 feet/60–80 meters. It was 8 feet/2.7 meters thick at its base, and 20–26 feet/6–8 meters high. Chains supported by pontoons blocked entry to the city from the river at night. The western chain stretched between the Tour de Nesle on the Left Bank and the Louvre. The eastern chain stretched from the Tour Barbeau on the Quai des Célestins on the Right Bank across an island in the Seine to the Tour de la Tournelle on the Quai de la Tournelle on the Left Bank. A ditch was dug across the island to accommodate the chain, creating two islands: the Île aux Vaches (Cow Island) and the Île Notre-Dame. None of the towers exists today. A *Histoire de Paris* plaque marks the location of the Tour Barbeau between 30 and 32 Quai des Célestins, 4ᵉ.

The wall on the Right Bank was built first, because of its greater strategic importance, between 1190 (at the beginning of the Third Crusade) and 1209. Along the Rue des Jardins Saint-Paul, 4ᵉ, is the most impressive remnant of the wall—260 feet/80 meters long—which was uncovered in 1946 and restored in 1998. The Tour de Jean-sans-Peur (John the Fearless Tower, 20 Rue Étienne Marcel, 2ᵉ) was built against the inside of the wall in 1408. There is a narrow house at 148 Rue Saint-Honoré, 1ᵉʳ, that was built where the wall used to be. In the Archaeological Crypt of the Louvre Museum are the foundations of the enormous circular keep (*donjon*) at the center of the medieval Louvre Fortress.

---

* The same size as London's Hyde Park and Kensington Gardens.

** The first wall to encircle the Marais, the so-called "Wall of the Eleventh Century," was a wooden palisade that enclosed the *bourgs* of Saint-Gervais and Saint-Merri. Nothing of it remains today, but its eastern boundary was probably along the Rue des Barres.

The wall on the Left Bank was built between 1200 and 1215, starting on the west end at the Tour de Nesle, which stood on the site of the present-day Institut de France, and continuing parallel to what is now the Rue Mazarine (formerly Rue des Fossés [ditches, or moat] de Nesle). Stones from the Roman amphitheater were probably used to build the Philippe-Auguste Wall. The Porte de Buci, which opened onto the Rue Saint-André-des-Arts, was the principal gate to the west, leading to the Abbey of Saint-Germain-des-Prés along what is now the Rue de Buci. A remnant of a tower is visible at 4 Passage de Commerce Saint-André, between the Rue Saint-André-des-Arts and the Boulevard Saint-Germain in the 6th arrondissement, behind the picture window of a restaurant. From there the trace of the wall follows the Rue de l'École de Médecine, Rue Monsieur-le-Prince (former Rue des Fossés Monsieur-le-Prince), and Rue Soufflot. The Porte Saint-Jacques (at 172 Rue Saint-Jacques, 5e) was the most important gate in the south of Paris, located near the top of the Montagne Sainte-Geneviève. The trace of the wall continues east along the Rue des Fossés Saint-Jacques, Rue Clovis (where there is a vestige of a rampart), and Rue du Cardinal Lemoine (former Rue des Fossés Saint-Victor). The most important gate on the east end of the Left Bank was the Porte Saint-Victor (at 2 Rue des Écoles), so-called because the Abbaye Saint-Victor was just beyond the eastern gate to the city, in the area around the present-day Place Jussieu. The trace continues along the Rue des Fossés Saint-Bernard. At 7 bis Boulevard Saint-Germain is a narrow building that was built in the space once occupied by the wall.

THE CHURCH

The Church was the dominant institution throughout Europe in the Middle Ages, during which popes competed with monarchs for power. The two most important monastic orders during the Middle Ages—the Benedictines and the more austere Cistercians—both started in Burgundy and then spread across France and Europe.

Following the destruction caused by the Vikings in the ninth century, during the eleventh and twelfth centuries there was a dramatic increase in the construction and reconstruction of monasteries, both in and especially

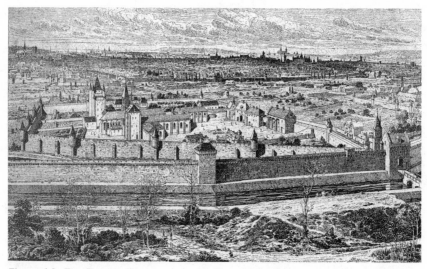

Figure 10. The Temple Enclosure in the fifteenth century, behind the Charles V Wall. RECONSTITUTION BY T. J. H. HOFFBAUER.

around Paris, and the building of churches and chapels within the city's expanding neighborhoods. In the twelfth and thirteenth centuries, a large number of convents were established on the Right Bank in the Marais. The growth of the cult of the Virgin in Western Europe at this time resulted in the extraordinary number of churches in Paris and elsewhere dedicated to *Notre Dame* (Our Lady) in her honor.

Paris was literally surrounded by monasteries, including, among others (clockwise):

On the Right Bank:

- Abbaye Montmartre (built by Louis VI le Gros/the Fat [1081/1108–1137] in 1134).
- Le Prieuré Saint-Martin-des-Champs (founded during the Merovingian era; destroyed by the Vikings; rebuilt in 1067 by Henri I [1008/1031–1060], and rebuilt again in the twelfth century, when it was surrounded by a wall with 17 towers).

- L'Enclos du Temple (built by the Knights Templar [*les Templiers*]* in 1152 on land donated by Louis VII).
- Le Prieuré Sainte-Catherine du Val des Écoliers, also known as the Couvent Sainte-Catherine (whose church was consecrated in 1228 in memory of the Battle of Bouvines in 1214; the site of the monastery is now the Place du Marché Sainte-Catherine, 4ᵉ).
- Couvent des Grands Augustins (established in 1259 outside the Porte Saint-Eustache).

On the Left Bank:

- Abbaye Saint-Victor (founded in 1114).**
- Abbaye Sainte-Geneviève (founded 506, rebuilt in 1147; the Tour de Clovis still stands inside the walls of the Lycée Henri IV).
- Abbaye Saint-Germain-des-Prés (founded in 558, rebuilt and reconsecrated in 1163; the biggest monastery of all).

Inside the new city walls, under the reign of Louis IX (Saint Louis), were founded:

- Couvent des Cordeliers (built in 1234–1571 on a former vineyard; specialized in medical studies, it became the site of the Faculté de Médecine [Medical School]; the refectory is all that remains today, at 15 Rue de l'École de Médecine, 6ᵉ).
- Couvent des Mathurins (1219; a remnant of a vault can be seen at 7 Rue de Cluny, 6ᵉ, across the street from the Hôtel de Cluny).

---

* The order was named the Templars because their headquarters in Jerusalem were next to the Temple of Solomon. After the fall of the kingdom of Jerusalem in 1244 and of the city of Acre, the last stronghold of the Crusader states, in 1291, the Templars returned to Europe and Paris became their headquarters.

** To provide the abbey with fresh water, the Victorins dug a canal from the Bièvre (Beaver) river, which flowed into the Seine near where the Gare d'Austerlitz stands today, parallel to the Seine to the abbey, and then into the Seine near today's Rue de Bièvre, 5ᵉ.

Outside the eastern end of the Philippe-Auguste Wall near the river on the Right Bank, Louis IX established the Couvent des Carmes in 1254. After the Couvent des Carmes moved near the Place Maubert on the Left Bank in 1319, the Couvent des Célestins occupied its former premises in 1352. Its grounds were bordered by the Rue du Petit-Musc to the west, Rue de l'Arsenal to the east, Rue de la Cerisaie to the north, and the Quai des Célestins and Rue de Sully to the south. The monastery was just inside the Charles V Wall, whose construction was completed in 1383.

In 1293, the Grands Augustins took possession of the Couvent des Frères Sachets on the Left Bank of the Seine, in the faubourg Saint-Germain-des-Prés. Between 1368 and 1453, their monastery was constructed alongside the river. The Mint (Hôtel des Monnaies) was built at the western end of its grounds in the eighteenth century.

Ever since the founding of the Hôtel-Dieu next to Notre-Dame in the seventh century, hospitals were closely associated with churches and monasteries since the sick and the poor were looked after by monks and nuns whose orders were sometimes known as *hospitaliers* (hospitallers).

Around 1260, the *Hospice des Quinze Vingts*[*] was founded by Louis IX (the future Saint Louis) on the Rue Saint-Honoré near the Louvre, outside the Philippe-Auguste Wall. Its three hundred beds (15 x 20) were intended for the blind. The hospital moved to its current location at 28 Rue de Charenton, 12e, in 1779.

Most monasteries were surrounded by fields that were cultivated by the monks and nuns who sold their produce to Parisians. Over the centuries the abbeys and convents ended up selling their fields for development of the expanding city. The monasteries, both inside and outside the city, disappeared altogether at the time of the Revolution.

LA CITÉ/THE CITY (THE ISLAND)
In 1163, Bishop Maurice de Sully began construction of the Cathédrale Notre-Dame de Paris on the site of the old Cathédrale Saint-Étienne

---

[*] The vigesimal numeral system, which was in use in the Middle Ages, is based on twenty, the same way that the decimal system is based on ten. While the decimal system is ubiquitous now, the French still say *quatre-vingts* (four twenties) for eighty and *quatre-vingt-dix* (four twenties ten) for ninety, whereas the French-speaking Swiss say *huitante* (formerly *octante*) et *nonante*.

Figure 11. The Île de la Cité, from the map of Paris known as the Plan de Bâle by Olivier Truschet and Germain Hoyau, 1553. The Cathédrale Notre-Dame de Paris is at the top; the Palais de la Cité is at the bottom.

built by the Merovingian king Childebert I; it was completed 182 years later, in 1345. The cathedral was the second church to be built in the new Gothic style that was to define the Middle Ages, after the Basilique Saint-Denis, which was built by Abbot Suger between 1132 and 1144.* Notre-Dame is 416 feet/127 meters long, 130 feet/40 meters wide, and 108 feet/33 meters high—nearly twice the size of the cathedral it

---

* The third was the Cathédrale Notre-Dame de Chartres (1194–1250), 50 miles/86 kilometers southwest of Paris.

replaced. The tympanum above the Portail Sainte-Anne (the portal on the right side of the western façade of the cathedral; Saint Anne was the mother of Mary)—which was the first portal installed, around 1200—came from the Saint-Étienne Cathedral, which explains why its sculpture is more archaic than the sculpture above the two other portals and why the tympanum does not completely fill the peaked space above the lintel. During the Middle Ages, all of the statues on the west façade were painted, but this custom disappeared with time. Before its roof was destroyed by fire on April 15, 2019, Notre-Dame was the most visited monument in Paris—and the world—with a record 13.6 million visitors in 2015.

Around 1190, Philippe II Auguste established his court at the Palais de la Cité at the western end of the island. His Capetian predecessors had started to transform the old Gallo-Roman fortress located there into a palace. At the beginning of the twelfth century, Louis VI built a massive new *donjon* known as the *Grosse Tour*, which existed until it was demolished in 1776 after a fire. Between 1243 and 1248, Louis IX (Saint Louis) built the Sainte-Chapelle, a royal chapel, in the Rayonnant style of Gothic architecture to house relics. In 1250, Louis also built the crenellated tower overlooking the Seine, which at one time was called the Tour Saint-Louis but was nicknamed the Tour Bonbec in the sixteenth century when it was used as a torture chamber. (To have a "bon bec"—"bec" meant "mouth" in Old French—meant to confess after torture.) The tower was restored in 1868, when a new floor was added.

Between 1301 and 1314, Philippe IV le Bel/Philip IV the Fair (1268/1285–1314) started to rebuild the Palais de la Cité of Philippe-Auguste in order to group together all the administrative functions of the kingdom. The Conciergerie with its impressive *Salle des gens d'armes* (Hall of the Soldiers)—the largest surviving medieval hall in Europe—and twin towers (the Tour César to the east and the Tour d'Argent to the west) that we see today date from this period. Philippe IV also built the *Grande Salle* (Great Room) above the *Salle des gens d'armes*; it was the largest hall in Europe at the time, but burned down in 1618. The square Tour de l'Horloge (Clock Tower) was built by Jean II le Bon/John II the

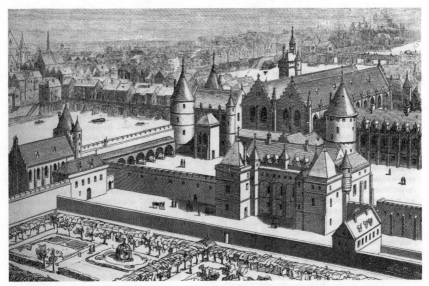

Figure 12. The Palais de la Cité in the fourteenth century, looking northeast toward the Right Bank. Note the four towers along the river Seine, which are still there. The lower Tour Saint-Louis (later renamed the Tour Bonbec) is on the left; the twin towers are in the middle; the top of the Clock Tower is on the right behind the Grande Salle. RECONSTITUTION BY T. J. H. HOFFBAUER.

Good between 1350 and 1353; the clock was installed by Charles V in 1371.

In 1312, Philippe IV began the construction of the Quai des Grands Augustins, next to the monastery on the Left Bank, which was the first quai in Paris.

In 1314, Philippe IV accused the wives of two of his three sons and two French knights of engaging in adultery in the Tour de Nesle, the old guard tower at the western end of the Philippe-Auguste Wall on the Left Bank of the Seine (where the Institut de France stands today). The women were found guilty of adultery and imprisoned; after being tortured, the men confessed to adultery and were therefore found guilty of the crime of *lèse majesté* (meaning "to do wrong to majesty," or an offense against the crown), which brought with it a particularly grisly death. The scandal became known as the "*Affaire de la Tour de Nesle.*"

Figure 13. The view from the Right Bank in the fourteenth century with, from left to right, the Tour de Nesle at the end of the Philippe-Auguste Wall (the site is now occupied by the Institut de France), the Pré aux Clercs, and the Abbey of Saint-Germain-des-Prés with the three steeples of its church. RECONSTITUTION BY T. J. H. HOFFBAUER.

Philippe IV is perhaps best known, however, for pressuring the French Pope Clément V (1264/1305–1314) to move the papal court to Avignon, creating the Avignon Papacy (1309–1377), and then to have the Inquisition try the wealthy Templars and convict them of heresy. He personally ordered their Grand Master Jacques de Molay to be burned at the stake on the Île aux Juifs at the western tip of the Île de la Cité in 1314. Philippe had hoped to use the Templars' wealth to finance his wars and construction projects, but Clément V transferred the Templars' assets to their rival military order, the Knights Hospitallers.

Jacques de Molay reportedly cursed the pope, Philippe IV, and Philippe's descendants from his execution pyre. It is true that Clément V and Philippe both died within a year of Jacques de Molay's execution. Philippe's three sons then died in quick succession between 1314 and 1328, bringing an end to the Capetian dynasty.*

---

* This series of events is the subject of *Les Rois Maudits* (*The Accursed Kings*), a popular series of six historical novels written by Maurice Druon between 1955 and 1977, which was turned into two French television miniseries in 1972 and 2005.

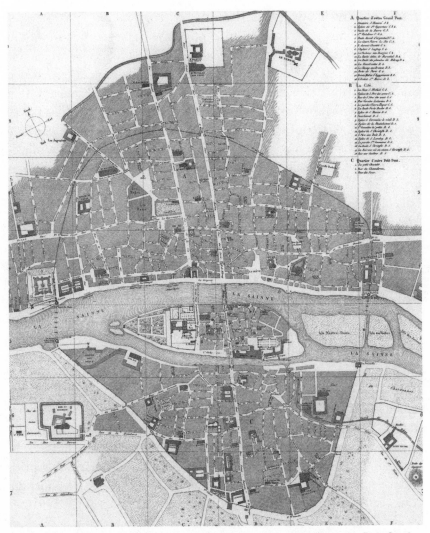

Figure 14. Paris from 1285 to 1314, during the reign of Philippe Le Bel. On the Right Bank, the city has expanded outside the Philippe-Auguste Wall. Outside the wall, the Priory of Saint-Martin-of-the-Fields and the Temple Enclosure are at the top left and right, respectively; the Abbeys of Saint-Germain-of-the-Fields and Saint-Victor are at the lower left and right, respectively. MAP BY ALBERT LENOIR & H. GIRAUD.

LA VILLE/THE TOWN (THE RIGHT BANK)

After the Viking raids in the ninth century, the Right Bank continued to dry out. The best site was the *monceau* (mound) *Saint-Gervais*, which was high enough to avoid flooding and had been inhabited since Merovingian times. On the left side of the Église Saint-Gervais-Saint-Protais at 4-14 Rue François-Miron between the Rue de Brosse and the Rue des Barres stand eleven adjacent houses originally built to be rented out (*maisons à loyer*) by *la Fabrique Saint-Gervais* (the council responsible for administering the financial affairs of the church of the same name) between 1733 and 1734.* The high steps leading from the street to the front of the long building suggest just how high the *monceau* was before it was "leveled" by Haussmann in the second half of the nineteenth century.

During the Middle Ages, development of the *Quartier Saint-Gervais* extended east from around the *monceau Saint-Gervais* along the Rue François-Miron and the Rue Saint-Antoine (formerly the Roman road leading to Melun and on to Sens) to around the Rue Beautreillis, which is just south of the Place des Vosges today. Two churches marked the western and eastern boundaries of the *quartier*: the Église Saint-Gervais-Saint-Protais (sixth century; rebuilt starting in the fifteenth century; named after twin martyrs), and the Chapelle Saint-Paul-des-Champs (632–642; replaced by the Église Saint-Paul in 1125, which was demolished in 1796, although a section of its wall can be seen at the corner of the Rue Saint-Paul and the Rue Neuve Saint-Pierre), respectively. During the Middle Ages, the Carrefour de l'Orme, the small square around the elm tree in front of the Saint-Gervais-Saint-Protais Church, was the meeting place where debts were paid: "*Attendez-moi sous l'orme*" ("Wait for me under the elm"). In 1702, the Quartier Saint-Gervais was divided into the Quartier de Grève to the west and the Quartier Saint-Paul to the east.

The Port de Grève developed from the twelfth century and was the principal port for Paris. It was next to the Place de Grève (renamed the Place de l'Hôtel de Ville in 1803), which was where the market was held

---

* An even more impressive row of twenty-four *maisons à loyer* or *maisons de rapport* with shops on the ground floor, built by the chapter of Saint-Germain-l'Auxerrois between 1669 and 1678, is found at 2-14 Rue de la Ferronerie, 1er, one block south of the Fontaine des Innocents on the street where Henri IV was assassinated in 1610.

Figure 15. Bird's-eye view of Quartier de l'Hôtel de Ville between 1765 and 1778. The new Hôtel de Ville in the center is overlooking the Place de Grève, which is next to the Port de Grève. Behind it is the Church of Saint-Gervais-Saint-Protais. The end of the Pont Notre-Dame leading to the Île de la Cité, with houses lining its sides, is at the bottom right. RECONSTITUTION BY T. J. H. HOFFBAUER.

and was the commercial center of medieval Paris. "*Grève*" meant a river-bank covered with gravel. "*Faire grève*" originally referred to the men who would congregate on the Place de Grève in search of work. The expression later evolved to mean to stop working to go on strike.

The Maison aux Piliers (1357) was the first city hall. It was replaced by the Hôtel de Ville, built between 1533 and 1628.

In 1137, Louis VI moved the market from the Place de Grève to the new Marché des Champeaux, future site of Les Halles. Between 1181 and 1183, Philippe-Auguste enlarged and improved the market, constructing two long buildings known as "*halle*," from the German word *Halle* meaning covered market. Three more *halles* were built in the thirteenth century.

The market area was surrounded by neighborhoods inhabited by the artisans who worked there and belonged to guilds that built and supported local churches. For example, between 1509 and 1523 the butchers' guild built the church Saint-Jacques-de-la-Boucherie. The church later fell into ruin and was demolished during the Revolution—all but the tower, that is, known by all as the Tour Saint-Jacques.

L'UNIVERSITÉ/THE UNIVERSITY (THE LEFT BANK)

Starting from the time of the philosopher and theologian Pierre Abélard (1079–1142, lover of Héloïse and father of the exotically named Astrolabe) in the early twelfth century, Paris became a great center of learning. The first schools were located next to Notre-Dame, but teachers and students soon moved to the Left Bank. By 1140, twelve schools had been built around the Abbaye Sainte-Geneviève.

In 1204, Philippe-Auguste chartered the University of Paris. It was Europe's second oldest university after Bologna. The University of Paris was an autonomous body under the control of the pope and subject to ecclesiastical law, recognizing the separate status of scholars (clerics, or *clercs*), with their own rights and privileges. This sometimes led to violent clashes between students and monks.

Between 1245 and 1250, the Collège des Bernardins was constructed (it was remodeled in 1338) to educate future Cistercian monks. Until the Revolution the college occupied all the land between the Seine and the Rues du Cardinal-Lemoine, des Bernardins, and Saint-Victor. All that remains is the magnificent refectory, which has been beautifully restored and since 2008 can be visited at 20 Rue de Poissy, 5ᵉ.

In 1253, Robert de Sorbon (1201–1274) founded the Collège de Sorbon. Later, the University of Paris became commonly known as "the Sorbonne," but *la Sorbonne* was from the beginning one of many colleges within the University of Paris, even if it was the most distinguished among them. The present building of the Sorbonne along the west side of the Rue Saint-Jacques south of the Rue des Écoles was built between 1885 and 1901, and replaces seventeenth-century college buildings constructed by Cardinal de Richelieu, a former student at the Sorbonne, on the site of the original Collège de Sorbon. Richelieu also built the Chapelle de la Sorbonne (architect Jacques Lemercier), where he is buried; it is the only building left from this period. The very discreet entrance to the impressive *cour d'honneur* and chapel is at 17 Rue de la Sorbonne. On the paving stones of the courtyard of honor is an outline of the first chapel, which was consecrated in 1326.

By 1400, the University of Paris had become the largest center of learning in Europe, attracting some five thousand students; in the sixteenth century, there were up to forty thousand students. Since instruction was in Latin—the *lingua franca* of the educated throughout Europe—the area was called the *Quartier Latin* (Latin Quarter).

In 1470, twenty years after Johannes Gutenberg invented the movable type printing press, the first printing presses were set up at the University of Paris. At the time only 5 percent of the population could read and students were a primary market. One of the first printers, Robert Estienne, was located at 17 Rue de Beauvais, 5ᵉ. Even today, there are reportedly 135 publishing houses and bookshops in the Latin Quarter.

By the sixteenth century, the University of Paris was made up of up to sixty-five colleges, including eight or nine colleges for foreign students. The first, the Collège de Danemark (College of Denmark), was established in the middle of the twelfth century. The Collège des Ecossais (College of the Scots) was established in 1326; it has been located at 65 Rue du Cardinal Lemoine, 5ᵉ, since 1665.

In 1530, François Iᵉʳ founded the Collège Royal (the future Collège de France), where professors lectured in Greek, Hebrew, and Latin.

In 1563, the Collège de Clermont was founded by Jesuits in the Paris residence of the bishop of Clermont, across from the Sorbonne at 123 Rue Saint-Jacques, 5ᵉ. Its name was changed to Louis-le-Grand in 1682. The lycée was rebuilt between 1885 and 1888 and it now incorporates many neighboring colleges. Former students, who are known as "*magnoludoviciens*," include writers Molière, Victor Hugo, and Charles Baudelaire; philosophers Voltaire and Denis Diderot; revolutionaries Maximilien Robespierre and Camille Desmoulins; artists Eugène Delacroix and Edgar Degas; as well as seven former presidents of the French Republic. The equally distinguished Lycée Henri IV was established in 1796 in the former Abbaye Sainte-Geneviève behind the Panthéon at 23 Rue Clovis, 5ᵉ.

Between 1661 and 1688, the Collège des Quatre Nations (now the Institut de France) was built by Le Vau pursuant to a bequest from Cardinal Mazarin. The college was intended to educate students from the four territories that had come under French rule through the Peace of Westphalia (1648) and the Treaty of the Pyrenees (1659): Flanders, Alsace, Roussillon, and the Papal States.

CHAPTER 4

The House of Valois (1328–1589)

The House of Valois was named after its founder, Charles, Comte de Valois, brother of the Capetian king Philippe IV and father of the first Valois king, Philippe VI. When Philippe VI was crowned king in 1328, the population of Paris was 250,000; 80 percent of Parisians lived in *la Ville*, 11.5 percent in *l'Université*, and 8.5 percent in *la Cité*.

The Maison de Valois ruled France during a period of tremendous upheaval that straddled the end of the Middle Ages and the beginning of the Renaissance. It began with the Hundred Years War between the French and the English (1337–1453) and the Black Death (1348–1349), which killed a quarter to a third of Frenchmen and caused the Valois kings to leave Paris for their châteaux in the Loire Valley, and ended with more plagues (1498, 1562) and the Wars of Religion between Catholics and Protestants (1562–1598).

Two bright spots for Paris during the Valois dynasty's 261 years in power were the reigns of Charles V le Sage/the Wise and François Ier.

CHARLES V (1338/1364–1380)

To defend Paris against English invaders during the Hundred Years War, between 1365 and 1420 (fifty-five years) first Charles V, and then his son and successor Charles VI, constructed a new wall on the Right Bank, outside the Philippe-Auguste Wall. It followed the old course of the Seine for 3 miles/4.8 kilometers, enclosing (from west to east) the Louvre, Saint-Martin-in-the-Fields, the Temple Enclosure, and the Marais. Charles V built the Bastille fortress (1370–1383) to protect the eastern entry to Paris just outside the royal residences the Hôtel Saint-Pol and

Figure 16. Map of Paris circa 1530 by Sebastian Munser (1572) showing the new Charles V Wall on the Right Bank (on the left side of the map) and the old Philippe-Auguste Wall on the Left Bank (on the right side of the map). The Bastille fortress is at the top.

Figure 17. The Bastille fortress in 1575. REPRODUCTION BY T. J. H. HOFFBAUER OF A DRAWING BY ARCHITECT JACQUES I ANDROUET DU CERCEAU (1510–1584).

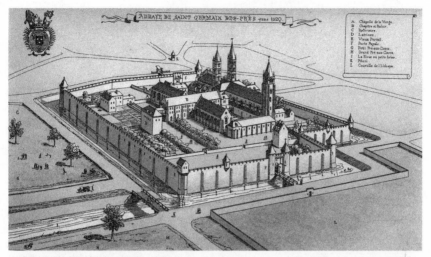

Figure 18. The Abbey Saint-Germain-des-Prés, circa 1520. Since it was outside the Philippe-Auguste Wall, it was surrounded by its own wall with a moat filled with water from the Seine. RECONSTITUTION BY T. J. H. HOFFBAUER.

the Hôtel des Tournelles, which once faced each other across the Rue Saint-Antoine but are both now long gone.

Since the Left Bank had not experienced the growth of the Right Bank and still largely consisted of monasteries and colleges surrounded by fields and vineyards, Charles V did not build a new wall on the Left Bank, but did dig a steep moat or ditch (*fossé*) outside the Philippe-Auguste Wall. The moat was dry since the wall was on a hill. In 1368, Charles V ordered the abbot of Saint-Germain-des-Prés to build a defensive wall around the abbey, surrounded by a moat that was filled with water from a channel from the river known as the *Petite Seine*. The channel was filled in around 1540 and is now the site of the Rue Bonaparte.

With the new wall on the Right Bank, the surface area of the city increased from 620 acres/250 hectares to 1,062 acres/430 hectares and its population grew to 275,000.

In 1358, Charles V left the Palais de la Cité for the Louvre. After Charles's departure, the Palais de la Cité was never again used as a royal residence. Charles left a *concierge* with judicial authority in charge of the palace, which eventually became known as the *Conciergerie* and is now part of the Palais de Justice, or Law Courts.

In the 1370s and 1380s, now that it was inside the new wall and no longer needed for defensive purposes, Charles V transformed the old Louvre Fortress into the new Louvre Palace. His architect was Raymond du Temple, the *maître des ouvrages de maçonnerie du roi*. All that remains of Charles's palace are its foundations.

Beginning in 1361, Charles V sometimes resided in the Hôtel Saint-Pol (also spelled Saint-Paul) orginally built on the site of the village of the same name in the Marais outside the Phillippe-Auguste Wall, and the Château de Vincennes in the Bois de Vincennes. The Hôtel Saint-Pol comprised a group of buildings with a garden and zoo located between the Rue Saint-Antoine and the Seine, none of which survive.

In 1388, Charles V's chancellor, Pierre d'Orgemont, constructed the Hôtel des Tournelles across the Rue Saint-Antoine from the Hôtel Saint-Pol, where the Place des Vosges stands today.

At the Château de Vincennes, Charles resided in the 170-foot/52-meter-high *donjon* (central tower or keep), the tallest medieval fortified structure in Europe, which was beautifully restored in 2007. Philippe VI

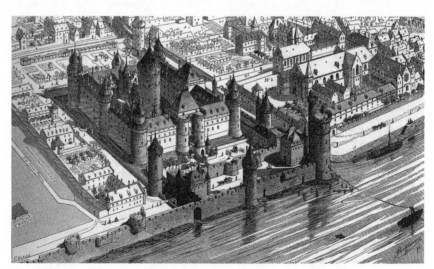

Figure 19. The Louvre Palace of Charles V in 1380. RECONSTITUTION BY T. J. H. HOFFBAUER.

BUILDINGS FROM THE MIDDLE AGES

The churches, chapels, monasteries, and convents are the best monuments to the Middle Ages. The religious buildings and secular structures from the Middle Ages that can still be seen in Paris include:

- 1001–1163: Église Saint-Germain-des-Prés, 6ᵉ.
- 1135–1145: Basilique Saint-Denis, in the northern suburb of Saint-Denis. It was the first Gothic church.
- 1163–1345: Cathédrale Notre-Dame de Paris, on the Île de la Cité.
- 1170–1240: Église Saint-Julien-le-Pauvre, Rue Saint-Julien-le-Pauvre, 5ᵉ.

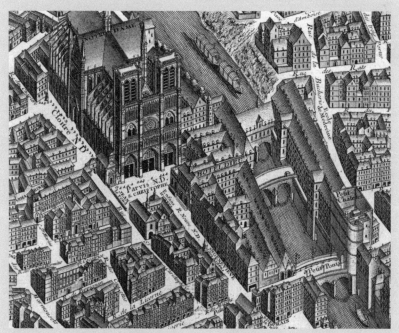

Figure 20. Extract of sheet 11 of the Plan Turgot (1739) showing the Cathedral of Notre-Dame de Paris, with the Hôtel Dieu in front of it on both banks of the river, and the Petit Pont leading to the Petit Châtelet on the Left Bank in the lower right.

- 1190: Foundations of the Donjon du Louvre, in the lower level of the Louvre Museum, 1er.
- 1190–1215: Remnants of the Philippe-Auguste Wall, at Rue Charlemagne/Rue des Jardins Saint-Paul, 4e, and at Rue Clovis, 5e, among other places.
- 1243–1248: Sainte-Chapelle, 8 Boulevard du Palais, on the Île de la Cité.
- 1301–1314: Conciergerie, 2 Boulevard du Palais and Quai de l'Horloge, on the Île de la Cité. Its *Salle des gens d'armes* (Hall of the Soldiers) and four towers along the Seine (the Tour Bonbec [1250], the twin Tour César and Tour d'Argent [1314], and the Tour de l'Horloge [1353]) are all that remain of the medieval Palais de la Cité.
- 1340–1410: Donjon du Château de Vincennes, on the edge of the Bois de Vincennes to the east of Paris.
- 1356–1383: Remnants of the base of the Charles V Wall and moat, in the underground area below the Carrousel du Louvre leading to the Louvre Museum.
- 1369–1383: La Bastille. The fortress was demolished in 1789, but its outline is traced in brass medallions on the Place de la Bastille and Rue Saint-Antoine, 4e. Part of a tower was discovered when excavating for the métro in 1900 and moved to the Square Henri-Galli at the bottom of Boulevard Henri IV, 4e, near the Seine.
- 1380: Porte de Clisson, 58 Rue des Archives, 3e. It is all that remains of the Hôtel de Clisson.
- 1407: Maison de Nicolas Flamel, 51 Rue de Montmorency, 3e. The house is considered to be the oldest in Paris.
- Fourteenth Century: Two medieval half-timbered houses, 11 and 13 Rue François-Miron, 4e.*
- 1409–1411: Tour Jean-sans-Peur (John the Fearless Tower), 20 Rue Étienne Marcel, 2e. The tower, 69 feet/21 meters high, was built against the Enceinte de Philippe-Auguste. It is the last remaining vestige of the former Hôtel des Ducs de Bourgogne, owned by the Dukes of Burgundy.

---

* The best half-timbered houses in France are found in Troyes, in Champagne, southeast of Paris, and in Dinan, in Brittany.

- 1475–1507: Hôtel de Sens, 1 Rue du Figuier, 4e. Now the Bibliothèque de Forney, it was the Paris home of the archbishop of Sens, who was the superior of the bishop of Paris until 1622.
- 1485–1510: Hôtel de Cluny, 6 Place Paul Painlevé, 5e. Now the Musée de Cluny–National Museum of the Middle Ages, it was the Paris residence of the abbots of the Cluny monastery in Burgundy.
- Thirteenth and Fifteenth Centuries: Église Saint-Séverin, Rue des Prêtres-Saint-Séverin, 5e. The church was substantially rebuilt in its present form and Flamboyant Gothic style between 1452 and the 1470s following damage or neglect suffered during the Hundred Years War. It is famous for its *"pilier tors"* ("twisting pillar").
- Fifteenth Century: Église Saint-Germain-l'Auxerrois, Place du Louvre, 1er, across from the Colonnade du Louvre.
- 1492–1626: Église Saint-Étienne-du-Mont, Place Sainte-Geneviève, 5e, behind the Panthéon.
- 1494–1657: Église Saint-Gervais-Saint-Protais, Place Saint-Gervais, 4e, behind the Hôtel de Ville.

began the construction of the *donjon* around 1337. His grandson Charles V started to build the large rectangular wall around the *donjon*, which was completed by Charles VI around 1410. In 1379, Charles V began the construction of the Sainte-Chapelle de Vincennes, whose design was based on the Sainte-Chapelle in Paris. While it took Louis IX (Saint Louis) only five years to complete the Sainte-Chapelle in the Palais de la Cité, the Sainte-Chapelle de Vincennes was not inaugurated until 1552.

With the construction of the Hôtel Saint-Pol, the Bastille, and the Château de Vincennes, the center of gravity of the city moved from the Île de la Cité and the Louvre east to the Marais, where it remained until the middle of the seventeenth century.

After Charles V, the Valois kings abandoned Paris, preferring to live in their châteaux in the Loire Valley—Amboise, Blois, Chenonceaux, Chaumont, all four royal *demeures* (residences) since the fifteenth century, culminating in François Ier's magnificent Chambord (1519–1547). During this period Louis XI (1461–1483) annexed Burgundy and eliminated the apanages, and France took on roughly the hexagonal shape that it has today. Not until François Ier's arrival on the throne 135 years later did another king reside in Paris and building works resume.

FRANÇOIS IER (1494/1515–1547)

With the coronation of François Ier/Francis I at the Cathédrale Notre-Dame de Reims on January 1, 1515, the Middle Ages ended and the French Renaissance began. The population of Paris had been reduced from 280,000 in 1400 to around 200,000 by the plague and the Hundred Years War.

François Ier's reign was dominated by the Italian Wars (1494–1559) with the Holy Roman emperor Charles V of the House of Hapsburg (known as Charles Quint to distinguish him from Charles V of France). François Ier was a great patron of the arts who brought many Italian artists to France to decorate his palaces. After François Ier's victory over the Swiss at the Battle of Marignano in 1515 (a date forever etched in the memories of French schoolchildren) and conquest of the Italian city-state of Milan, less than nine months after his coronation, the twenty-one-year-old king invited the sixty-three-year-old Leonardo da Vinci (1452–1519) to spend his final years as his guest at the manor house Clos Lucé, near the king's residence at the Château d'Amboise. Leonardo brought with him his unfinished masterpiece the Mona Lisa, which François Ier acquired after Leonardo's death. The portrait is thought to be of Lisa Gherardini, the wife of Francesco del Giocondo. "Mona" is a contraction of "madonna" in Italian, meaning *madame* in French. The painting is known as "*la Gioconda*" in Italy and "*la Joconde*" in France.

In an attempt to court England as an ally against the Hapsburgs, in June 1520 François Ier (then twenty-five years old) invited Henry VIII (twenty-eight years old) to a tournament known as the "Field of the Cloth of Gold" ("*Camp du Drap d'Or*") near Calais in northern France. In the end Henry supported François Ier's rival Charles Quint.

In 1525, François Ier was captured during the Battle of Pavia and was held prisoner in Madrid for nearly a year before being ransomed.

Building Works

In 1528, François Ier decided to reside in and around Paris, and he was the first king since Charles V, who died in 1380, to undertake important building works in the city. He had a long reign (thirty-two years), and he was a builder. His many projects in the Loire Valley included the renovation of the Château d'Amboise; the addition of a monumental spiral staircase to the Château de Blois; and especially the construction of Château de Chambord between 1519 and 1547, with its 426 rooms, 365 fireplaces, and 280 chimneys, whose grounds cover an area nearly as big as the city of Paris today.*

Outside Paris, François Ier converted the Château de Fontainebleau, 34 miles/55 kilometers southeast of Paris, from a medieval castle to a Renaissance château between 1528 and 1547. It was his favorite residence. In 1539, François Ier undertook the reconstruction and expansion

Figure 21. The court façade of the Lescot Wing of the Louvre Palace. ENGRAVING BY ARCHITECT JACQUES I ANDROUET DU CERCEAU (1510–1585) FROM *LE PREMIER VOLUME DES PLUS EXCELLENTS BASTIMENTS DE FRANCE* (1576).

---

* In the 1530s, François Ier also confiscated the Château de Chenonceau (1515–1521), built over the Cher tributary, from the son of Thomas Bohier for unpaid debts, and the Château d'Azay le Rideau (1518–1527) from the *financier* Gilles Berthelot who had fled the country for fear of being arrested for corruption.

Figure 22. The Hôtel de Ville in 1617. Drawing by Claude de Chastillon (1559–1616). ENGRAVING BY MATTHÄUS MERIAN (1593–1650).

of the Château de Saint-Germain-en-Laye, 12 miles/19 kilometers west of Paris; the château was subsequently expanded several times.

Within Paris, François Ier started to rebuild the Louvre Palace of Charles V in the Renaissance style—razing the medieval keep in 1528 and starting in 1546 the construction of what is now the southern section of the west wing of the Cour Carrée, which was completed in 1551, four years after his death. The so-called "Lescot wing" ("*aile Lescot*"), named after its architect, is the oldest part of the Louvre today. Pierre Lescot also built the Hôtel Carnavalet (1545–1572), one of the earliest and most magnificent of the *hôtels particuliers* constructed in the Marais and now the Historical Museum of the City of Paris.

In 1533, François Ier began the construction of the Hôtel de Ville on the Place de Grève in the Renaissance style; it was not completed until 1628. The original architect was the Italian Domenico da Cortona, known as *Le Boccador* (Golden Mouth), and the Renaissance façade of the Hôtel de Ville was known as the "*façade du Boccador*." It replaced the Maison aux Piliers (the Pillar House), which had served as the city hall since 1357.

Also in 1533, François Ier ordered the demolition of all the gates in the Philippe-Auguste Wall on the Right Bank. The roads outside these gates were—and still are—noticeably wider than the roads inside the gates.

Between 1547 and 1549, architect Pierre Lescot built the Fontaine des Innocents next to the Cimetière des Innocents. It was relocated to a square next to Les Halles (now the Place Joachim du Bellay) in 1858 after the cemetery was closed. The original fountain was attached to a wall. When it was relocated, a fourth side was added. The high base was added in 1865.

❧

Three very different parish churches around Les Halles were started or finished during the reign of François Ier:

- The Église Saint-Jacques-de-la-Boucherie (1509–1523), on the Rue Saint-Honoré, between Les Halles and the Place de Grève. Built by the butchers' guild (*corporation*) as their parish church, replacing an earlier church built in the thirteenth century, it was the starting point for the *Chemin de Compostelle*, leading to the Cathedral of Santiago de Compostela in northwestern Spain. The church was closed and confiscated during the Revolution, and all but the famous Tour Saint-Jacques was sold as a stone quarry in 1797. In 1862, Haussmann transformed the church's old bell tower into a stand-alone monumental tower in the Flamboyant Gothic style with the assistance of architect Théodore Ballu, and built a small park (*square*) around it. The 177-foot/54-meter-high tower was beautifully restored a second time between 2000 and 2009, and opened to the public for the first time during the summer months in 2012.
- The intimate Église Saint-Merri (1515–1612), built in the Flamboyant Gothic style, just south of the Centre Pompidou; its western façade has recently been renovated. The Saint-Merri quarter, which was crowded with craftsmen, was the setting for the climactic street battle during the June Rebellion of 1832 in Victor Hugo's novel *Les Misérables*.

- The imposing Église Saint-Eustache (1532–1640), just north of Les Halles. Les Halles parish was the biggest in Paris, and Saint-Eustache was—and remains—the second largest church in Paris after Notre-Dame, after which it was modeled. Its exterior is in the Gothic style while its interior is in the Renaissance style.

THE END OF THE HOUSE OF VALOIS

In 1550, Paris was still the largest city in Europe, with a population of 275,000.

François Ier was succeeded by his son Henri II (1519/1547–1559), who died in the Palais des Tournelles from an injury sustained while jousting in a tournament on the Rue Saint-Antoine.

Between 1564 and 1572, his widow, Catherine de Médicis (1519–1589), built the Tuileries Palace, outside the Charles V Wall, a quarter-mile/500 meters downriver from the Louvre. The architect was Philibert Delorme.

On the advice of her personal astrologer, Cosimo Ruggieri, who predicted that she would die near Saint Germain, which was just across the Seine from the Tuileries Palace, Catherine never lived in the Palais des Tuileries. Instead, between 1574 and 1584 Catherine built the Hôtel de Soissons (architect Jean Bullant), known as the Hôtel de la Reine when Catherine resided there. The residence was constructed on the site of the Hôtel de Nesle, then the home of the Convent of the Repentant Daughters, near the Église Saint-Eustache. Catherine built a 98-foot/30-meter-high fluted tower with a caged platform at the top, now called the Medici Column, in the courtyard of the *hôtel*. It may have been used for astrological observations. The Hôtel de Soissons was demolished to make way for the Halle au Blé (now the Bourse de Commerce), which was finished in 1767. All that remains of it today is the *colonne Médicis*.

Henri II was succeeded by his three sons: François II (1544/1559–1560), who was briefly married to Mary Stuart, Queen of Scots; Charles IX (1550/1560–1574); and Henri III (1551/1574–1589). François II and Charles IX both died young of natural causes. Henri III was assassinated by the fanatical Dominican monk Jacques Clément in retaliation for Henri III's assassination seven months earlier at the Château de Blois of Henri I, Duc de Guise, who had formed the Catholic League in 1576 and posed a threat to Henri III's throne. Like his brothers, Henri III died without an heir—the last of the Valois kings—and his brother-in-law Henri de Navarre became Henri IV—the first Bourbon king.

CHAPTER 5

The Bourbons (1589–1791)

HENRI IV (1553/1589–1610)

On August 18, 1572, at the Cathédrale Notre-Dame de Paris, King Henri III de Navarre (the future King Henri IV of France), a Huguenot (French Protestant), married Marguerite de Valois (the future Reine Margot, 1552–1615), daughter of the late King Henri II and Catherine de Médicis, and sister of the late king François II, Charles IX (then king

Figure 23. Plan de Mérian (1615), showing Paris after the building works of Henri IV.

of France) and Henri III (the future king of France). The wedding took place during the French Wars of Religion (1562–1598), which pitted the Catholic League led by Henri I, Duc de Guise, against the Huguenots led by Admiral Gaspard de Coligny. During the ten years leading up to the wedding, there had been three outbreaks of civil war and attempts by Huguenot nobles to seize power in France, and tensions between the two camps were high. Four days after the wedding, Coligny was shot and wounded. Fearing Huguenot reprisals and taking advantage of the presence in Paris of a large number of the Huguenot nobility to celebrate the royal wedding, Catherine de Médicis, a fervent Catholic, convinced her twenty-two-year-old son King Charles IX to make a preemptive strike against the Protestant leaders. Six days after the wedding, on St. Bartholomew's Day, upon the ringing of the bells at the Église Saint-Germain-l'Auxerrois across from the Louvre Palace, Coligny was killed by a group led by the Duc de Guise himself, setting off the widespread massacre of three thousand Huguenots in Paris over the next three days, and of ten to thirty thousand (estimates vary) French Protestants in twelve other cities in France with large Protestant minorities over the next weeks.* Henri de Navarre was spared.

In 1589, after his brother-in-law Henri III died without an heir, King Henri III de Navarre became King Henri IV of France, the first Bourbon king by reason of his descent from Louis IX. The name of the House of Bourbon is derived from the lordship—and later dukedom—of Bourbon in the Auvergne, a historical region in the center of France.

The Catholic League refused to accept Henri IV as their king since he was Protestant, and waged a four-year-long civil war to overthrow him.

In 1590, Henri IV laid siege to Paris, which was still the largest city in Europe, but with a smaller population of 220,000. Thousands died from starvation or disease before the siege was lifted.

After other failures to take Paris, on July 25, 1593, Henri IV finally converted to Catholicism at the Basilique de Saint-Denis, reportedly saying that "*Paris vaut bien une messe*" ("Paris is well worth a mass").

On March 22, 1594, Henri IV entered Paris.

---

* *La Reine Margot*, written by Alexandre Dumas in 1845, and the eponymous film by Patrice Chéreau, released in 1994, both recount the story of the St. Bartholomew's Day Massacre.

In 1598, Henri IV promulgated the Edict of Nantes, which guaranteed religious freedom to Protestants, effectively ending the Wars of Religion.

In 1600, Henri IV's childless marriage to Marguerite de Valois was annulled, and he wed Marie de Médicis (1575–1642), a distant cousin of Catherine de Médicis, who bore him six children.

In 1601, Henri IV's gardener Jean Robin planted an acacia tree in what is now the Square René Viviani, next to the medieval church Saint-Julien-le-Pauvre. It is now the oldest tree in Paris.

Building Works

Henri IV, ably assisted by his chief minister Maximilien de Béthune, Duc de Sully (1559–1641), transformed Paris during his reign. Unlike other kings, he did not just build royal palaces and he built no churches. His projects included squares, a bridge, roads, and a hospital—all built on open land in and around Paris. In 1600, he introduced zoning laws by banning the construction of timber houses and overhanging structures (*encorbellements*). Over the next decade he built (or had built by private investors) the Grande Galerie du Louvre and the Pavillon de Flore; the Pont Neuf, Rue Dauphine, and Place Dauphine; the Place Royale; and the future Hôpital Saint-Louis. He built sixty-eight new streets in Paris and commissioned the development of the Île Saint-Louis. For all of this, Henri IV is rightly considered to be Paris's first city planner (*urbaniste*).

In 1594–1595, Henri IV drew up his *Grand Dessein* to develop the Louvre, which then was a new Renaissance palace with a single wing (the Lescot Wing) started by François Ier and finished by his son Henri II in 1551, plus the three remaining walls of the medieval Louvre Fortress, a quarter-mile/500 meters upriver from the new Tuileries Palace built perpendicular to the Seine by Catherine de Médicis twenty years earlier. The Grand Dessein envisaged the construction of the *Cour Carrée* (Square Courtyard) first conceived by Henri II, which was four times the size of the existing courtyard, a waterside gallery to connect the Louvre Palace and the Tuileries Palace, and a northern gallery opposite the waterside gallery, enclosing a vast courtyard between the Louvre and the Tuileries, in a space where many buildings then stood.

Figure 24: The Grand Dessein du Louvre of Henri IV. MURAL BY LOUIS POISSON (?–1613).

On and off between 1595 and 1610, Henri built the quarter-mile/450-meter-long Grande Galerie, or Galerie du Bord de l'Eau (Waterside Gallery), with the Pavillon de Flore at its western end, connecting the Louvre with the Tuileries. It would be another 250 years before Henri's Grand Dessein would finally be completed by Napoléon III.

At the western end of the Île de la Cité, across from the Louvre, Henri IV undertook three related projects.

First, between 1599 and 1606 Henri IV finished the construction of the Pont Neuf, which had been initiated by Henri III in 1578 but had stopped in 1588 due to the Wars of Religion. It was the first stone bridge in Paris, with 12 arches; the first bridge without houses lining its sides; and the first bridge with sidewalks. The consoles on its sides were

Figure 25. The Palais de la Cité at the western end of the Île de la Cité in 1560, before the construction of the Pont-Neuf and the Place Dauphine. The spire of the Sainte-Chapelle and the towers of Notre-Dame are in the background. RECONSTITUTION BY T. J. H. HOFFBAUER.

decorated with 381 different *mascarons* (grotesque masks).* In 1608, the *pompe de la Samaritaine*, a building housing a hydraulic pump to supply water to the Louvre and the Tuileries, was constructed next to the downstream side of the second arch from the Right Bank, in front of today's La Samaritaine department store. The name *La Samaritaine* (the Samaritan woman) came from a bas-relief above the entrance to the pump house depicting the Samaritan woman drawing water from a well for Jesus, as described in the fourth chapter of John's Gospel. *La pompe de la Samaritaine* was demolished in 1813. In 1614, the equestrian statue of Henri IV was erected on the Place du Pont Neuf. It was destroyed during the Revolution; the present statue dates from 1818.

The Pont Neuf was the favorite place for Parisians to promenade for more than a century, with unobstructed views downriver of the Louvre and the Grande Galerie. The Pont Neuf (New Bridge) is now the oldest existing bridge in Paris.

---

* All of the original *mascarons* were replaced with new ones when the Pont Neuf was restored between 1852 and 1855. Some of the originals can be seen at the Musée du Moyen Âge and the Musée Carnavalet.

HÔTEL DE LA REINE MARGOT

In 1609, Henri's former wife Marguerite de Valois (la Reine Margot), who had spent eighteen years in exile in the Auvergne, moved into the Hostel de la Reine Marguerite that she had built on the Left Bank, just outside the Philippe-Auguste Wall and west of the Rue de Seine. She died there in 1615. The *hôtel*'s extensive gardens stretched along the Seine opposite the Tuileries Garden. After Queen Marguerite's death, it was on these grounds that many nobles built their *hôtels particuliers*.

In 1608, Queen Margot built the small *Chapelle des Louanges* (Chapel of Praises) in her garden, and brought in monks to sing all day long in praise of God, Jacob, and Jesus. The monks built the *Couvent des Petits-Augustins* between 1609 and 1619 on the

Figure 26. Extract from the Plan de Mérian (1615) of the faubourg Saint-Germain showing, from left to right, the Pont Neuf, the Tour de Nesle anchoring the western end of the Philippe-Auguste Wall on the Left Bank, the rectangular Hôtel de la Reine Margurite (next to, and perpendicular to, the Seine) with the circular Chapelle des Louanges in the middle of its garden alongside the Seine, and the walled Abbey of Saint-Germain-des-Prés with its church with three steeples, surrounded by a wall. REPRODUCTION BY T. J. H. HOFFBAUER.

land belonging to the Hôtel de la Reine Margot between the Rue des Saint-Pères and the Rue des Petits-Augustins (now the Rue Bonaparte). In 1618, the chapel was incorporated into the *Église des Petits-Augustins*. Following the abolition of the monastic orders in 1791, the convent was confiscated and used as a depot for royal sepulchres and statues. In 1795, the Musée des Monuments Français was established on the site by Alexandre Lenoir in order to preserve the architectural heritage of France after the destruction of royal monuments ordered during the Revolution. Lenoir salvaged fragments of the Château d'Anet (1548) of Diane de Poitiers, the courtesan of Henri II, Queen Margot's father, which was vandalized during the Revolution, and affixed them to the façade of the Église des Petits-Augustins. In 1816, the site was transferred to the École des Beaux Arts (School of Fine Arts). Starting in 1832, the current building of the École des Beaux-Arts was constructed on the 5 acres/2 hectares of grounds of the convent; all that remains of the convent is the church, which forms part of the north side of the courtyard, whose entrance is at 14 Rue Bonaparte, 6ᵉ.

Second, in 1607 Henri IV built the new, straight, and paved Rue Dauphine (33 feet/10 meters wide), named after his son the Dauphin, the future Louis XIII. The Rue Dauphine led from the south end of the Pont Neuf to the Porte de Buci in the Philippe-Auguste Wall on the Left Bank, on fields acquired from the Convent of the Grands Augustins and the Abbey of Saint Denis. Henri IV also built the Rue d'Anjou (now de Nesle) and Rue Christine (named after his second daughter) leading from the Rue Dauphine. Lots on either side of the Rue Dauphine were sold for residential and commercial use. This *percée* opened up for development the faubourg Saint-Germain between the Philippe-Auguste Wall and the Abbey of Saint-Germain-des-Prés.

Finally, between 1607 and 1610 the triangular Place Dauphine was constructed by Jean Androuet de Cerceau next to the Pont Neuf in the former gardens of the Palais de la Cité. Henri IV gave the land to Achille de Harlay, who in exchange was required to build out the square within three years in accordance with plans approved by Henri IV. Harlay sold the lots to merchants and lawyers who built forty-five houses of varying sizes on twelve lots behind a common façade of brick and cut stone, which was later to define the Louis XIII style of architecture. With the proceeds of the sales, Harlay built eighteen houses on the east side of Rue de Harlay (also given to him by Henri IV), which he rented out. Due to its central location, the Place Dauphine was the most sought-after property in Paris, and was much more expensive than Henri's next square, the Place Royale. In the eighteenth century, additional floors were built on most houses on the Place Dauphine, new windows were pierced in the façade, and the brick was covered with plaster. Only the two houses facing the Pont Neuf retain their original design; their brick and stone façades were restored in 1945 and again in 2016.

At the eastern edge of Paris, just inside the Charles V Wall and near the Bastille, between 1605 and 1612 (two years after Henri IV's death) the Place Royale was constructed on the site of the former Palais des Tournelles, where Henri II and Catherine de Médicis had resided. After Henri II died there from an injury sustained while jousting, Catherine razed the palace. Each side of the square was 350 feet/108 meters long and comprised nine lots. Henri gave the lots on three sides of the square to high-ranking nobles on the condition that they construct pavilions on their lots in accordance with Henri's design. Henri IV himself built the nine pavilions on the north side of the square (where silkworks were

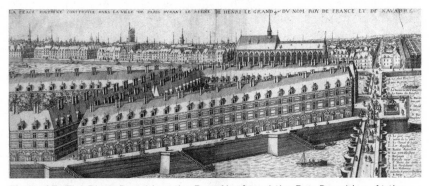

Figure 27. The Place Dauphine, the Pont Neuf, and the Rue Dauphine. At the top right is the Couvent des Grands Augustins on the Left Bank. PRINT BY CLAUDE DE CHASTILLON (1559–1616).

Figure 28. The new Place Royale (later renamed the Place des Vosges) during the sumptuous festivities on April 5–7, 1612, known as "*le carrousel des Chevaliers de la gloire*," following the announcement of the future marriage between Louis XIII and Anne d'Autriche. PAINTING BY UNKNOWN ARTIST.

originally located) between 1608 and 1610. The thirty-six residences, designed by the architect Claude Vellefaux, all had matching brick and stone façades, similar to the Place Dauphine. Most owners rented out their buildings.

The Place Royale was, along with the Place Dauphine, the first square built in Paris after the Place de Grève, and enclosed the first public garden in Paris, which originally was treeless and gateless. In 1682, the garden was covered with grass, surrounded by a fence with locked gates, and made into a private garden for the square's residents. Two rows of linden trees were planted in 1783.

The Place Royale and the Place Dauphine were the first two "royal squares" in Paris—so named because a statue of a king stood at their center; three others would be built before the Revolution.

In 1800, Napoléon Ier changed the name of the square to the Place des Vosges to reward the first department in France to pay taxes supporting a campaign of the Revolutionary Army. Among other distinguished residents, Victor Hugo lived there; his apartment at 6 Place des Vosges is now the Victor Hugo Museum.

Unlike today's more modest Place Dauphine, the elegant Place des Vosges has retained its architectural integrity and is the best surviving example of the Louis XIII style of architecture. Indeed, an equestrian statue of Henri IV's son and successor stands at the center of the square.

Henri IV built the Maison Royale de Santé (later renamed the Hôpital Saint-Louis), also in the Louis XIII style, on a site to the north of the Charles V Wall, between the Porte Saint-Martin and the Porte du Temple. Construction began in 1607 and finished two years after Henri IV's death, in 1612. Like the Place Royale, it was designed by Claude Vellefaux. The historic and austere buildings around the quadrangle (*le quadrilatère*, each side nearly 400 feet/120 meters long) represent some of the best seventeenth-century architecture in Paris today. The enclave was—and still is—surrounded by a wall. The hospital, with many modern additions, continues to operate today.

On May 14, 1610, the day after the coronation of Marie de Médicis as queen of France, Henri IV was assassinated by the Catholic fanatic François Ravaillac on the Rue de la Ferronerie. A stone rendering of Henri's shield as the king of France and Navarre is embedded in the road to mark the spot. Ravaillac was tortured, drawn, and quartered (the manner of execution reserved for the crime of *lèse-majesté*) on the Place de Grève.

Figure 29. The Maison Royale de Santé (later renamed the Hôpital Saint-Louis), 1608. Drawing by Claude de Chastillon (1559–1616). ENGRAVING BY JACQUES POINSSART.

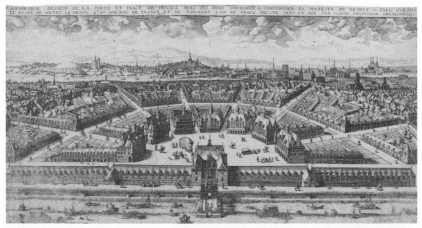

Figure 30. The plan for the Place de France, 1610, which was never built. Drawing by Claude de Chastillon (1559–1616). ENGRAVING BY JACQUES POINSSART.

Before he died, in 1608 Henri IV planned to build an even more impressive square, to be called the Place de France, in the shape of a fan in the fields near the Temple known as the *couture du Temple*. Before his assassination put an end to the project, Henri built the following streets in the north part of the Marais as part of the plan: Rues Debelleyme (in part), de Bretagne (in part), du Poitou, Charlot, de Santonge, and du Perche. The Rue Debelleyme traces the distinctive semicircle shape that the Place de France was intended to have. Bretagne, Poitou, Santonge, and Perche are all names of former provinces of France, fittingly intended to lead to the Place de France.

In 1609, Henri IV granted the engineer Christophe Marie the commission to create a residential island from two uninhabited islands just east of the Île de la Cité: the Île Notre-Dame and the Île aux Vaches. The project was delayed by Henri's assassination as well as by financial and technical problems, but in the 1620s and 1630s Marie and his partners François Le Regrattier and Lugles Poulletier (after whom cross streets on the island are named) finally filled in the space between the two islands, building quais around the new island and a street down the middle (Rue Saint-Louis-en-l'Île), with lots on either side for sale. He also built the Pont Marie (now the second oldest bridge in Paris, after the Pont Neuf) connecting the island to the Right Bank between 1614 and 1635, and the Pont de la Tournelle leading to the Left Bank in 1656. Like most bridges at the time (except the Pont Neuf), the Pont Marie was originally lined with two rows of houses. Mainly in the 1640s, 120 private residences (*hôtels particuliers*) were built on the island. The most desirable lots were on the north side of the island, facing the Marais, where the aristocrats lived. The most outstanding *hôtels* today, both closed to the public, are:

- Hôtel Lambert (1640–1644; architect Louis Le Vau), behind a high wall at the northeastern tip of the Île Saint-Louis, next to the Pont de Sully. It was purchased from Baron Guy de Rothschild in 2007 by the brother of the emir of Qatar and completely restored between 2010 and 2018.
- Hôtel de Lauzun (1657; architect Charles Chamois), 17 Quai d'Anjou. It is owned by the Ville de Paris and has also been beautifully restored.

Three months after Henri IV's death, his first wife, la Reine Margot, laid the first stone of the façade of the Église Saint-Étienne on the

Figure 31. The Pont Marie with the west end of the Île Saint-Louis on the right, 1757. A flood carried away the right two arches of the Pont Marie and twenty houses in 1658; the bridge was rebuilt in 1670, but not the houses. PAINTING BY NICOLAS JEAN-BAPTISTE RAGUENET (1715–1793).

Figure 32. The Collège Royal (the future Collège de France) built during the reign of Henri IV. PRINT BY CLAUDE DE CHASTILLON (1559–1616).

Montagne Sainte-Geneviève, which had been under construction since 1517 under François Ier. It was consecrated in 1626 and is best known for its Renaissance rood screen (*jubé*).

Finally, in 1612, two years after Henri IV's death but at his instigation, construction of a new building to house the Collège Royal, founded by François 1er in 1530, got underway across from the Sorbonne on today's Rue des Écoles on a site selected by the founder's son and successor, Henri II. Only the western wing and the first section of the southern wing of the college designed by Charles de Chastillon were built. One hundred fifty years later, the building around the main courtyard (the Chalgrin building, named after its architect Jean-François Chalgrin) was constructed by Louis XV between 1772 and 1778. The college was enlarged by architect Paul Letarouilly between 1834 and 1841, taking on its final form. In 1870, its name was changed to the Collège de France. Today the Collège de France is considered to be France's most prestigious research establishment.

Louis XIII (1601/1610–1643)

The Dauphin was only eight when he became King Louis XIII after the assassination of his father, so the Queen Mother Marie de Médicis governed in his name as regent until he came of age.

In 1615, at age fourteen, Louis XIII married Anne of Austria (a Spanish princess). In 1617, at age sixteen, Louis took power and briefly exiled Marie to Blois, before reconciling with her.

In 1624, Louis appointed Cardinal Arnaud Jean du Plessis, Duc de Richelieu (1585–1642), as his chief minister. In 1630, the Queen Mother pressured Louis to replace Richelieu, but Louis supported the wily Richelieu and again exiled his mother—this time permanently—in the *"journée des dupes"* ("day of the fools"). In 1635, Richelieu founded the Académie Française. When he died in 1642, Pope Urban VIII reputedly declared: "If there is a God, the Cardinal de Richelieu will have much to answer for. If not . . . well, he had a successful life."*

In 1637, the French philosopher René Descartes (1596–1650) published *Discours de la Méthode/*Discourse on the Method (which included the famous dictum, *cogito ergo sum/je pense, donc je suis/*I think, therefore I am)—considered by many to mark the beginning of the Age of Enlightenment, which ended with the French Revolution. One explanation for why Paris is called the *Ville Lumière* (City of Light) is because during the eighteenth century it was the center of the Enlightenment (*les Lumières*) movement led by Voltaire and Jean-Jacques Rousseau. Another explanation is the early presence of public lighting in the city dating back to the seventeenth century.

Building Works
After the death of Henri IV, a former Protestant who converted to Catholicism to become king, there was a strong Catholic resurgence as France belatedly embraced the Counter-Reformation (1545–1781) and a large number of churches were built in Paris in the new baroque style, many with domes, including:

- Façade of the Église Saint-Gervais-Saint-Protais (1615–1621, architect Salomon de Brosse), 13 Rue des Barres, 4ᵉ. Construction of the church began in 1494 in the Gothic style, but was delayed by the Wars of Religion and lack of funds. The façade, with its

---

* This period is recounted in the historical novel *The Three Musketeers* by Alexandre Dumas, which was serialized in 1844.

three levels of Doric, Ionic, and Corinthian columns, was the first to be built in Paris in the new baroque style.

- Église de l'Oratoire (1621–1630, Clément II Métezeau and Jacques Lemercier; 1740–1745, Pierre Caqué), 145 Rue Saint-Honoré, 1ᵉʳ. It has been a Protestant church since 1844.

- Église Saint-Louis (1627–1641), 99 Rue Saint-Antoine, 4ᵉ. The church was later renamed Saint-Paul-Saint-Louis in memory of the nearby Église Saint-Paul, which had been built in 1125 at the corner of today's Rue Saint-Paul and Rue Neuve-Saint-Pierre (replacing the Chapelle Saint-Paul-des-Champs built on the same site around 632–642) and was demolished in 1797.

- Église Sainte-Marie de la Visitation (1632–1634, François Mansart), 17 Rue Saint-Antoine, 4ᵉ. It has been a Protestant church since 1802, and is now known as the Temple du Marais.

Figure 33. Reproductions of elevations by Jacques-François Blondel (1705–1774) of baroque façades of churches built in Paris between 1616 and 1739.

- Chapelle de la Sorbonne (1635–1644, Jacques Lemercier), Place de la Sorbonne, 5ᵉ. Cardinal Richelieu, a former student at the Sorbonne, constructed the chapel along with other college buildings (that no longer exist) around a large courtyard. The chapel has two façades, one facing the Place de la Sorbonne and the other facing the courtyard of the Sorbonne, and features the first church dome in Paris. Richelieu's tomb lies in the chapel.

In 1612, the Queen Mother Marie de Médicis purchased the Hôtel de François de Luxembourg outside the Philippe-Auguste Wall, and some adjacent properties. Between 1615 and 1631, she had the Palais du Luxembourg constructed on the grounds by Salomon de Brosse. Its distinctive *façade aux bossages* features horizontal stonework reminiscent of the Pitti Palace in Marie's hometown of Florence.* Brosse cleverly aligned the dome-topped entrance at the end of the Rue de Tournon, which was built one hundred years earlier on land acquired from the Abbaye Saint-Germain-des-Prés, thus providing an impressive approach to the palace. The original garden was much smaller than it is today, bordered on the south by the Enclos des Chartreux, a Carthusian monastery founded by Louis IX in 1257. To irrigate the garden, in 1609 Marie rebuilt the Aqueduc d'Arcueil constructed by the Romans. In 1621, Rubens decorated the galleries of the palace with twenty-four vast and extravagant portraits that celebrated the main events of Marie's marriage to Henri IV and her regency after his death, which can now be seen in a dedicated room in the Louvre.

In 1618, the Cours-la-Reine, a long promenade and garden, was constructed in honor of Marie de Médicis along the Right Bank of the Seine between the Palais des Tuileries and today's Place de l'Alma. The garden was rebuilt in 1723, and the embankment was constructed in 1769.

Starting in 1624, Louis XIII demolished part of the medieval north wing of the Louvre Palace and extended the Lescot Wing to the north by adding a central pavilion and a new wing the same size as the Lescot Wing, which copied Lescot's façade, thus starting the process of quadrupling the

---

* The same horizontal stonework is also found at the Loire Valley Château de Cheverny (1624–1630), designed by Jacques Bougier, a student of Salomon de la Brosse.

Figure 34. The Palais and Jardin du Luxembourg, with the Couvent des Chartreux in the upper right. EXTRACT FROM THE PLAN DE TURGOT (1739).

size of the palace and the courtyard. His architect, Jacques Lemercier,
completed the wing by around 1642. The central pavilion between the
Lescot Wing and the new Lemercier Wing became known as the *Pavillon de l'Horloge* after a clock was added in 1857; it is now known as the
Pavillon Sully. Lemercier also began construction of the first part of the
north and south wings heading east.

In 1628, the Hôtel de Ville (City Hall), started by François Ier in 1533,
was finally completed, replacing the Maison aux Piliers.

Between 1629 and 1639, the Palais-Cardinal was built by Jacques
Lemercier for Cardinal Richelieu. Upon Richelieu's death in 1642, the
palace became the property of the Louis XIII. It acquired the new name
Palais-Royal when the regent Anne d'Autriche and the young Louis XIV
resided there between 1643 and 1649. In 1692, Louis XIV deeded the
Palais-Royal to his younger brother the Duc d'Orléans, and the palace
remained in the Orléans family until 1848. Since the end of the nineteenth century it has housed the Conseil d'Etat, France's highest administrative court.

Figure 35. The Palais-Royal, circa 1660, after the extensive garden was added behind it following the demolition of the west end of the Charles V Wall. ENGRAVING BY ADAM PÉRELLE (1638–1695).

Between 1634 and 1647, the Louis XIII Wall (also known as "*les Fossés jaunes*" or "Yellow Moat," possibly because of the yellowish color of the soil) was built, extending the western part of the Charles V Wall to enclose the Jardin des Tuileries up the Rue Royale to la Madeleine (together with the Charles V Wall, now occupied by the Grands Boulevards).

In 1635, the royal medicinal herb garden (the future Jardin des Plantes) was completed and put under the direction of the king's physicians.

Louis XIV (1638/1643–1715)

In 1638, at the age of thirty-seven and after twenty-three years of childless marriage to Louis XIII, Anne d'Autriche gave birth to a son, Louis Dieudonné (Louis the God-given). In 1640, Anne gave birth to a second son, Philippe I, who became Duc d'Orléans upon the death of his uncle in 1660 and founded the modern House of Orléans. During the reign of Louis XIV he was known simply as *Monsieur*, the traditional style at the court of France for the younger brother of the king.

Louis was four years old when his father died in 1643, and the Queen Mother Anne of Austria was made regent, with Cardinal Jules Mazarin (1602–1661) serving as chief minister between 1642 and 1661.

In thanks for Louis's unexpected birth, after she became regent Anne constructed a magnificent church in the French Baroque style with an adjoining convent on the grounds of the Abbaye du Val-de-Grâce that was run by Benedictine nuns in the faubourg Saint-Jacques, just south of the Philippe-Auguste Wall and east of the Rue Saint-Jacques. Seven-year-old Louis XIV laid the first stone in 1645, and then completed the project in 1669, three years after his mother's death at the abbey. The architects were François Mansart, Jacques Lemercier, Pierre Le Muet, and Gabriel Le Duc. The church can be visited today as part of a guided tour of the Musée du Service de Santé des Armées (Museum of the Army Medical Corps).

In 1648, the Thirty Years War finally ended with the Peace of Westphalia, named after the region in northwestern Germany where the three peace treaties that constituted the settlement were negotiated. The conflict started as a religious war between Catholic and Protestant states in the fragmented Holy Roman Empire, but developed into a more general war involving the great powers of Europe. France allied itself with the Protestant states against its traditional rivals, the Hapsburgs of the Holy Roman Empire (based in Austria) and Spain. While the war devastated Central Europe, France was largely spared. The Peace of Westphalia granted increased autonomy to the German-speaking states of the Holy Roman Empire, recognized the independence of the Dutch Republic (marking the beginning of the Dutch Golden Age), and transferred Alsace from the Holy Roman Empire to France.

In France, the Thirty Years War was followed by the Fronde, a series of civil wars led by nobles throughout France between 1648 and 1653 in response to taxes levied by Mazarin in the king's name to defray the costs of the war. After his generals finally repressed the revolt, Louis XIV was crowned in Reims in 1654 at age sixteen, when he reportedly declared, "*L'État, c'est moi*" ("I am the state").

Along with his father Louis XIII, Louis XIV—le Roi Soleil (the Sun King)—reigned during the *Grand Siècle* (Great Century)—the seventeenth century—when France became the dominant military and cultural power in Europe. Louis XIV transformed France into an absolute monarchy, and Versailles became the model for Europe's other royal courts, which adopted French language, art, fashion, and literature.

France was the largest country in Europe, with a population of eighteen million, compared with fourteen million in Russia, 6.5 million in Austria, six million in Spain, and 5.5 million in England. The population of Paris was four hundred thousand.

In 1659, Louis XIV signed the Treaty of the Pyrenees ending France's ongoing wars with Spain, its nemesis since the days of François I and Charles Quint. To seal the peace, Louis married his cousin the Infanta Maria Theresa at Saint-Jean-de-Luz, on the border between France and Spain. When they made their grand entrance into Paris along the impressive new Cours de Vincennes at the eastern edge of the city in August 1660, a large throne was erected on what was then known as the Place du Trône (now Place de la Nation).

On August 17, 1661, Nicolas Fouquet (1616–1680), Louis XIV's superintendent of finance since 1653, invited Louis to an extravagant gala at his magnificent new château Vaux-le-Vicomte, 34 miles/55 kilometers southeast of Paris. (It was built between 1656 and 1661 by the architect Louis Le Vau [1612–1670], landscape architect André Le Nôtre [1613–1700], and painter/decorator Charles Le Brun [1619–1690].) Three weeks later he was arrested by the legendary d'Artagnan of the Three Musketeers for embezzlement, and Vaux-le-Vicomte was placed under sequestration for the benefit of the state. Fouquet spent the rest of his life in prison.

After Mazarin died in 1661, Louis XIV appointed Jean-Baptiste Colbert (1619–1683) as his intendant of finances, succeeding the disgraced Fouquet. While he never held the title of chief minister, as Richelieu and Mazarin had, through his diligence and competence Colbert accumulated many other important responsibilities over the next twenty-two years.

Under Colbert, France's economy thrived. Among many other initiatives, in 1664 Colbert purchased the Gobelins tapestry manufactory (*la Manufacture des Gobelins*), located alongside the Bièvre river in the faubourg Saint-Marcel south of Paris, where the Gobelin family and other dyers and tanners had worked since the fifteenth century, and reorganized the Savonnerie carpet manufactory (*la Manufacture de la Savonnerie*), both originally promoted by Henri IV. The Manufacture de la Savonnerie, which was originally located in an old soap factory in the village of Chaillot, was merged into the Manufacture des Gobelins in 1821. Since 1937, the national factories of both Gobelins and Savonnerie belong to the Mobilier National (National Furniture Collection), part of the Ministry of Culture. The combined manufactory is still operating in period buildings behind an impressive new brick and cut stone gallery (1914) located at 42 Avenue des Gobelins, 13ᵉ, which is open to the public.

Having been forced to flee Paris by the Fronde, Louis resolved to establish his court outside the city and built Versailles between 1664 and 1710. Louis employed Le Vau, Le Nôtre, and Le Brun, who had all worked on Vaux-le-Vicomte for Fouquet. Jules Hardouin-Mansart, who studied under his renowned great-uncle François Mansart, also worked as an architect on the project.

In 1682, Louis and his court moved to Versailles, 12 miles/20 kilometers southwest of Paris, which remained the seat of government until 1789. Life at court was recorded in the letters written by Madame de Sévigné (1626–1696) and the *Mémoires* of Louis de Rouvroy, Duc de Saint-Simon (1675–1755).

During Louis XIV's reign, France fought three major wars: the Franco-Dutch War (1672–1678), the War of the League of Augsburg (1689–1697), and the War of the Spanish Succession (1702–1712). The first confirmed Louis XIV as the most powerful monarch in Europe and ended with France's acquisition of Franche-Comté; the second resulted in France's loss of Lorraine; and the third nearly bankrupted France and marked Britain's emergence as a global power.

Throughout his marriage with Maria Theresa, Louis had numerous mistresses who bore him thirteen illegitimate children. The most notable were Louise de la Vallière; Athénaïs de Montespan (who was removed after thirteen years and seven children as a result of *l'Affaire des Poisons*); Marie-Angélique de Fontanges (who, according to Madame de Sévigné, was "*belle comme une ange, sotte comme un panier*" ["beautiful as an angel, dumb as a basket"]); and finally, Françoise Scarron, later known as Madame de Maintenon (ex-governess to the children of Louis and Madame de Montespan), whom Louis secretly married after the queen died in 1683.

It was largely at the urging of the devout Madame de Maintenon, supported by Louis's confessor Père La Chaise, that Louis revoked the Edict of Nantes in 1685, causing four hundred thousand Protestants (Huguenots) to flee France.

Louis was a great patron of the arts. The composer Jean-Baptiste Lully (1632–1686), author Jean de la Fontaine (1621–1695), philosopher Blaise Pascal (1623–1662), and playwrights Corneille (1606–1684), Jean Racine (1639–1699) and Molière (1622–1673) all lived—and died—during his long reign.

As the British historian Alistair Horne summed it up, Louis's seventy-two-year reign began with the brutal Frondes; in the 1660s and 1670s, Louis made important reforms and France enjoyed considerable prosperity, thanks largely to Colbert, who died in 1683. From 1682 onward, following his move to Versailles, Louis was preoccupied with foreign wars and romantic affairs; from 1700 onward, his reign was in decline until his death in 1715, four days before his seventy-seventh birthday.

Building Works

Between 1661 and 1683, Colbert served as superintendent of buildings, in charge of all royal architectural projects. At the instigation of Colbert, who believed that the king should mark his reign not only by the wars that he fought but by the buildings that he constructed, Louis XIV founded the Royal Academy of Architecture in 1671 with the mission of making Paris, not Rome, the artistic and architectural model for the world.

Louis XIV not only built Versailles; thanks to Colbert he also built in Paris. As Alistair Horne put it, "Louis XIV inherited a city of brick and left it marble."

Like so many kings before him, Louis improved the Louvre, creating the magnificent *Cour Carrée*, which was first envisioned by Henri II and was included in Henri IV's Grand Dessein. Between 1660 and 1678, he doubled the length of the north wing of the palace and the width of the south wing; built an east wing to enclose the square courtyard; built

Figure 36. The Cour Carrée of the Palais du Louvre. Note that the north and east wings are roofless. EXTRACT OF THE PLAN DE TURGOT (1739).

Figure 37. The Collège des Quatre Nations (the future Institut de France), circa 1660. DRAWING AND ENGRAVING BY ADAM PÉRELLE (1638–1695).

new interior and exterior façades of the Cour Carrée; and constructed the magnificent Colonnade on the exterior façade of the east wing of the Cour Carrée, creating a monumental new entrance to the Louvre (architect Claude Perrault). Unfortunately, Louis XIV abandoned the project before it was finished when he moved to Versailles, leaving it to Louis XV to complete the Cour Carrée in 1754.

On the Left Bank, opposite the Cour Carrée, Louis XIV demolished the Tour de Nesle (at the beginning of the west end of the Philippe-Auguste Wall) so that the Collège des Quatre Nations could be built by the architect Le Vau between 1661 and 1688, pursuant to a bequest from Cardinal Mazarin. According to the original design, there was supposed to be a bridge between the Cour Carrée and the Collège des Quatre Nations, but it was only in 1804 that the Pont des Arts was built by Napoléon Ier.

But Louis XIV's greatest building works were outside the city's walls, which he demolished. On the Right Bank, he laid out avenues and boulevards that came to epitomize Paris. On the Left Bank, he initiated enormous projects alongside the Seine at both the eastern and western outskirts of the city.

Between 1670 and 1690, Louis demolished the Charles V/Louis XIII Wall—making Paris an "open city" for the first time since Philippe-Auguste built his wall five hundred years earlier—and had the architect Pierre Bullet build in its place wide *boulevards* (now the *Grands Boulevards*) lined with parallel rows of elm trees, which served as a *cours* where Parisians would promenade.

The word *boulevard* (in the beginning sometimes spelled *boulevart*) is derived from "*bollwerk*," a Middle Dutch or German word meaning the top of a military rampart, or bulwark. It was originally used by the French to designate a rampart converted to a promenade, and then to circular roads built on former fortifications, but later was used to mean any large road.

In 1672, a monumental *arc de triomphe* (triumphal arch) was built on the boulevard on the site of the former Porte Saint-Denis (architect Jacques-François Blondel). In 1674, another monumental *arc de triomphe* was built on the site of the former Porte Saint-Martin (architect Pierre Bullet, based on the design by Jacques-François Blondel).

Figure 38. The newly erected Arc de Triomphe de la Porte Saint-Denis, circa 1662. ENGRAVING BY ADAM PÉRELLE (1638–1695).

Louis XIV planned to build similar boulevards on the southern city limit on the Left Bank, known as the *Boulevards du Midi*, but the project was only carried out starting in 1760.

Paris was able to become the first "open city" in Europe thanks to the expansion of France's territories as a result of Louis XIV's wars and the construction of a ring of three hundred forts along the borders of France by the military engineer Sébastien Le Prestre de Vauban (1633–1707), and the corresponding reduction of the risk of attack by its enemies.[*] As a result, Paris was able to develop outside the old city walls for one hundred years until the construction of the Farmers General Wall around 1790.

On the Right Bank, at the western end of the city, between 1665 and 1679 André Le Nôtre, in addition to redesigning the Jardin des Tuileries and the Cours-la-Reine, laid out the Avenue des Tuileries, leading west from the Jardin des Tuileries through fields to the top of the Butte Chaillot, in the direction of the Château de Saint-Germain-en-Laye, where Louis XIV was born and resided between 1666 and 1681. Two hundred

---

[*] Twelve of these fortifications were added to the list of UNESCO World Heritage Sites in 2008.

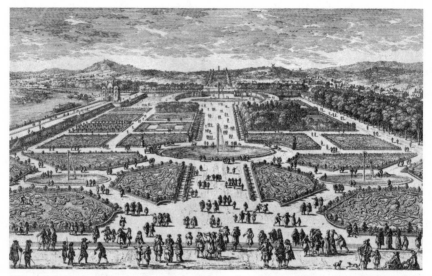

Figure 39. View of the Jardin des Tuileries, circa 1660, looking west up the Avenue des Tuileries (the future Avenue des Champs-Élysées). DRAWING AND ENGRAVING BY ADAM PÉRELLE (1638–1695).

years later this became the Avenue des Champs-Élysées, leading to the Place de l'Étoile (now Place Charles-de-Gaulle), and defining the "Historic Axis" that we know today.

On the Left Bank, at the eastern end of the city beyond the Jardin des Plantes, between 1670 and 1677 Louis XIV built the Hôpital de la Salpêtrière (hospital by Louis Le Vau, chapel by Libéral Bruant) on the site of a former gunpowder factory (saltpeter was used to make gunpowder) built by Louis XIII. The gunpowder factory was opposite the Arsenal on the Right Bank, a collection of buildings next to the Couvent des Célestins that had been used to make cannons and other weapons since the time of François Ier. The Hôpital de la Salpêtrière was enlarged in 1684 and by the time of the Revolution it was the world's biggest hospital, with a capacity of ten thousand patients. The Hôpital de la Pitié, founded by Marie de Médicis in 1612, was moved next to the Hôpital de la Salpêtrière in 1911 and was merged with it in 1964 to form the Groupe Hospitalier Pitié-Salpêtrière, a general teaching hospital. It is the largest hospital in France today.

Figure 40. Hôpital de la Salpêtrière, as seen from the river Seine, circa 1660.
ENGRAVING BY ADAM PÉRELLE (1640–1695).

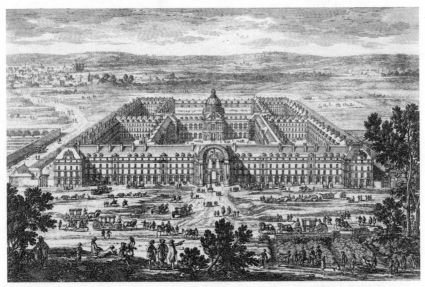

Figure 41. The Hôtel des Invalides, circa 1660, before the construction of the Dome Church. DRAWING AND ENGRAVING BY ADAM PÉRELLE (1635–1695).

At the western end of the city, between 1671 and 1676 Louis XIV built the Hôtel des Invalides (architect Libéral Bruant) to house seven thousand *anciens combattants* (veterans). Between 1679 and 1708, he added the Dome Church of the Hôtel des Invalides (Église du Dôme des Invalides, architect Jules Hardouin-Mansart), and laid out the Place Vauban in front of the church, along with the Avenue de Breteuil (half a mile/840 meters long and 230 feet/70 meters wide), which opened in 1680. Around 1780, the Avenue de Ségur (half a mile/815 meters long and 138 feet/42 meters wide) and the Avenue de Villars (188 yards/172 meters long and 130 feet/40 meters wide) were built, radiating from the Place Vauban on either side of the Avenue de Breteuil.

Between 1685 and 1689, Louis built the Pont Royal (architect Jules Hardouin-Mansart), connecting the Tuileries Palace with the Left Bank. It was the first bridge in Paris that was not connected to the Île de la Cité or the new Île Saint-Louis, and opened up the western end of the Left Bank for development. Nevertheless, after Louis XV most of the development of Paris took place on the Right Bank.

A partial list of other buildings constructed in Paris during Louis XIV's long reign includes:

- 1641–1649: Palais-Mazarin (now the "*site Richelieu*" of the Bibliothèque Nationale de France), 58 Rue Richelieu, 2ᵉ.
- 1646–1745: Église Saint-Sulpice (*place* 1754; fountain 1844–1848), Place Saint-Sulpice, 6ᵉ.
- 1653–1690: Église Saint-Roch (Jacques Lemercier), 284 Rue Saint-Honoré, 1ᵉʳ.
- 1656–1660: Hôtel de Beauvais (Antoine Le Pautre), 68 Rue François-Miron, 4ᵉ.
- 1664–1702: Église Saint-Louis-en-l'Île (François Le Vau), 19 bis Rue Saint-Louis-en-l'Île, 4ᵉ.
- 1667–1672: Observatoire de Paris (Charles Perrault), 14ᵉ.
- 1670–1676: Église Notre-Dame de l'Assomption (Charles Errard), 263 bis Rue Saint-Honoré, 1ᵉʳ (now the Polish church in Paris).

- 1671: Hôtel de Lully (Daniel Gittard), 45 Rue des Petits-Champs, 1ᵉʳ.
- 1682–1683: Église Saint-Thomas d'Aquin (Pierre Bullet), 7ᵉ.
- 1685–1692: Place des Victoires (Jules Hardouin-Mansart), 1ᵉʳ, built by private developers.
- 1686–1699: Place Vendôme—originally Place Louis-le-Grand (Jules Hardouin-Mansart), 1ᵉʳ, built by private developers.

With the creation of an "open city," bigger and even more magnificent *hôtels particuliers* could be built outside the old city walls.

THE DEVELOPMENT OF THE ARISTOCRATIC QUARTIERS OF PARIS AND THEIR *HÔTELS PARTICULIERS*

To finance his many wars, Louis borrowed enormous amounts of *livres* (the French currency from 781 to 1794) from private *financiers*, who with their new fortunes built magnificent *hôtels particuliers* in the new neighborhoods around the Louvre and in Saint-Germain-des-Prés, outside the former city walls.

The development of the *hôtel particulier*, which started in the Marais in the last quarter of the sixteenth century, reached its apogee during the reign of Louis XIV, when it was characterized by a mansion built between a courtyard and a garden (*la séquence cour-logis-jardin*).

Like nobles everywhere, the French aristocrats wanted to live near the king. So when Charles V left the Palais de la Cité for the Louvre in 1358, the nobility followed. And when he started to build the Hôtel Saint-Pol in the Marais in 1361, they followed again and the geographical center of gravity of the city moved to the east. Even more nobles moved to the Marais after the construction of the Place Royale (now Place des Vosges) initiated by Henri IV in 1605 and inaugurated in 1612, two years after his death, by his son and successor Louis XIII.

When Louis XIII resided in the Louvre, his chief minister Cardinal de Richelieu built his palace, known as the Palais-Cardinal, on the other side of the Rue Saint-Honoré between 1633 and 1639, and the nobility—as well as some of the new *financiers* who had made their fortunes lending money to the king—followed, building their residences near the king and his first minister in what came to be known as the Quartier Richelieu. During the two Richelieu decades (1624–1642), the center of gravity of Paris moved westward, away from the overcrowded Marais. After Richelieu died, the palace became the property of Louis XIII. When the four-year-old Louis XIV and his mother Anne of Austria moved into the palace in 1643, it was renamed the Palais-Royal.

In the 1640s, other aristocrats and *financiers* moved onto the new Île Saint-Louis; still others moved to the faubourg Saint-Germain, first along the Seine next to the former palace of Queen Marguerite de Valois (la Reine Margot), the first wife of Henri IV, where she lived from 1609 until her death in 1615, and then on the streets leading from the faubourg Saint-Germain to the Hôtel des Invalides, built by Louis XIV between 1671 and 1676.

The move westward in search of more space and cleaner air continued with the development of neighborhoods in the faubourg Saint-Honoré, the Chaussée-d'Antin, and Poissonière. During the Second Empire, the Champs-Élysées and Avenue Montaigne were developed, and after the city was enlarged to include eight new arrondissements in 1860, new neighborhoods were developed around the Parc Monceau and, finally, in the 16th arrondissement, which was as far west as one could go and still be within the city limits. The expansion continued into the western suburbs of Paris, out to Versailles and beyond.

In all these neighborhoods (*quartiers*) the aristocrats and the haute bourgeoisie built magnificent *hôtels particuliers*, many of which are still standing today. They were called *hôtels* to denote an urban residence grander than a house (*maison*) but less grand than a palace (*palais*)—a term usually reserved for a royal residence (some notable exceptions being the Palais-Cardinal and the Palais-Mazarin). Beginning in the nineteenth century, the modifier *particuliers* (individual) was added to *hôtels* to distinguish these private residences from other *hôtels* intended for public use, such as the *Hôtel de Ville* (City Hall) or the *Hôtel-Dieu* (House of God, another name for a hospital).

LOUIS XV (1710/1715–1774)

In 1711, Louis XIV's son the Dauphin died of smallpox. His grandson, the new Dauphin, died in 1712 of measles, as did the new Dauphin's first son. As a result, when Louis XIV died in 1715, he was succeeded by his great-grandson Louis, age five, with Louis XIV's nephew Philippe, Duc d'Orléans, as regent. Louis XV lived at the Palais des Tuileries until the regent died in 1723, whereupon he moved back to Versailles.

Louis XV fought two wars of the Austrian Succession against Frederick II of Prussia, starting in 1740 and ending in defeat in 1748 (but including a victory won by the Maréchal de Saxe at the Battle of Fontenoy in the Netherlands in 1745), and the Seven Years War (1756–1763), which ended with the Peace of Paris, whereby France lost to Great Britain her empire in Canada, the Mississippi territory, and India. Closer to home, Lorraine and Corsica came under French control.

Louis XV was a weak and unpopular king. Between 1726 and 1743, the government was run by Louis's former tutor, Cardinal de Fleury; between 1758 and 1770, it was run by Étienne-François, Duc de Choiseul. In 1725, Louis married Marie Leszczyńska (1725–1768), a Polish princess who bore him ten children. Like his great-grandfather, Louis XV had many mistresses, including Mademoiselle Poisson (1721–1764), who became the Marquise de Pompadour and was also known as Madame de Pompadour; she was Louis's official mistress (*maîtresse-en-titre*) between 1745 and 1751 and remained an influential advisor on matters of state and the arts until her death, when she bequeathed her residence, the Palais de l'Élysée, to France. It was thanks to Madame de Pompadour that Louis XV bought the Manufacture de Sèvres porcelain manufactory in 1757. After Madame de Pompadour died, Jeanne Bécu, the Comtesse du Barry (1743–1793), was Louis's mistress until his death in 1774. She was beheaded during the Revolution.

Louis XV's long reign took place during the Age of Enlightenment (or the Age of Reason), led in France by the great philosophers Voltaire, Montesquieu, and Rousseau, which produced Diderot's Encyclopedia. But the decadence of the regime also produced the Marquis de Sade and *Les Liaisons Dangereuses* (1782) by Choderlos de Laclos.

The British historian Norman Davies described Louis XV's long reign—at nearly fifty-nine years, the second longest after that of

Figure 42. The Plan de Turgot by cartographer Louis Bretez (16?–1738). In 1734, the *prévôt des marchands* Michel-Étienne Turgot commissioned Louis Bretez to draw the famous map of Paris in twenty panels known as the Plan de Turgot. The map, which was completed in 1739, gives a bird's-eye view of Paris during the reign of Louis XV. Many extracts appear throughout this book.

Louis XIV—as "one of debilitating stagnation," which made the monarchy more vulnerable to the revolution that came fifteen years after his death. Nonetheless, during his long reign Louis XV and his favorite architect Ange-Jacques Gabriel made some important contributions to the urban landscape of Paris, embracing the neoclassical style.

Building Works

The provost of the merchants, Michel-Étienne Turgot, in addition to commissioning the famous map of Paris, is credited with the construction between 1739 and 1745 of the Fontaine des Quatre-Saisons at 57-59 Rue de Grenelle, 7ᵉ, between the Boulevard Raspail and the Rue du Bac. The monumental fountain was sculpted and built by the royal sculptor Edmé Bouchardon. It was the largest and most ornate of the 30 public fountains built in Paris in the eighteenth century to provide drinking water to the city's residents.

From approximately 1732 until his death in 1766, the Italian architect Jean-Nicolas Servandoni designed and built the west façade of the Église Saint-Sulpice, whose first stone was laid by Anne d'Autriche in 1646. He planned to build a large square in front of the church, 394 feet/120 meters wide and 682 feet/208 meters long, but was unable to carry out his plan due to the presence of a Jesuit seminary built by parish priest Jean-Jacques Olier in 1645. Servandoni was only able to construct the building at 6 Place Saint-Sulpice, which suggests how grand Servandoni's square would have been. The current square, which was completed in 1754, is 262 feet/80 meters wide and 344 feet/105 meters long. The destruction of the seminary in 1808 permitted the construction of the Fountain of the Four Bishops in 1848.

On the Right Bank, in 1754 Louis XV finished the work on the Cour Carrée of the Louvre begun by Louis XIV but abandoned when he moved to Versailles.

In 1759, Louis XV undertook the demolition of the Hôtel du Petit Bourbon in order to clear the area in front of the Colonnade du Louvre; work was only completed in 1776, although the space that exists today dates from the Second Empire.

Between 1757 and 1774, Louis XV constructed the Place Louis XV, together with the Rue Royale, west of the Tuileries Garden (renamed Place de la Révolution in 1792, Place de la Concorde in 1795, Place Louis XV again in 1814, Place Louis XVI in 1826, and finally Place de la Concorde once again in 1830) and the neoclassical façades on its north side, now housing the Hôtel de Crillon and the Hôtel de la Marine; the architect was Ange-Jacques Gabriel.* It was the last of the five royal squares with the statue of a king at their center built in Paris.**

---

* The buildings themselves were built later. For example, architect Louis-François Trouard bought the westernmost lot at auction and built a sumptuous mansion that was purchased by the Comte de Crillon in 1788. His descendants lived there until 1904. In 1906, the Société des Grands Magasins et des Hôtels du Louvre bought the mansion and two adjacent buildings; the Hôtel de Crillon opened in 1909. It reopened after four years of extensive renovations in 2017.

** The other four are the Places Dauphine, Royale (now des Vosges), Louis-le-Grand (now Vendôme), and des Victoires.

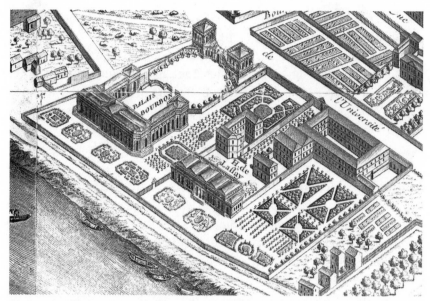

Figure 43. The Palais Bourbon and the Hôtel de Lassay. EXTRACT FROM THE PLAN DE TURGOT (1739).

From 1750, when the Grands Boulevards became fashionable for carriage rides and people-watching, *hôtels particuliers* were built by nobles and the wealthy bourgeoisie at the west end, while theaters, dance halls, and circuses were built on the Boulevard du Temple at the east end.

Between 1763 and 1767, Louis built the circular *Halle au Blé* (Wheat Market) for grain storage on the site of the former Hôtel de Soissons built by Catherine de Médicis. Originally, six roads radiated from the Rue de Viarmes, which encircled the hall; only the Rue de Viarmes exists today. In 1783, a laminated wooden dome was built over the central courtyard; it was destroyed by fire in 1802 and replaced by a cast-iron dome in 1813.

On the Left Bank, between 1722 and 1728 the Duchesse de Bourbon, the legitimized daughter of Louis XIV and Madame de Montespan, built the Palais Bourbon across the river from the future Place Louis XV. She sold some of her land to her lover, the Marquis de Lassay, who built the Hôtel de Lassay next door.

Between 1752 and 1770, southwest of the Invalides on the Plaine de Grenelle, Louis XV constructed the École Militaire (architect

Figure 44. Eastern façade of the École Militaire with the Champ de Mars behind.
LITHOGRAPH BY JULES ARNOULT (1814–1868).

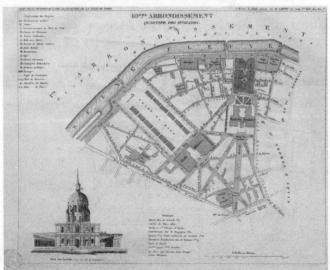

Figure 45. The Quartier des Invalides (1834), with the Champ de Mars behind the École Militaire at ten o'clock, and the Esplanade des Invalides in front of the Hôtel des Invalides at twelve o'clock.

Figure 46. The Panthéon, between 1880 and 1900. PHOTOGRAPH BY NEURDEIN FRÈRES.

Figure 47. The Hôtel des Monnaies, between 1865 and 1900. PHOTOGRAPH BY
ÉDOUARD DONTENVILLE OR DONTENVILL (1846–19?).

Ange-Jacques Gabriel), with the Place de Fontenoy (named after the battle of 1745) in front and the Champ de Mars (a military parade ground,
104 acres/42 hectares) behind. The vast complex is even larger than the
Hôtel des Invalides. Louis also built the Avenue de Saxe (named after
the general who won the Battle of Fontenoy) to connect with the Place
de Breteuil and the Avenue de Lowendal (named after another of Louis's
generals) to connect with the Invalides, and the Avenues de Suffren, de la
Bourdonnais, and de la Motte-Picquet around the Champ de Mars.

Further east on the Left Bank, Louis XV started to build the Panthéon (1757–1790, architect Jacques-Germain Soufflot), which was
originally a church dedicated to Sainte Geneviève, and the neighboring Faculté de Droit (Law School, 1771–1774) at the top of the Montagne Sainte-Geneviève, then the highest point in Paris; the Hôtel
des Monnaies (the Mint) on the Quai de Conti (1767–1777, architect

Jacques-Denis Antoine), whose neoclassical façade recalls the Colonnade du Louvre across the river started one hundred years before by Louis XIV and finished by Louis XV; and the École de Chirurgie (later the École de Médecine, or Medical School), with another neoclassical façade, near the Carrefour de l'Odéon (1769–1774, architect Jacques Gonduin), which was extended after the construction of Boulevard Saint-Germain (1878–1905, architect Léon Ginain).

Finally, starting in 1760 Louis built the *Boulevards du Midi* ("*le Midi*" means the South of France) on the southern edge of the city, as envisioned by his great-grandfather Louis XIV. Starting at the Hôtel des Invalides and heading east, they comprised the Boulevards des Invalides, du Montparnasse, d'Enfer (today the part of the Boulevard Raspail between Boulevard Montparnasse and Place Denfert Rochereau), and the Boulevards Saint-Jacques, Auguste-Blanqui (leading to Place d'Italie), and de l'Hôpital (ending at the Seine). The Boulevards du Midi were 138 feet/42 meters wide, whereas the Grands Boulevards were 118 feet/36 meters wide.

LOUIS XVI (1754/1774–1792/1793)

Unlike his grandfather Louis XV, Louis XVI was religious and he had no mistresses. While he meant well, he could not bring himself to make the reforms necessary to redress the grievances of the French people. As a result, he was blamed for the regressive policies and obduracy of the Ancien Régime.

In 1770, Louis XVI married Marie-Antoinette, daughter of Empress Maria Theresa of Austria; he was fifteen years old and she was fourteen. Eight years later, she bore him the first of four children. As a result of her lavish spending and frivolous conduct, she was deeply unpopular with the French people.

Still stung by France's recent defeat by Great Britain during the Seven Years War (1756–1763), Louis XVI supported the American Revolution, which began in 1776 and ended with the Treaty of Paris in 1783, but put France into debt to do so. To make matters worse, harvests were poor and the price of bread began to rise. Since bread was the people's staple diet— most workers consumed about 3 pounds/1.4 kilos of bread each day and spent half their wages on it—the price increase and the threat of famine led to violent riots, setting the stage for the Revolution.

On April 27, 1784, Beaumarchais's masterpiece *Le Mariage de Figaro* (originally called *La Folle Journée*) was first performed at the new Théâtre Français on the Place de l'Odéon. The play, which had been banned since it was first written in 1778, three years after Beaumarchais's *Le Barbier de Séville*, mocked the excesses of the Ancien Régime. Figaro pointedly asked the nobles seated in the audience, "*Qu'avez-vous fait pour tant de biens? Vous vous êtes donné la peine de naître, et rien de plus!*" ("What have you done for so much wealth? You took the trouble to be born, and nothing more!"). The play was a triumph, with twelve curtain calls. It also sounded the death knell for the society of birth represented by the Ancien Régime and presaged the society of merit introduced by the Revolution and the First Empire. When in exile on Saint Helena, Napoleon Ier said that *Le Mariage de Figaro* started the Revolution.

Building Works
Significant building works carried out in Paris during Louis XVI's reign include:

- 1775: Construction of La Bagatelle (The Trifle), a *maison de plaisance* (a small pleasure palace) built in the neoclassical style by the Comte d'Artois, Louis XVI's brother, in the Bois de Boulogne (architect François-Joseph Bélanger). It was constructed in only sixty-four days to win a bet with Marie-Antoinette.
- 1776: Opening of the Cour du Commerce Saint-André along the trace of the former Philippe-Auguste Wall, 6e. Le Procope, the oldest café in Paris, having been first established in 1686 by Francesco Procopio dei Coltelli, who had immigrated from Sicily to France in 1670, opened there in 1784. It later became a center of the Enlightenment, patronized by such celebrities as Voltaire and Rousseau.
- 1777–1782: Construction of today's Cour de Mai and the eastern façade of the Palais de Justice on the Île de la Cité (architect Pierre

Desmaisons). The front gate of the palace was built by the master locksmith Bigonnet in 1781.

- 1777–1782: Construction of the Théâtre Français and the semicircular Place de l'Odéon in front of it (architects Joseph Peyre, Charles de Wailly), and some of Paris's first sidewalks on the Rue de l'Odéon, 6ᵉ, all built on the grounds of the former Hôtel du Prince de Condé. The theater is the oldest in Paris and the first with seats. It was built to be the theater of the Comédie-Francaise, created by Louis XIV in 1780. It was renamed the Théâtre de l'Odéon in 1797 and the Théâtre de l'Europe in 1990.

- 1779: Completion of the Parc Monceau by Philippe d'Orléans, 8ᵉ.

- 1782: Demolition of the Petit Châtelet fortress at the end of the Petit Pont, 5ᵉ.

Figure 48. The eastern façade of the Palais de Justice, circa 1865. PHOTOGRAPH BY CHARLES SOULIER (1840–1875).

Figure 49. The Saint-Sulpice Church with its mismatched towers, circa 1841.
After the death in 1766 of Jean-Nicolas Servandoni, the principal architect
of the façade, which was inspired by the façade of Saint Paul's Cathedral in
London, Oudot de Maclaurin erected the twin towers according to Servandoni's
baroque design. Between 1777 and 1780, Servandoni's pupil Jean Chalgrin
rebuilt the north tower (on the left) making it 16 feet/5 meters higher than
the south tower and more neoclassical in style. The Revolution interrupted the
works and the south tower was never rebuilt. VERY EARLY PHOTOGRAPH BY ARMAND-
HIPPOLYTE-LOUIS FISEAU (1819–1896).

- 1782–1787: Construction of the Hôtel de Salm (architect Pierre
  Rousseau) for the German prince Frederick III von Salm-Kyrburg
  (now the Palais de la Légion d'Honneur), 7ᵉ.*

- 1782: Opening of the Théâtre de la Comédie Italienne (now the
  Opéra Comique; architect Jean-François Heurtier), on what is

---

* Thomas Jefferson modeled Monticello on the Hôtel de Salm.

now the Place Boïeldieu, 2ᵉ, built in the garden of the Hôtel de Choiseul.

- 1786–1790: Construction of the Théâtre du Palais-Royal, later known as the Théâtre Français, the Théâtre de la Comédie-Française, and the Salle Richelieu (architect Victor Louis), 2 Rue de Richelieu, 1ᵉʳ. It housed republican members of the Comédie-Francaise at the new Théâtre Français on the Place de l'Odéon who at the beginning of the Revolution split from the original company, which remained royalist. Since 1799 it has been the principal theater of the Comédie Française and was most recently renovated in 2014.

- 1786: Transfer of bones from the Cimetière des Innocents next to Les Halles to former quarries at Montsouris, now called *les Catacombes* (the Catacombs), in the Place Denfert-Rochereau, 14ᵉ.

- 1786–1791: Construction of the Pont Louis XVI (now the Pont de la Concorde).

Three developments during the reign of Louis XVI deserve special mention.

Redevelopment of the Palais-Royal

Between 1781 and 1786, the Duc de Chartres (future Duc d'Orléans, who during the Revolution adopted the name Philippe-Égalité), who needed money to pay off his debts, rebuilt the Palais-Royal around the central garden, adding shopping arcades with 174 identical archways, with three floors of residences above (architect Victor Louis).* From 1786 until 1830 (when it was superseded by the Grands Boulevards), the Palais-Royal was the most popular place for Parisians to promenade. The success of the Palais-Royal inspired the arcades along the Rue des Colonnes in 1792 and especially the Rue de Rivoli, which was built from the Place de la Concorde to the Louvre between 1802 and 1835, and was extended east to the Rue Saint-Antoine between 1849 and 1856.

---

* The same Duc d'Orléans created the Parc Monceau.

Farmers General Wall

Between 1785 and 1791, Paris was once again surrounded by a wall: the *Enceinte des Fermiers Généraux* (Farmers General Wall). Unlike previous walls, its purpose was not defensive, but to collect taxes. As a result, the wall was only 10–13 feet/3–4 meters high and 3 feet/1 meter thick. The new wall was 15 miles/24 kilometers long, with 62 toll barriers and 55 customs houses known as *"barrières."* All construction within 110 yards/100 meters of the wall (reduced to 65 yards/60 meters in 1789) was forbidden. The primary gates to Paris were the Barrière de l'Étoile (later the Place de l'Étoile) to the west and the Barrière d'Enfer (later the Place Denfert-Rochereau) to the south. Surviving remnants include the Rotonde (formerly, Barrière) de la Villette, the Rotonde (formerly, Barrière) du Parc Monceau, identical customs houses at the Place Denfert-Rochereau (formerly, Barrière d'Enfer), and the Barrière du Trône at the Place de la Nation. The architect was Claude-Nicolas Ledoux.*

First Apartment Buildings

Finally, during the reign of Louis XVI the bourgeoisie, who would replace the aristocracy as the dominant class in the nineteenth century, developed the apartment building, or *maison de rapport*, which had the same exterior size and appearance as an *hôtel particulier*, but was of course divided into separate apartments that could be rented out to generate income. It was wider than the *maisons bourgeoises* that it largely replaced. The first modern apartment buildings (*immeubles d'appartements*) were built around the Palais-Royal by the architect Victor Louis in 1784. The same idea was used by architects Percier and Fontaine when they designed the first stretch of the Rue de Rivoli in 1802. Fifty years later, rows of apartment buildings would line the streets built by Baron Haussmann as part of his *Grands Travaux*, when they would become better known as *immeubles de rapport* and *immeubles haussmanniens* (see Chapter 8).

---

* Parisians' hostile reaction to the Tax Wall led to the famous epigram *"le mur murant Paris rend Paris murmurant"* ("The wall walling Paris keeps Paris wailing/murmuring").

THE POLICY OF ALIGNMENT*

Because the expanding city of Paris had developed behind walls ever since the Middle Ages, its streets were narrow and congested. Even on major roads, such as the Rue Galande on the Left Bank, two coaches were often unable to pass because buildings encroached on the street. In the 1670s, the municipal authorities adopted *la politique du retranchement* to deal with the problem, which allowed them to demolish the façade of an encroaching building and rebuild a new façade set back from the street (*retranchée*). But this aggressive approach was complicated and costly since the city had to indemnify the owner for the loss of part of his property.

The "policy of retrenchment" was replaced by *la politique de l'alignement* promulgated in a royal decree of 1783, which required that all existing streets be gradually widened whenever the buildings along them were rebuilt. The decree also ordered that *plans d'alignement* be drawn up for every street in Paris.

In 1796, the government established uniform widths for each of the four categories of street in Paris, ranging from 20 feet/6 meters for the smallest (which was the width of the largest streets in the Middle Ages) to 46 feet/14 meters for the largest. The alignment plans for all the streets of Paris were finally published in 1813. In the 1830s, the required width of certain streets was increased. For example, in the Marais the width of the smallest streets was increased from 20 feet/6 meters to 33 feet/10 meters.

The obvious problem with the "policy of alignment," which remained in force until the 1970s, was that it could only be implemented upon the reconstruction of the buildings along the street in question. Since many buildings were never rebuilt, this resulted in the situation found on many streets in Paris today where newer buildings are set back from the street and older buildings are not. (The Rue Saint-André-des-Arts, 6ᵉ, which dates back to the Middle Ages, is just one example among many.) This phenomenon was aggravated outside the historic center by a regulation passed in 1967 that in effect provides that the farther a building is set back from the street, the higher the building can be.

---

* Principal source: *Paris—La Forme d'une Ville*, by Michaël Darin, Parigramme, 2016.

The difficulty in achieving the desired alignment within a reasonable time was one of the main reasons why Rambuteau and Haussmann preferred building new streets through old neighborhoods (*percées*), as discussed in Chapters 7 and 8.

CHAPTER 6

The Revolution and Napoléon Ier (1789–1815)

THE REVOLUTION (1789–1799)

In 1789, the population of Paris was 630,000, and the population of France was twenty-five million.

Following the storming of the Bastille on July 14, 1789, and the Declaration of the Rights of Man and the Citizen on August 26, 1789, the

Figure 50. The taking of the Bastille fortress on July 14, 1789. RECONSTITUTION BY T. J. H. HOFFBAUER.

First Republic was proclaimed by the National Assembly in 1792. The Ancien Régime of the Bourbon kings was over.

In 1790, France was divided into eighty-three *départements*. In 1795, Paris and its suburbs, within a range of 7.5 miles/12 kilometers, were assigned to the *département de la Seine*. The city was governed by the Commune.

In Paris, places with royal names were given revolutionary names: Place Louis XV was renamed Place de la Révolution; the Pont Louis XVI (now de la Concorde) became the Pont de la Révolution; Place Vendôme became Place des Piques; Place Royale became Place Nationale; Place du Trône (Square of the Throne) became Place du Trône Renversé (Square of the Overturned Throne); the Hôtel Royal des Invalides became the Hôtel National des Invalides; the Palais Royal became Palais Égalité, etc.

In 1792, the Assembly was replaced by the Convention when the radical Jacobins seized power from the relatively moderate Girondins. In 1793, Louis XVI (then called Citizen Louis Capet) and Marie-Antoinette went to the guillotine in the Place de la Révolution and the Reign of Terror began, led by Maximilien de Robespierre and the Committee of Public Safety. During the next ten months three thousand people were beheaded in Paris and another fourteen thousand elsewhere in France.

Three sites in Paris were witness to some of the bloodiest chapters of the Revolution: the Église Saint-Joseph-des-Carmes (70 Rue de Vaugirard, 6ᵉ), the Place de la Révolution, and the Place du Trône Renversé.

In August 1792, the Saint-Joseph-des-Carmes church was transformed into a prison for clerics who opposed the Revolution. On September 2, 116 priests were massacred in the garden of the church for refusing to swear to uphold the anti-religious revolutionary constitution. It was the first of what came to be known as the September Massacres where more than one thousand other prisoners—half the prison population of Paris—were summarily executed by "*septembriseurs*" ("Septembreakers"), presaging the violence of the Terror.

A single guillotine was used to carry out most of the political executions in Paris during the Revolution. Between January 21, 1793, and June 9, 1794, the guillotine was located at the Place de la Révolution.

During those sixteen and a half months 1,119 victims, including Louis XVI, Marie-Antoinette, and the Girondins, were beheaded. Their bodies were buried in a common grave in the former cemetery of a parish church where Louis XVIII later built an expiatory chapel in memory of his brother (29 Rue Pasquier, 8ᵉ).

On June 14, 1794, the guillotine was moved to the Place du Trône Renversé (now the Place de la Nation). During the next six weeks—until the Terror ended on July 27, 1794—1,306 men, women, and children, from all walks of life, were beheaded there. Their bodies were buried in two common graves nearby at what is now the Picpus Cemetery (35 Rue de Picpus, 12ᵉ). The names of the victims and their backgrounds (nobles, military, monks, nuns, commoners) are listed on the walls of a neighboring chapel (built in 1841), including the names of sixteen Carmelite nuns aged from twenty-nine to seventy-eight who mounted the scaffold, one after the other, singing hymns. In 1803, a separate cemetery was opened next to the common graves by a group of relatives of the aristocrats who were buried there, for their families. The Marquis de Lafayette (1757–1834) is buried there because his mother- and sister-in-law were among the victims.

Sick of the executions, on 9 Thermidor Year II of the French Revolutionary Calendar (July 27, 1794) the National Convention arrested Robespierre, beginning what became known as the Thermidorian Reaction. On July 28, the guillotine was moved back to the Place de la Révolution, where Robespierre and 104 of his supporters were executed over the following three days.

In 1795, the Convention approved a new constitution that vested executive authority in a five-member Directory (*Directoire*) appointed by parliament, and the Place de la Révolution was renamed Place de la Concorde. The worst of the Revolution was over.

During the Directory's four years in power, France was continuously at war with foreign coalitions and its economy was collapsing. The directors increasingly relied on the army—and especially on the popular young general Napoléon Bonaparte—to remain in power.

Building Works

The streets built during the Revolution were all constructed by private investors. On the Left Bank, in 1790 the Comte de Provence (the future Louis XVIII), owner of the Palais de Luxembourg, subdivided the western third of the Jardin du Luxembourg and built the Rues Madame, de Fleurus, and Jean Bart in the 6th arrondissement. (The neighboring Rue Guynemer had been built in 1778.) On the Right Bank, the Rue Mandar (1792–1795, architect Charles-François Mandar) and the Rue des Colonnes (1793–1795), the latter in the Greek Revival style, were both built in subdivisions in the 2nd arrondissement.

Apart from the highly symbolic demolition of the Bastille, which began the day after its fall on July 14, 1789, and took more than two years to complete, the principal impact of the Revolution on the architecture of Paris resulted from the confiscation of property by the government, now in the hands of the Third Estate (commoners, who represented 98 percent of the population), in retaliation against the First Estate (the clergy) and the Second Estate (the nobility).

Between 1789 and 1790, the new Assembly voted first to close the churches and monasteries and suppress the monastic orders and then to confiscate and sell off their lands and property. The "de-Christianization" of France followed. All the great abbeys that had been built around the historic center of Paris during the Middle Ages disappeared. Churches and monasteries were vandalized and became Temples of Reason or warehouses, or were put to other public use.

On the Île de la Cité, Notre-Dame was used to store provisions and the Sainte-Chapelle to store archives.

On the Left Bank, the Église Saint-Germain-des-Prés was used to store saltpeter; the Abbaye Sainte-Geneviève became the Lycée Henri IV (located behind the Panthéon); the Val-de-Grâce Church became a military hospital; the Couvent des Petits-Augustins became the Museum of French Monuments and later the School of Fine Arts (*l'École des Beaux Arts*); and the Église Saint-Sulpice became a place of worship of the Supreme Being (*l'Être Suprême*). The fields of the Enclos des Chartreux, a Carthusian monastery immediately to the south of the Luxembourg Palace, were added to the Luxembourg Garden, opening up an imposing view all the way to the Observatory—a distance of nearly 1 mile/1.5 kilometers.

In 1791, the National Assembly voted to transform the recently completed Église Sainte-Geneviève into a "Temple of Great Men" where the remains of distinguished French citizens should be buried, modeled on the Pantheon in Rome, which had been used as a mausoleum since the sixteenth century. It also approved a new text to be engraved over the entrance: "*Aux Grands Hommes La Patrie Reconnaissante*" ("To the Great Men, the Grateful Homeland"). Soon thereafter the windows in the façade were bricked up to make the interior darker and more solemn. The first person *panthéonisé* was Honoré Gabriel Riqueti, comte de Mirabeau, a moderate leader during the early stages of the Revolution who tried and failed to persuade Louis XVI to accept a constitutional monarchy. Mirabeau was buried in the Panthéon only three days after his death in 1791, but his remains were removed in 1794 when the political winds shifted and he was declared an enemy of the people. The same thing happened with the remains of martyred revolutionary Jean-Paul Marat. To prevent a recurrence, in 1795 the new Convention decreed that no one should be placed in the Pantheon who had not been dead for at least ten years. The building was restored to the Catholic Church by Louis XVIII in 1816.

On the Right Bank, the cloister of the Couvent des Célestins was used first to store wood during the Revolution and then as a *caserne de gendarmerie* (police barracks) under the Consulate. (The current Caserne des Célestins de la Garde Républicaine at 18 Boulevard Henri IV, 4ᵉ, with its stables and riding ring, was built on the site of the former monastery between 1895 and 1901, following the construction of Boulevard Henri IV in 1879.) The church of the Couvent des Minimes (built in 1623 on part of the land occupied by the Hôtel des Tournelles, thanks to Marie de Médicis) was demolished in 1801; in 1813, the cloister was made into a *caserne de gendarmerie* (which was rebuilt in 1925). During the Revolution, Louis XVI and his family were imprisoned in the *donjon* of the Temple Enclosure. In 1794, the venerable Abbaye Saint-Martin-des-Champs became the *Conservatoire* (now *Musée*) *des Arts et Métiers* (Conservatory of Arts and Trades, a museum dedicated to industrial design, located at 60 Rue Réaumur, 3ᵉ). Of all the monasteries and convents from medieval Paris, Saint-Martin-des-Champs is the only one that still has the look and feel of a monastery.

Many more churches and monasteries were demolished and the land they were on was subdivided by *speculateurs* for development over the course of the nineteenth century, transforming the urban landscape of Paris. As just two examples among many, the cloister of the Dominican monastery located at today's Place Saint-Thomas-d'Aquin, 7ᵉ, was first used to store weapons and later became the Hôtel de l'Artillerie. It was acquired by the prestigious École des Sciences Politiques from the Ministère de la Défense in 2016 and is now being transformed into a new campus scheduled to open in 2022. In the Enclos du Temple, which dated back to the twelfth century, Napoléon Iᵉʳ demolished the *donjon*, the church, and the wall surrounding the enclosure in 1808, but the abbot's palace and outbuildings were used as a Benedictine convent until 1848 and then as army barracks. Those buildings were demolished in 1853 and the land was subdivided. On the site of the Temple Enclosure were constructed the Square du Temple in 1857, along with five roads, the town hall (*mairie*) for the 3rd arrondissement, a nursery school (*école maternelle*), a market (*le marché du Carreau du Temple*), and several apartment buildings. There is nothing left of the original Enclos du Temple.

On February 9, 1792, the Assembly confiscated the property of aristocrats who had fled the country. Their *hôtels particuliers*—especially in the 7th arrondissement—became the seat of the Senate (the Palais du Luxembourg), the seat of the National Assembly (the Palais Bourbon), and many ministries, and later the residences of the president of France (the Palais de l'Élysée), the prime minister (the Hôtel de Matignon), and the president of the National Assembly (the Hôtel de Lassay, adjoining the Palais Bourbon). When Louis XVI was imprisoned on October 10, 1792, his property was also confiscated, including the Louvre Palace.

On August 14, 1792, the Assembly decreed that all royal statues, bas-reliefs, and other monuments be removed, unleashing what one author described as "the Saint Bartholomew's Day of royal statues." Among the many "victims" were the equestrian statues of Henri IV on the Pont Neuf, of Louis XIII in the Place des Vosges, of Louis XIV in the Place Louis-le-Grand (now Vendôme) and the Place des Victoires, and of Louis XV in the Place Louis XV (then de la Révolution and now de la Concorde). A year later the Commune ordered the destruction of the twenty-eight statues of kings in the gallery above the three great doors of Notre Dame Cathedral, which was promptly carried out by the people, not realizing that the statues were not of kings of France but of Israel and Judah.

On October 10, 1793, one year after the imprisonment of Louis XVI, the Grande Galerie du Louvre, along the Seine, opened as the *Musée Central des Arts de la République*—the precursor of today's Louvre Museum. Under the First Empire, the museum was renamed the *Musée Napoléon*, in recognition of the priceless contributions to its collection from art seized during his many military campaigns, and the palace was known as the *Palais des Arts*. Until 1855, the primary purpose of the museum was to train artists by allowing them to copy the masterpieces in the museum's collection; the public was only admitted on Sundays.

Also in 1793, the *Musée Nationale d'Histoire Naturelle* opened in the newly dubbed *Jardin des Plantes* (formerly the *Jardin Royal des Plantes Médicinales*, established by Louis XIII in 1635).

First Consul—Bonaparte (1799–1804)

After his success at the head of the French army in Italy in 1797, culminating in his decisive victory over the Austrians at the Battle of Rivoli, and his failure in Egypt in 1798, when the French fleet was destroyed by Horatio Nelson at the Battle of the Nile (also known as the Battle of Aboukir Bay), General Napoléon Bonaparte (1769–1821) returned to Paris in 1799 to stage a coup d'état and seize power as first consul of the three-member Consulate (*Consulat*), ending the French Revolution and beginning the Napoleonic era in which France would come to dominate most of continental Europe.

When Napoléon won the Battle of Marengo in the Piedmont region of Italy in June 1800, the population of Paris had declined to 547,000, and the population of France had increased to thirty-three million.

Streets in Paris named after Napoléon's victories in Italy include the Rue de Rivoli (1ᵉʳ, 4ᵉ), Rue de Marengo (1ᵉʳ), Rue du Pont-de-Lodi (6ᵉ), and the Pont d'Arcole between the Hôtel de Ville and the Île de la Cité. Napoléon III added the Boulevard Magenta (10ᵉ) and the Rue de Solférino (7ᵉ), named after his victories in Italy in 1859.

During the rare period without war between 1800 and 1805, Napoléon Ier focused on reforming France. His initiatives during that period included:

- 1800: New *départements* set up during the Revolution were placed under the charge of prefects appointed by the central government; Paris was included within the *département de la Seine*, administered by a *préfet* who replaced the mayor of Paris.
- 1801: Introduction of the metric system.*
- 1802: The Concordat with Pope Pius VII reestablished the Roman Catholic Church as "the religion of the greater majority of Frenchmen," with the state responsible for all churches.**
- 1802: New national police force established.
- 1802: Reform of the *lycées* (state secondary schools), École Polytechnique (founded 1794), École Normale Supérieure (founded 1794); reopening of the Sorbonne, which was closed during the Revolution, in 1808.
- 1802: Establishment of the Légion d'Honneur, headquartered in the Hôtel de Salm since 1804.
- 1804: Introduction of the Code Civil (later known as the Code Napoléon), followed by the Codes of Civil Procedure, Commercial Law, Criminal Procedure, and the Penal Code.

THE FIRST EMPIRE—NAPOLÉON IER (1804–1814)

In 1804, Napoléon Ier crowned himself "Emperor of the French" at the Cathédrale Notre-Dame de Paris at age thirty-five, and then began the Napoleonic Wars against various coalitions of European powers. In 1805,

---

* One of two surviving marble meters, out of the 16 standard meters installed throughout Paris in 1796–1797 in order to familiarize Parisians with the new unit of measurement, is still affixed to the wall at the end of the arcade at 36 Rue de Vaugirard, 6e.

** In 1907–1908, ownership of all churches and chapels was transferred to the municipalities where they were located, with responsibility for their maintenance and repair. The state retained ownership of the eighty-seven cathedrals in France.

Napoléon Iᵉʳ defeated the Austrians at Ulm, and the Austrians and Russians at Austerlitz, which brought about the collapse of the Holy Roman Empire. In 1806, he defeated the Prussians at Iéna and Auerstaedt. In 1807, he won the Battles of Eylau, Friedland, and Tilsit in East Prussia. On July 5-6, 1809, Napoléon Iᵉʳ won the Battle of Wagram (near Vienna) against the Austrians. It was his last victory. Paris avenues, streets, squares, and bridges are named after all these victories.

Napoléon Iᵉʳ had conquered nearly all of continental Europe. Austria and Prussia were nominally allied with France, as were the thirty-six German states that made up the Confederation of the Rhine formed at Napoléon Iᵉʳ's instigation following his victory at the Battle of Austerlitz. Russia, at war with the Ottoman Empire, was neutral. Only Britain, Sicily, and Sweden held out against Napoléon Iᵉʳ. Three of his brothers were kings—of Spain (Joseph), Holland (Louis), and Westphalia (Jérôme).

In 1810, Napoléon Iᵉʳ divorced Josephine, whom he had married in 1796 but who bore him no heir, in order to marry Archduchess Marie-Louise of Austria (1791–1847). In 1811, Napoléon II (*l'Aiglon*, the king of Rome) was born. He died of tuberculosis in Vienna in 1832.

In 1811, the twelve *communes* of Paris during the Revolution were made into one, divided into twelve *arrondissements* and administered by a prefect appointed by the emperor.

On June 24, 1812, Napoléon Iᵉʳ invaded Russia with an army of six hundred thousand soldiers and two hundred thousand horses. It was the largest army ever mobilized in Europe. Half the soldiers were French; the rest were Italian, Austrian, Polish, and German. On September 7, Napoléon Iᵉʳ narrowly won the pyrrhic and inconclusive Battle of Borodino, where the Grande Armée suffered thirty thousand casualties, including forty-three generals. According to Talleyrand, it was "the beginning of the end." With the Grande Armée approaching, the Russians evacuated Moscow. After the French entered Moscow on September 14, the Russians set the city on fire, destroying it, to deprive the French army of shelter and provisions. After waiting in vain for Czar Alexander to surrender, Napoléon Iᵉʳ began his retreat on October 19, but the exhausted and starving Grande Armée was relentlessly pursued by both the Russian army and the Russian winter. After a final desperate battle to cross the

Berezina River at the end of November,* what was left of the Grande Armée was finally able to escape Russia on December 14, bringing an end to the disastrous Russian Campaign. Fewer than one hundred thousand soldiers survived.

The Russian Campaign marked the turning point in the Napoleonic Wars. Prussia and Austria soon broke their imposed alliance with France and joined Russia, the United Kingdom, Portugal, Sweden, Spain, and a number of German states in the War of the Sixth Coalition. On October 19, 1813, Napoléon Ier was decisively defeated by the Sixth Coalition armies at Leipzig, in Saxony, and was compelled to return to France. The Confederation of the Rhine was dissolved, and Napoléon Ier lost control of the territories east of the Rhine.

Following their victory at Leipzig, the Russian, Austrian, and German armies invaded France. After three months of fighting, on March 31, 1814, the Russians, led by Czar Alexander, captured Paris and Cossacks camped on the Champs-Élysées.** On April 6, Napoléon Ier abdicated. On April 28, he was exiled to Elba, 12 miles/20 kilometers off the coast of Tuscany. Louis XVI's young son, the titular Louis XVII, having died in prison in June 1795, his brother the Comte de Provence was restored to the throne as Louis XVIII after twenty-three years in exile.

Not quite one year later, on February 26, 1815, Napoléon Ier escaped from Elba and returned to Paris, arriving on March 20. Louis XVIII fled to London. Napoléon Ier was defeated at Waterloo by the armies of England, under the command of the Duke of Wellington, and Prussia, led by General Gebhard Blücher, on June 18 and abdicated a second time on June 22, ending the period known as "the 100 Days." He was imprisoned on Saint Helena in the South Atlantic, one of the most remote islands in the world.

On July 6, 1815, Louis XVIII entered Paris for the second time, earning the nickname *"Louis deux-fois-neuf"* ("Louis two times nine").***

---

* In French, *"Bérézina"* is a synonym for "disaster."

** Some say that the name of the French *bistro* or *bistrot* originated during the Russian occupation of Paris in 1814, when Cossacks who wanted to be served quickly in restaurants would shout *"bystro!"* which means "quickly" in Russian.

*** Due to his fondness for oysters, Louis was also known as *"Louis des huîtres."*

The Congress of Vienna met between September 1814 and June 1815, ending twenty years of French revolutionary wars and Napoleonic wars, which had left two million people dead, and establishing a new balance of power in Europe. It marked the beginning of Britain's "imperial century," which lasted until 1914.

Napoléon Ier died on Saint Helena on May 5, 1821.*

Building Works

As might be expected, Napoléon Ier built many monuments to commemorate his military accomplishments, including:

- 1806–1810: Vendôme Column in the Place Vendôme, modeled on Trajan's Column in Rome, in commemoration of the Battle of Austerlitz in 1805. The column is 144 feet/44 meters high and was cast from bronze melted down from cannons captured by the Grande Armée.
- 1806–1809: Arc de Triomphe du Carrousel (architects Charles Percier and Pierre Fontaine). The triumphal arch was erected on the Place du Carrousel in front of the Tuileries Palace, which was named after a military horse parade (*carrousel*) conducted there by Louis XIV in 1662.
- 1806–1814: Creation of an Imperial Court of Honor (*cour d'honneur*) between the front of the Palais des Tuileries (the eastern façade) and the Place du Carrousel, and start of construction of the Arc de Triomphe de l'Étoile (completed by Louis-Philippe between 1833 and 1836).

Napoléon Ier also ordered the construction of a colossal 78-foot/24-meter-high bronze elephant to be cast from cannons captured at the Battle of Friedland and placed at the center of the Place de la Bastille, where it was to serve as a public fountain. Pending construction of the bronze

---

* The artist whose work best epitomizes the Revolutionary and Napoleonic periods is Jacques-Louis David (1748–1825). His monumental paintings of Napoléon Ier, Marat, and so many others line the walls of the Louvre.

Figure 51. The Place Vendôme, with the Opéra Garnier in the distance. The Vendôme Column has the third of four statues of Napoléon Ier on top. The first statue was taken down during the Restoration and replaced with the royal flag of the fleur de lys. The second statue, of Napoléon Ier in his trademark redingote and bicorne hat, with his hand slipped into his vest, was installed by Louis-Philippe in 1833. In 1863, Napoléon III replaced it with the statue in the photograph above of Napoléon Ier in a Roman toga; the second statue of Napoléon Ier in his army uniform now overlooks the Cour d'Honneur at the Hôtel des Invalides. After the column was pulled down during the Commune in 1871, it was rebuilt with the current statue—a copy of the original—in 1874. *PARIS ET SES ENVIRONS—* COLLECTION GEORGES SIROT (PHOTOGRAPH CIRCA 1890–1900).

Figure 52. The Arc de Triomphe du Carrousel in front of the Palais des Tuileries, between 1854 and 1870. PHOTOGRAPH BY ÉDOUARD DONTENVILLE OR DONTENVILL (1846–19?).

elephant (which never happened), a plaster and wood full-scale model was built and installed on the Place de la Bastille in 1814, where it remained until 1846, when it was finally removed due to its dilapidated condition. Its circular base, however, was used for the current July Column.

Beyond monuments to his military victories, Napoléon Ier's priority was to improve the dire state of the city's infrastructure. Major engineering projects initiated by Napoléon Ier—some of which were only completed years after his defeat at Waterloo—included:

- Construction between 1802 and 1835, of the first part of the Rue de Rivoli, from the Place de la Concorde alongside the Jardin des Tuileries to the Palais des Tuileries (Charles Percier and Pierre Fontaine), as well as of the neighboring Rues de Castiglione, Cambon, de Mondovi, and du Mont-Thabor, on land confiscated from convents during the Revolution. All but the Rue de Cambon were named after battles won in the Italian and Egyptian campaigns. Napoléon Ier incorporated arcades in the buildings alongside the Rue de Rivoli, reflecting their popularity in the Palais-Royal. It was planned to extend the Rue de Rivoli as far as the Hôtel de Ville.

- Construction of 15 fountains throughout the city, including the Fontaine du Palmier (1806–1808) in the new Place du Châtelet, and the Fontaine de Mars (1806–1808) at 129 Rue Saint-Dominique, 7e, near the Champ de Mars.

- Construction of the Pont des Arts (the first pedestrian bridge and first metal bridge in Paris) in 1804,[*] the Pont d'Austerlitz in 1805, and the Pont Saint-Louis and Pont d'Iéna in 1813 (increasing to 15 the total number of bridges in Paris).

- Construction of nearly 2 miles/3 kilometers of embankments (*quais*). Following severe flooding during the winter of 1801–1802, the quais surrounding the Île de la Cité were completed (except in front of the Hôtel-Dieu) and quais were built on the Left Bank from the Pont Royal west to the École Militaire.

- Construction of seven covered markets, including the Marché Saint-Germain (1813–1818), built on the site where the fair known as *la Foire Saint-Germain* had been held every year from 1176 until it closed in 1786.[**]

- Construction of the Marché aux Fleurs (Flower Market) on the Quai de la Corse on the Île de la Cité in 1808, on the site of a demolished church.

- Construction of five slaughterhouses in a ring around Paris.

- Opening in 1804 of the Père Lachaise Cemetery, the first cemetery established on the outskirts of Paris for health reasons (followed

---

[*] The original bridge was damaged when it was hit by a boat in 1979 and had to be rebuilt between 1982 and 1984.

[**] The current Marché Saint-Germain was built between 1976 and 1996 on a portion of the original fairgrounds, which extended to the future Rue de Tournon. The small courtyard in front of the restaurant at 8 Rue Mabillon, 6e, which is 10 feet/3 meters below today's street level, shows the level of the original fairgrounds.

by the Montparnasse Cemetery in 1824 and the Montmartre Cemetery in 1825).

- Construction of a series of enormous warehouses, known as *la Halle aux Vins*, on the Quai Saint-Bernard, 5^e, on the site of the former Abbaye Saint-Victor (where the Jussieu campus of the University of Paris has stood since 1960).

Figure 53. Extract from the Plan de Turgot (1739) showing the collection of buildings between the Cour Carrée and the Palais des Tuileries (which Napoléon III would finally remove), before Napoléon Ier began the construction of the first section of the Rue de Rivoli and the first section of the northern gallery of the Louvre Palace alongside it. Note the Palais-Royal on the left.

Figure 54. The first section of the Rue de Rivoli built by Napoléon Ier from the Place de la Concorde alongside the Jardin des Tuileries to the Palais des Tuileries. *PARIS ET SES ENVIRONS*—COLLECTION GEORGES SIROT (PHOTOGRAPH CIRCA 1890–1900).

Figure 55. The Pont des Arts and the Institut de France. PHOTOGRAPHER UNKNOWN.

By far Napoléon Ier's most ambitious infrastructure project was the construction of the Canal de l'Ourcq, which began in 1802 but was not completed until 1825. Prior to Napoléon Ier, the drinking water of Paris came primarily from the Seine and from 55 fountains in public squares that were supplied by two large hydraulically powered pumps next to the Pont Neuf and the Pont Notre-Dame dating back to the seventeenth century—known as *la Samaritaine* and *la Notre-Dame*, respectively—and two large steam pumps installed in 1781 at Chaillot and Gros Caillou. Soon after taking power, Napoléon Ier told the minister of interior Jean-Antoine Chaptal, "I want to do something great and useful for Paris." Chaptal replied immediately, "Give it water." The result was the Canal de l'Ourcq (engineer Pierre-Simon Girard), 63 miles/101 kilometers long, connecting the River Ourcq in Picardy to the Bassin de la Villette and the Canal Saint-Martin (3 miles/4.5 kilometers long, leading to the Bassin de l'Arsenal and the Seine), and to the Canal Saint-Denis (4 miles/6.6 kilometers long, leading to the suburban towns of Saint-Denis and Aubervilliers). The canals not only provided much-needed drinking water to Paris, they were also used for transportation of goods by horse-drawn barge, making La Villette one of the most important ports in France and industrial areas in Paris.

Other changes to the urban landscape of Paris during the Napoleonic period include:

- 1800: Opening of the Passage des Panoramas (the first covered *passage* in Paris).
- 1802–1808: Demolition of the Grand Châtelet (originally a fortress but at the time a collection of buildings last rebuilt by Louis XIV in 1684 that included a court and a prison, among other functions related to the administration of justice) and construction of the first Place du Châtelet in its place, with the Fontaine du Palmier (with its palm trunk) at its center.
- 1806–1810: Construction of a new portico on the Palais Bourbon to match the classical portico of the unfinished Madeleine across the Seine at the top of the Rue Royale. Napoléon Ier planned to

Figure 56. The Grand Châtelet in 1750, before its demolition in 1802. The Pont au Change, lined with buildings, is behind it. RECONSTITUTION BY T. J. H. HOFFBAUER.

Figure 57. The first Place du Châtelet in 1851, just before its demolition by Haussmann. PHOTOGRAPH BY LOUIS ADOLPHE HUMBERT DE MOLARD (1800–1874).

Figure 58. The Chambre des Députés (formerly the Palais Bourbon, now the Assemblée Nationale), between 1860 and 1870. PHOTOGRAPH BY PIERRE EMONTS OR EMONDS (1831–1870).

Figure 59. The Bourse de Paris. *PARIS ET SES ENVIRONS*—COLLECTION GEORGES SIROT (PHOTOGRAPH CIRCA 1890–1900).

erect a *Temple de la Gloire de la Grande Armée* (Temple to the Glory of the Great Army), but work stopped when he was deposed.

- 1806–1813: Reconstruction after a fire of the Halle au Blé (Wheat Market, architect François-Joseph Bélanger), which would become the Bourse de Commerce (Commodities Exchange) in 1889.
- 1807–1813: Construction of the Bourse de Paris (Stock Exchange, architect Alexandre-Théodore Brongniart).

The triumphal arches, victory columns, and temple-like porticoes of the Palais Bourbon, the Madeleine, and the Bourse de Paris all reflect Napoléon Ier's ambition to transform Paris into a "new Rome."

Napoléon Ier had more plans for Paris, but he ran out of time. His grandest plan, drawn up by the architect Auguste Hibon in 1811, was to build a vast palace to be called the Palais du Roi de Rome, after the title that he had given to his son, on the site of the current Palais de Chaillot on the Place du Trocadéro, with extensive grounds and administrative and military buildings stretching from the École Militaire to the Bois de Boulogne.

CHAPTER 7

The Restoration and the July Monarchy
(1814–1848)

THE BOURBON RESTORATION (1814–1830)

Louis XVIII (1755/1814–1824) returned to Paris for the second time in 1815, after the Battle of Waterloo. He died in 1824 without an heir

Figure 60. "Liberty Leading the People" in commemoration of the July Revolution of 1830. DRAWING AND LITHOGRAPH BY ADOLPHE MOUILLERON (1820–1881).

and was succeeded by his younger brother, the former Duc d'Artois, who became Charles X (1757/1824–1830/1836). The new Bourbon regime of the Restoration was a constitutional monarchy, unlike the absolutist Ancien Régime before the Revolution.

In 1824, the population of Paris was 715,000. Approximately two-thirds of Parisians lived on the Right Bank, and one-third on the Left Bank.

As a result of Charles X's repressive policies, the "July Revolution" took place on July 27, 28, and 29, 1830 (dubbed *"Les Trois Glorieuses"* ["The Glorious Three"] by Balzac). Charles abdicated and went into exile in Britain.

On the cultural front, the novel became the predominant form of Western literature in the nineteenth century. French authors described the age: *Le Rouge et le Noir* (*The Red and the Black*), written by Stendhal (1783–1842) and published in 1830, depicts French society under the Bourbon Restoration (1814–1830). *Le Père Goriot*, written by Honoré de Balzac (1799–1850) and published in 1835, portrays Parisian society in 1819, during the reign of Louis XVIII. *Les Misérables*, written by Victor Hugo (1802–1885) and published in 1862, takes place in Paris between 1815 and the uprising on June 5 and 6, 1832 ("the June Rebellion," discussed below).

Building Works

Louis XVIII was determined to restore the prestige of the Bourbon dynasty. First, he transferred the remains of Louis XVI and Marie-Antoinette from the former cemetery of the parish church la Madeleine (unrelated to the Église de la Madeleine at the top of the Rue Royale that was finally consecrated in 1842), where they had been buried after their beheading on the Place de la Révolution in 1793, to the Basilica of Saint-Denis, where all but three French kings had been buried since the tenth century. Then, on January 21, 1815—twenty-two years to the day after Louis XVI's execution—Louis XVIII laid the first stone for an Expiatory Chapel (*Chapelle Expiatoire*) dedicated to his brother and sister-in-law to be constructed on the site where they had been buried. The chapel, which was designed by Pierre Fontaine and is located at 29 Rue Pasquier, 8ᵉ, was inaugurated in 1826. The chapel and the former cemetery, where the bodies of many of the 1,119 people guillotined on the Place de la Révolution between 1792 and 1794 were buried in the same common grave as the king and queen, are now situated in the Square Louis XVI (created by Haussmann in 1862), the only public place in Paris to bear the monarch's name.

In 1816, Louis issued a decree ordering the replacement of the royal statues destroyed during the Revolution, and began a long campaign to remove Napoleonic emblems from the monuments and buildings of Paris. Perhaps most famously, he removed the bronze statue of Napoléon Ier as Marcus Aurelius from the top of the Vendôme Column and replaced it with the royal flag of the fleur de lys.

Between 1822 and 1825, the Canal Saint-Martin was completed, finishing a project begun by Napoléon Ier in 1802, along with its 9 foot-bridges and 9 locks to account for the 89-foot/27-meter difference in height between the Bassin de la Villette and the Bassin de l'Arsenal, next to the Seine.

Between 1823 and 1836, the Église Notre-Dame-de-Lorette was built in the neoclassical style at 18 bis Rue de Châteaudun, 9e. The architect was Hippolyte Lebas.

The Restoration also saw the beginning of large property development projects on the outskirts of Paris.

In 1819–1820, the financier Jean-Joseph Lapeyrière and the architect Auguste Constantin started to create the subdivision in the Quartier des Porcherons in what in 1860 would become the 9th arrondissement. The neighborhood bordered by the Rues des Martyrs, de La Rochefoucauld, and Saint-Lazare was soon dubbed "*la Nouvelle Athènes*" ("New Athens") because of the architectural style of its buildings deemed by some to be reminiscent of Ancient Greece. Through the Second Empire it was popular with writers, actors, musicians, and painters, and became the center of the Romantic movement in Paris, which developed in France and the rest of Europe in response to the rationality of the Enlightenment and the changes brought by the Industrial Revolution.

In 1824, Jacques-Léonard Violet purchased 260 acres/105 hectares on the Plaine de Grenelle, which in 1860 became part of the 15th arrondissement, now the most populous arrondissement in Paris. The land was originally owned by the Abbaye Saint-Germain-des-Prés, but was confiscated during the Revolution. It was situated in the agricultural village of Vaugirard, whose name was derived from the first name of one of the abbey's monks, Gérard de Moret (*Val Girard*). Violet and his associate Alphonse Letellier subdivided the property and effectively created a new town complete with residential, commercial, and industrial districts, that they named Beau-Grenelle. It was the largest development in Paris to date. In 1830, Grenelle became a village in its own right.

In 1827, the long and narrow Île aux Cygnes (Isle of Swans), an artificial island in the Seine off the 15th arrondissement, was created to protect the brand-new Pont de Grenelle. (The Île aux Cygnes should not be confused with an earlier Île des Cygnes, a natural island formed from five islets that was attached to the Champ de Mars at the end of the eighteenth century.)

LOUIS-PHILIPPE (1773/1830–1848/1850)

Louis-Philippe, Duc d'Orléans, was a member of the so-called junior (*cadet*) branch of the ruling House of Bourbon. The House of Orléans was founded by Philippe I, Duc d'Orléans, younger brother of Louis XIV. From Louis XV until Charles X, the kings of France came from the senior branch of the House of Bourbon who were direct descendants of Louis XIV. Normally, the cadet branch would succeed to the throne of France only if the senior branch died out. The abdication of Charles X presented an unforeseen scenario.

Louis-Philippe's father was Louis Philippe II, Duc d'Orléans, who supported the Revolution and changed his name to Philippe Égalité to make the point. He even voted for the execution of his cousin Louis XVI, which made him popular with the revolutionaries if not the nobles, but was himself beheaded during the Reign of Terror.

During the July Revolution, the Marquis de Lafayette (1757–1834) was appointed commander of the National Guard. Fearful that creating another republic would lead to civil war, he successfully persuaded the provisional government that Louis-Philippe, son of Philippe Égalité, had the right credentials to ascend to the throne of the "July Monarchy" as "King of the French" as opposed to "King of France." At age fifty-six, Louis-Philippe became the one and only Orléanist king, setting the stage for the competition between the two branches of the House of Bourbon as pretenders to the throne of France that continues to this day.

Louis-Philippe was also known as the "Citizen King" or the "Bourgeois King." To prove it, he was the first French king to wear trousers instead of *culottes* (breeches) and stockings. Indeed, it was during the July Monarchy that the bourgeoisie became the dominant class and capitalism became the dominant economic system in France. Louis-Philippe was married to Queen Marie-Amélie and they lived in the Palais des Tuileries.

On June 5 and 6, 1832, anti-monarchists revolted in an event known as the "June Rebellion." The insurrection was put down in less than a week.

In his role as the *"roi des Français,"* Louis-Philippe took several actions to reconcile the different constituencies of the French people with the July Monarchy.

In 1830, Louis-Philippe transformed the Église Sainte-Geneviève into the Panthéon for the second time, as an expression of his sympathy for revolutionary values. The crypt remained closed to the public, however, and no new remains were added. In 1851, physicist Léon Foucault (1819–1868) conducted a demonstration of diurnal motion by suspending a pendulum from the dome of the Panthéon. (A copy of Foucault's pendulum has hung from the dome of the Panthéon since 1995.) In 1852, Emperor Napoléon III restored the building to the Catholic Church, with the title of "National Basilica."

Between 1833 and 1836, Louis-Philippe completed the construction, begun by Napoléon Ier between 1806 and 1814, of the Arc de Triomphe de l'Étoile. It stands an impressive 164 feet/50 meters high and 148 feet/45 meters wide. Inside the arch are inscribed the names of 158 battles and 660 mostly military leaders of the Revolutionary and Napoleonic Wars.

In 1837, Louis-Philippe transformed the Château de Versailles into a museum *"dédié à toutes les gloires de la France"* ("dedicated to all the glories of France").

Figure 61. The Arc de Triomphe de l'Étoile. *PARIS ET SES ENVIRONS*—COLLECTION GEORGES SIROT (PHOTOGRAPH CIRCA 1890–1900).

Figure 62. The July Column commemorating the three days of the July Revolution. PHOTOGRAPHER UNKNOWN.

In 1840, Louis-Philippe had Napoleon Ier's body brought back to France for reinterment in the Dome Church, and erected the *Colonne de Juillet* on the Place de la Bastille in commemoration of the July Revolution.

Despite these efforts, Louis-Philippe became increasingly unpopular over the course of his eighteen-year reign, surviving seven assassination attempts.

～

Honoré de Balzac's series of books known as *La Comédie Humaine*, including *Les Illusions Perdues* (three volumes, 1836–1843), describes the period during Louis-Philippe's reign. The iconic caricatures of Honoré Daumier (1808–1879) were seen everywhere during the July Monarchy.

COUNT RAMBUTEAU—*PRÉFET DE LA SEINE* (1833–1848)

Just as Napoléon III had Baron Haussmann to carry out his plans to modernize Paris (as we shall see in the next chapter), Louis-Philippe had Count Rambuteau. But Napoléon III was an emperor with a grand vision who allowed Haussmann to incur enormous debt to modernize Paris, whereas Louis-Philippe was a constitutional monarch trying to appeal to his different constituencies who incurred no debt to fund his modernization plans. As a consequence, Rambuteau's accomplishments were more modest than Haussmann's *Grands Travaux*.

Between 1833 and 1848, Claude-Philibert Barthelot, Comte de Rambuteau (1781–1869), served as the prefect of the Seine *département* under Louis-Philippe, with administrative responsibility for Paris and the surrounding area. Having been appointed the year after nineteen thousand Parisians had died in a cholera epidemic, Rambuteau considered his first duty as prefect to be to provide Parisians with "air, water and shade."

The historic center of Paris—the Île de la Cité, the Marais, and the Latin Quarter—was still a medieval labyrinth of dark and dingy streets and alleys. The magnificent *hôtels particuliers* built in the Marais during the sixteenth and seventeenth centuries had been abandoned by the aristocrats during the Revolution and were now occupied by squatters or used for industrial purposes. What once was the grandest part of Paris was now the poorest and most prone to disease.

In 1837, Rambuteau cut two new, intersecting roads through the Île de la Cité in an effort to improve the sanitary environment of this overcrowded neighborhood: the Rue d'Arcole and the Rue de Constantine (where the Rue de Lutèce now stands).

In 1833–1834, he built the Pont Louis-Philippe, a suspension bridge at the west end of the Île Saint-Louis, and the short (246 yards/225 meters) Rue du Pont-Louis-Philippe between the bridge and the Rue de Rivoli, in a first attempt to penetrate, or pierce (*percer*), the Marais.

Between 1834 and 1839, Rambuteau built the Rue Rambuteau, 1er and 4^{e}—0.6 mile/1 kilometer long and 32 feet/13 meters wide and equipped with sidewalks, gutters, fountains, and *urinoirs*—connecting the neighborhood of Les Halles with the Rue des Francs-Bourgeois in the Marais and truly "piercing" the Marais.

Figure 63. View of the Boulevard de la Madeleine from the Place de la Madeleine with the Église de la Madeleine on the left. *PARIS ET SES ENVIRONS—*COLLECTION GEORGES SIROT (PHOTOGRAPH CIRCA 1890–1900).

Rambuteau also rebuilt the Grands Boulevards from the Place de la Madeleine to the Place de la Bastille, a distance of nearly 3 miles/4.4 kilometers, adding sidewalks and installing a public lighting system of gas lamps. As a result of these works, starting in the 1830s the Grands Boulevards became the place to see and be seen. Balzac described them as "*le coeur de Paris*" ("the heart of Paris"). There were fifty-nine cafés between the Place de la Madeleine and the Place de la République. Favorite haunts on the fashionable Boulevard des Italiens (the nickname of the nearby Opéra Comique), on the border between the 2nd and 9th arrondissements, included the Café Riche (at 16), the Café Tortoni (at 20), the Maison Dorée restaurant (at 22, built in 1841), and the Café Frascati (at the corner of the Boulevard Montmartre and the Rue de Richelieu).

Farther east, many theaters were built on the Boulevard du Temple, on the border between the 3rd and 11th arrondissements, which was nicknamed the Boulevard du Crime because of the many crime melodramas performed there. Most of the theaters were demolished during the construction of the Place de la République as part of Haussmann's *Grands Travaux*.

Following the success of the Grands Boulevards, the word *boulevard* became generic, applying to any large road. An *avenue* came to mean a street lined with trees.

The July Monarchy was also responsible for the restoration of three medieval churches (the Sainte-Chapelle, the Église Saint-Germain-l'Auxerrois, and the Cathédrale Notre-Dame de Paris) and one Renaissance era church (the Église Saint-Eustache), all Paris icons.

In 1836, Félix Durban (1797–1870) and Jean-Baptiste Lassus (1807–1857) were appointed to undertake the restoration of the Sainte-Chapelle. In 1840, they were joined by Lassus's lifelong associate Eugène Viollet-le-Duc (1814–1879), considered to be the world's first restoration architect. Work, which included the construction of a new spire in 1853, was only completed in 1867.

In 1837, Lassus was also given responsibility for restoring the Église Saint-Germain-l'Auxerrois, across from the Colonnade du Louvre.

Figure 64. The Sainte-Chapelle under restoration, with its new spire. PHOTOGRAPH BY X PHOT.

Figure 65. The Church of Saint-Germain-l'Auxerrois in 1856, after its restoration and after surrounding buildings had been cleared by Haussmann, but before the construction of the town hall of the 1st arrondissement and the belltower to its left, creating the Place du Louvre. PHOTOGRAPH BY ÉDOUARD BALDUS (1813–1889).

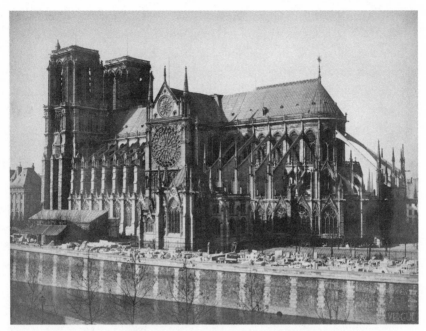

Figure 66. The Cathédrale Notre-Dame de Paris undergoing renovation, circa 1850. Note that there is no spire. PHOTOGRAPH BY GUSTAVE LE GRAY (1820–1884).

Figure 67. Notre-Dame after its renovation, with its new spire and statues on its western façade. *PARIS ET SES ENVIRONS*—COLLECTION GEORGES SIROT (PHOTOGRAPH CIRCA 1890–1900).

Between 1844 and 1866, Eugène Viollet-le-Duc and Lassus collaborated on the restoration of Notre-Dame, replacing the spire (1853–1859) which had fallen into disrepair and had been removed in 1786 and some of the bells, installing gargoyles, and replacing the twenty-eight statues of the kings of Judea and Israel. The heads of twenty-one of the statues that had been pulled down and decapitated during the Revolution were found in 1977 and are on display at the Musée de Cluny.*

Following damage suffered in a fire in 1844, architect Victor Baltard oversaw the complete restoration of the Église Saint-Eustache in Les Halles between 1846 and 1854.

Other construction projects undertaken during the July Monarchy, and related developments, include:

- 1832–1872: Construction of the École Nationale Supérieure des Beaux Arts (National School of Fine Arts), on the Quai Malaquais, 6ᵉ (entrance to courtyard at 14 Rue Bonaparte).

- 1833: Construction of the greenhouses (*serres*) in the Jardin des Plantes (architect Charles Rohault de Fleury), 5ᵉ.

- 1836: The thirty-three-hundred-year-old Luxor obelisk was erected in the Place de la Concorde, 1ᵉʳ. It took more than eight months to transport the obelisk from Egypt to Paris, and three hours to raise it upright on its granite pedestal in the center of the Place de la Concorde before two hundred thousand spectators. Diagrams showing how the obelisk was raised are engraved on its pedestal.

- 1836–1846: The Place de la Concorde was redesigned by Jacques-Ignace Hittorff, who added the 2 fountains and 8 stone monuments representing French cities (all restored in 2000).

* Viollet-le-Duc is also famous for his restoration of the medieval Château de Pierrefonds, on the edge of the Forest of Compiègne, northeast of Paris, and of the Cité de Carcassonne citadel, in the former Languedoc province in the south of France.

- 1838: The Champs-Élysées between the Rond-Point and the Étoile was transformed into an urban avenue soon to be lined with buildings.
- 1838–1851: Construction of the Sainte-Geneviève Library (Henri Labrouste), Place du Panthéon, 5ᵉ.
- 1839: Construction of the Orangerie (Alphonse de Gisors) in the Luxembourg Garden, 6ᵉ.
- 1840: Completion of the construction (begun in 1810) of the Palais d'Orsay (on the site of today's Musée d'Orsay), 7ᵉ, which was used to house the Conseil d'État (Council of State) and Cour des Comptes (Audit Office).
- 1842: Consecration of the Église de la Madeleine, 8ᵉ, modeled on the Roman temple *la Maison Carrée* in Nîmes. It was originally conceived by Napoléon Iᵉʳ in 1806 as a Temple to the Glory of the Great Army (*Temple à la Gloire de la Grande Armée*).

Figure 68. The Church of la Madeleine, circa 1860. PHOTOGRAPH BY ÉDOUARD BALDUS (1813–1889).

- 1844–1855: Construction of the Hôtel du Ministère des Affaires Étrangères (Jacques Lacornée), known as the *Quai d'Orsay*, in reference to its location, 7ᵉ.
- 1845: Law passed requiring sidewalks on all Paris streets.
- 1846–1857: Construction of the Basilique Sainte-Clotilde (named after the wife of Clovis), Rue Las Cases, 7ᵉ (with its imposing twin towers).
- 1847: The Île Louviers was connected to the Right Bank, just east of the Île Saint-Louis, 4ᵉ.

Three other significant changes to the urban landscape of Paris during Louis-Philippe's reign were the growing popularity of the *passage couvert* (gallery or arcade), the construction of the Thiers Fortifications, and the construction of the first railroad stations.

Passages

At 11 Boulevard Montmartre, 2ᵉ, is the entrance to the Passage des Panoramas, the oldest covered shopping arcade in Paris, which opened in 1800. It is 145 yards/133 meters long and is still full of shops and restaurants.

More than forty covered shopping *passages* or *galeries* were built on the Right Bank, mainly near the Grands Boulevards, between 1820 and 1850, often on the sites of former *hôtels particuliers*. Twenty *passages* were built in the 1820s alone; another nine were built between 1839 and 1847. The last *passage*, the Passage des Princes, was built in 1860.*

Haussmann's boulevards (all equipped with sidewalks) and the arrival of the *grands magasins* (department stores) led to the disappearance of most of the *passages*. Of the seventeen surviving *passages*, among the most interesting are (in order of arrondissement):

---

* The concept of the *passage* was adopted by other cities in France (for example, the impressive Passage Pommeraye in Nantes, built between 1841 and 1843) and abroad through the end of the nineteenth century. The Burlington Arcade in London, however, opened in 1819. The ultimate gallery is the enormous Galleria Vittorio Emanuele II in Milan (1867).

- Galerie Véro-Dodat (built in 1826), 19 Rue Jean-Jacques Rousseau, 1er.
- Galerie Vivienne (1823), 4 Rue des Petits-Champs, 2e.
- Galerie Colbert (1826), 6 Rue des Petits-Champs, 2e.
- Passage Vendôme (1827), 16 Rue Béranger, 3e.
- Passage des Panoramas (1800), 11 Boulevard Montmartre, 9e.
- Passage Jouffroy (1845), 10 Boulevard Montmartre, 9e—across from the Passage des Panoramas.
- Passage Verdeau (1846), 6 Rue de la Grange-Batelière, 9e—next to the Passage des Panoramas and the Passage Jouffroy.

Thiers Fortifications

Between 1840 and 1846, Prime Minister Adolphe Thiers constructed the last of Paris's 7 walls, known as the Thiers Fortifications. The wall was built for defensive purposes well outside the Farmers General Wall, which remained the city limit. He also built 16 detached forts located 1 to 3 miles/1.5 to 5 kilometers outside the fortifications.

The Thiers Fortifications were 21 miles/35 kilometers long, and covered 19,280 acres/7,802 hectares. First a moat and then a sloping area outside the wall, called a *glacis*, extended outward from the Thiers Fortifications to the location of today's Boulevard Périphérique. The fortifications were approximately 55 yards/50 meters wide; the surrounding "no-man's-land" known as *la Zone* on which all construction was forbidden, was approximately 275 yards/250 meters wide. The *Rue Militaire* (which was improved to become the *Boulevards des Maréchaux* [Boulevards of the Marshals] after the Annexation of 1860) was constructed just inside *les Fortifs*. The wall was demolished in stages between 1919 and 1929.

Railroads

The railway network of France went from almost nothing in 1840 to 11,000 miles/18,000 kilometers in 1870. During Louis-Philippe's reign, the following stations opened or were under construction:

- 1837: Gare Saint-Lazare; inauguration of first railway line, from Paris to Saint-Germain-en-Laye.
- 1840: Gare d'Austerlitz, Gare Montparnasse.
- 1846: Gare du Nord.
- 1846: Gare Denfert-Rochereau.
- 1847: Gare de Lyon.
- 1849: Gare de l'Est.

The stations were ringed around the city, just inside the Farmers General Wall, which was the city limit. The first train stations were called *"embarcadères"* (quays, or embarkation points); later they were named *"gares"* (stations).

THE REVOLUTION OF JUNE 1848

Despite Rambuteau's efforts to modernize the city, most Parisians still lived in squalid conditions with refuse clogging the streets and sewage running directly into the Seine. One percent of the population owned 80 percent of the wealth; half lived in poverty. Crime was rampant. The stage was set for Paris's third revolution in sixty years, which caused a chain reaction of revolutions in most of Europe and in parts of Latin America.

The Revolution of June 1848, from June 23 through June 26—the "June Days" (*"les journées de juin"*), with its famous barricades—led to the abdication of Louis-Philippe, who fled to England, where he lived until his death in 1850. He was the last king of France.[*] On November 4, 1848, the National Assembly of the Second Republic passed a new constitution stipulating that executive power should be exercised by a President of the Republic to be elected by the people.

---

[*] Descendants whom so-called *Orléaniste* monarchists consider to be the rightful pretenders to the throne hold the title Count of Paris, reviving the Carolingian title (e.g., the late Henri d'Orléans [1933–2019], Comte de Paris). Royalists who support the claim to the throne of descendants of Charles X are known as *légitimistes*.

CHAPTER 8

The Second Republic and the
Second Empire (1848–1870)

THE SECOND REPUBLIC (1848–1851)

After the death in Vienna in 1833 of Napoléon Ier and Marie-Louise's only son (and child), who as Napoléon II was the titular Emperor of the French for two weeks after his father abdicated following his defeat at Waterloo, his cousin Louis-Napoléon Bonaparte (1808–1873) became the de facto heir of the Bonaparte dynasty. Louis-Napoléon was the son of Napoléon Bonaparte's younger brother Louis (who was the king of Holland between 1806 and 1810) and Josephine de Beauharnais's daughter Hortense from her first marriage. After growing up in exile in Switzerland and Italy with his mother, who was estranged from his father, Louis-Napoléon made two failed attempts to seize power in France—first in Strasbourg in 1836 and then in Boulogne in 1840. After the first failed coup, Louis-Philippe exiled Louis-Napoléon to the United States. After the second, Louis-Philippe imprisoned him in the Ham fortress in northern France. While in what he called the "university of Ham," Louis-Napoléon wrote essays and published articles on a variety of subjects, and a book entitled *L'Extinction du Pauperisme* (1844), about the causes of poverty in the French industrial working class, with proposed solutions. The book was widely circulated in France and was largely responsible for the popular support he enjoyed in the future. In 1846, Louis-Napoléon escaped and fled to England.

Following the June Days uprising in 1848, Louis-Napoléon was elected to the National Assembly and returned to Paris on September 24. On December 10, he was elected to a four-year term as the first (and only) president of France under the Second Republic, winning 74 percent of the vote. On December 2, 1851, limited to a single term by the constitution, Louis-Napoléon staged a coup d'état and declared himself first consul, as Napoléon Ier had done in 1799. Exactly one year later, on December 2, 1852, Louis-Napoléon declared himself Emperor Napoléon III.

THE SECOND EMPIRE—NAPOLÉON III (1852–1870)

One of Napoléon III's first acts as emperor was to marry the Spanish aristocrat Eugénie de Montijo (1826–1920), with whom he had one child in 1856, a son who was killed in 1879 while fighting in the Zulu War in South Africa.

Like his uncle Napoléon Ier, Napoléon III was constantly at war in an effort to reestablish France as a world power. In Europe, he fought the Crimean War (1854–1856) alongside the British against the Russians, triumphing at the Siege of Sevastopol (commemorated by the Boulevard de Sébastopol, 1er, 2e, 3e, and 4e) and the Battle of Malakoff (a suburb just south of Paris), and conducted military campaigns against the Austrians in Italy in 1859, which led to French victories at the Battles of Magenta (Boulevard de Magenta, 8e and 10e) and Solferino (Rue de Solférino, 7e). Outside Europe, Napoléon III enlarged the French empire through military expeditions in Algeria (initiated by Charles X in 1830), Senegal (1854–1865), Gabon (1862), and Cochinchina (1858–1867). He also intervened in China (1858–1860), Syria and Lebanon (1860–1861), and Mexico (1862–1867).

Back home, the arrival of the Industrial Revolution was delayed by the Revolution and the Napoleonic Wars, but France soon caught up. In the first decade of the Second Empire, industrial production and foreign trade both doubled.

As a result of industrialization, the population of Paris (as well as of other big cities in France) grew dramatically, from 786,000 in 1831 to

1,053,000 in 1851 to 1,825,000 (including 400,000 following the Annexation of 1860) in 1866.

The news was not all good. In 1862, Haussmann wrote that over half the population lived "in poverty bordering on destitution." In 1866, cheap horse meat started to be sold at *boucheries chevalines*.

Building Works

Charles Marville (1813–1879) photographed Paris before and after Haussmann. His photographs, and those of his contemporaries including Gustave Le Gray (1820–1884)—many of which are reproduced here—are a vivid record of the transformational effect that the *Grands Travaux* had on Paris.

When Napoléon III came to power, he was determined to finish the job started by his uncle and continued by Louis-Philippe and Rambuteau, and turn Paris into a modern city. Over the previous eight hundred years Paris had grown organically, expanding in ever-wider concentric circles with the construction—and then demolition—of each of the city's walls. After Henri IV, new neighborhoods had mostly developed on greenfield sites to the west of the city, on both the Left and especially the Right Bank, but each neighborhood remained distinct and somewhat isolated. The Marais, the Île de la Cité, and the Latin Quarter—the oldest, poorest, and most crowded parts of the city—were also hotbeds of disease: After the cholera epidemic in 1832, which took nineteen thousand lives, nineteen thousand more Parisians died in another epidemic in 1849. Napoléon III wanted to reclaim the center of Paris and to provide all Parisians with a healthy environment.

In Napoléon III's words, he wanted to "*aérer, unifier, et embellir*" Paris—"to open up, tie together, and beautify" Paris. To tie the city together, he personally marked in blue, red, yellow, and green (in order of priority) the streets that he wanted to build on a map of Paris that he kept in his office in the Tuileries Palace. It was called the "colored plan," but unfortunately it has been lost.

Napoléon III's priority was to build a network of roads to connect the various neighborhoods of Paris and turn the city into a harmonious whole. In particular, he wanted to connect the new train stations on the edge of the old city, and the new neighborhoods annexed to Paris, with its center, to open up the city. To give Paris air and make it a healthier place to live, he wanted to build parks and *squares* (urban gardens), large and small, in and around the city, and to plant trees alongside his new, wide avenues and boulevards. Along with clean air, Napoléon III determined to give the city clean water. To beautify Paris, he resolved to open up space around its monuments to set them off to their best advantage. The new roads and the squares (*places*) that connected them should not only be functional, they should be beautiful.

Not since the Romans had anyone taken such an ambitious and comprehensive approach to planning the city. Napoléon III's model was London, where he had lived in exile, which had been entirely rebuilt since the Great Fire of 1666 and was then the most modern city in Europe.

Napoléon III conceived the master plan, and Haussmann translated it into hundreds of specific action plans that he and his team of architects and engineers then executed over his nearly seventeen prolific years as prefect of the Seine.

BARON HAUSSMANN—*PRÉFET DE LA SEINE* (1853–1870)
On June 22, 1853, Napoléon III appointed Georges-Eugène Haussmann (1809–1891), a Protestant from Alsace, prefect of the Seine and instructed him to carry out his ambitious plans for the modernization of Paris. The pharaonic works that followed were known as *les Grands Travaux* (the Great Works), which according to Haussmann's *Mémoires* (1893) took place in three phases.

First Phase: La Grande Croisée de Paris (1853–1859)
During the Middle Ages, visitors to Paris entered the city from the east, passing through the Porte de la Bastille in the Charles V Wall and proceeding along the Rue Saint-Antoine, which dated back to Roman times, to the Place de Grève, and then up the Rue Saint-Honoré to the Louvre, or across the Grand Pont to the Île de la Cité and the Palais de la Cité

(and later the Conciergerie) and Notre-Dame. Henri IV's construction of the Place Royale (des Vosges) just inside the Porte de la Bastille and the development of the Marais as an aristocratic quarter confirmed the importance of the eastern entrance to the city.

During the reigns of Louis XIV, XV, and XVI and the development of the Quartiers Richelieu, Saint-Honoré, Chaussée d'Antin, and Poissonière—all on the Right Bank—the primary entrance moved to the west side of the city. Visitors entered Paris through the Porte de l'Étoile in the Farmers General Wall, passed around the Arc de Triomphe before proceeding down the Champs-Élysées and around the Place de la Concorde, then down the new Rue de Rivoli (built by Napoléon Ier, which stopped at the Tuileries Palace), left on the new Rue de Castiglione to the Place Vendôme, and on to the Grands Boulevards. While the route was impressive, the straight section from the Arc de Triomphe to the Louvre only covered half the distance across the city, and the Grands Boulevards stopped at the Marais. A much more comprehensive network of roads was required to permit easier travel from north to south and from east to west.

La Grande Croisée de Paris, a great cross in the center of Paris, had been proposed by the Convention during the Revolution. Napoléon Ier had started it, and Napoléon III was determined to finish it. Its completion was the first phase of the renovation of Paris undertaken by Haussmann.

La Grande Croisée was not the first great cross to be built in Paris. During the Gallo-Roman era, the Romans built the Rue Saint-Jacques as their primary north-south road (*cardo maximus*) on the Left Bank, and the Rue Saint-Martin as the *cardo maximus* on the Right Bank (the Rue Saint-Denis was a second *cardo*). They built a road near today's Rue des Écoles as the primary east-west road (*decumanus maximus*) on the Left Bank, and the Rue Saint-Antoine (which was effectively extended to the west by the Rue Saint-Honoré) as the *decumanus maximus* on the Right Bank. Rather than simply widen the *cardo maximus* and *decumanus maximus* built by the Romans that were still the principal north-south and east-west roads in the center of Paris, Haussmann chose to make "*percées*" (openings)—new roads in built-up areas whose construction required the expropriation and demolition of existing streets and buildings.

The boulevards and streets that formed Haussmann's *Grande Croisée* were built parallel to the ancient Roman roads, in the heart of the historic center of Paris. On the Right Bank, Haussmann's *decumanus maximus* was the Rue de Rivoli (running parallel to the Rue Saint-Honoré and the western end of the Rue Saint-Antoine), which merged into the eastern end of the Rue Saint-Antoine. His *cardo maximus* was made up of the connecting Boulevards de Strasbourg and de Sébastopol (parallel to the Rue Saint-Denis), leading from the Gare de l'Est train station to the center of the city. On the Left Bank, Haussman's *cardo maximus* was the Boulevard Saint-Michel (parallel to the Rue Saint-Jacques). His *decumanus maximus* was the Boulevard Saint-Germain (parallel to the Rue des Écoles, which Napoléon III built between 1852 and 1855 but which Haussmann deemed inadequate to serve as the *decumanus maximus*).

The Great Cross on the Right Bank required the construction of the new Rue de Rivoli to connect the Place de la Concorde with the Place de la Bastille. Napoléon Ier built the first part of the Rue de Rivoli from the Place de la Concorde alongside the Jardin des Tuileries as far as the Palais des Tuileries, and Napoléon III ordered Haussmann to complete it before the opening of the Paris Universal Exposition of 1855, only two years later.

Haussmann's task was made easier by a new law adopted in February 1851 that gave the prefect of the Seine the authority to expropriate all the land on either side of a new street *"pour cause d'utilité publique"* ("for public use"). Moreover, he did not have to report to the Parliament, only to the emperor. While some funds for the construction of the Rue de Rivoli were provided by the state, additional financing was provided by a new investment bank, Crédit Mobilier, in exchange for the right to develop the real estate on either side of the new street. (Crédit Mobilier was created by brothers Émile and Isaac Pereire, whose grandfather had immigrated to France from Portugal in 1741.) This became the preferred method for financing the construction of most of Haussmann's many boulevards, avenues, and streets.

The huge sums required to fund the construction of the additions to the Louvre, practically all the building works on the Île de la Cité, the town halls, markets, schools, fire stations, and other public buildings

Figure 69. The Place du Louvre, with the new town hall and belfry to the left of the recently restored Church of Saint-Germain-l'Auxerrois. (Compare with the photograph of the church in Chapter 7 before the new buildings were constructed and the *place* was laid out.) PHOTOGRAPH BY CHARLES-HENRI PLAUT (1819–?).

throughout the capital; the city's new water supply and sewer networks; and the many new parks and squares were financed primarily through public borrowing, dramatically increasing the city's debt.

To meet Napoléon III's deadline for completion of the Rue de Rivoli, three thousand laborers worked on the new street day and night. The extension of the Rue de Rivoli was completed in less than two years, continuing the arcades that Napoléon Ier built on the first part of the street as far as the Rue du Louvre at the eastern end of the Palais du Louvre. The new Grand Hôtel du Louvre—the first of the *Grands Hôtels* built at Napoléon III's request—opened on the Rue de Rivoli on the site of today's Louvre des Antiquaires in time to welcome imperial guests to the Exposition. (The Grand Hôtel du Louvre moved to its present site on the west side of the Place du Palais-Royal in 1887, when its original premises were taken over by the Grands Magasins du Louvre department store.*) Along

---

* Les Grands Magasins du Louvre closed in 1974. Since 1978, the building has been occupied primarily by the Louvre des Antiquaires, a group of antique dealers that numbered 250 in the 1990s but has dwindled in recent years. In 2018, it was reported that the Fondation Cartier would take over the building and adapt it for use as contemporary art exhibition space.

the same route, Haussmann created a new square, the Place du Louvre, facing the Colonnade of the Louvre. After demolishing old structures, between 1858 and 1862 he constructed a town hall (*mairie*) mirroring the recently restored Église Saint-Germain-l'Auxerrois, inserted a belfry (*beffroi*) in between the two buildings and directly opposite the entrance to the Cour Carrée to balance them, and bracketed the ensemble with modern apartment buildings. The architect was Théodore Ballu. Haussmann also built the Avenue Victoria between the Hôtel de Ville and Place du Châtelet, and widened the Rue Saint-Antoine from where it merged with the Rue de Rivoli.

In 1855, Haussmann began work on the north-south axis, beginning with the Boulevard de Sébastopol and the connecting Boulevard de Strasbourg. The *percée* cut through the center of some of the most crowded and insalubrious neighborhoods in Paris, midway between the Rue Saint-Martin and the Rue Saint-Denis, where the 1849 cholera epidemic had been the worst. "It was the gutting (*éventration*) of old Paris," Haussmann wrote in his *Mémoires*, "of the neighborhood of riots, and of barricades, from one end to the other." The Boulevard de Sébastopol went north from the new Place du Châtelet. Heading south from the square, a new, replacement bridge, the Pont-au-Change, was constructed across the Seine in 1859–1860, leading to a new street, the Boulevard du Palais, that crossed the Île de la Cité in front of the Palais de Justice to the new, replacement Pont Saint-Michel, which was built in 1857. On the Left Bank, the north-south axis was continued by the Boulevard Saint-Michel (until 1867, named the Boulevard de Sébastopol Rive Gauche), which cut a straight line from the Seine to the Observatory, and then, as the Rue d'Enfer, extended all the way to the Route d'Orléans. The north-south axis was completed in 1860.

The two axes crossed at the Place du Châtelet—*la Grande Croisée*—making it the center of Haussmann's Paris. Napoléon Ier built the first Place du Châtelet fifty years earlier after demolishing the Grand Châtelet, originally built as a fortress in the ninth century to protect the Grand Pont from Viking attacks and most recently reconstructed in 1684. Haussmann completely rebuilt the square, demolishing all the buildings surrounding it, moving the Colonne du Palmier (also known as the Colonne

Figure 70. The old Pont Saint-Michel with the old Hôtel-Dieu and Notre-Dame (without a spire) behind it, in 1857. PHOTOGRAPH BY AUGUSTE HIPPOLYTE COLLARD (1812–1890).

Figure 71. The new Pont Saint-Michel, with "N" for Napoléon III, in 1859. Note that the new spire for Notre-Dame is under construction. All of the buildings on the left side of the bridge will soon be demolished to make way for the new Préfecture de Police, and the building to right of Notre-Dame (the old Hôtel-Dieu) will be demolished to enlarge the square in front of the cathedral. PHOTO-GRAPH BY AUGUSTE HIPPOLYTE COLLARD (1812–1890).

Figure 72. The new Place du Châtelet in 1859, with the new Boulevard de Sébastopol on the right. PHOTOGRAPH BY CHARLES MARVILLE (1813–1879).

du Châtelet or the Colonne de la Victoire), erected by Napoléon Ier, 40 feet/12 meters to the new center of the square, where it was placed on a new base. He then built two new theaters facing each other across the square: the Théâtre Impérial (now du Châtelet) and the Théâtre Lyrique (now de la Ville), both designed by the architect Gabriel Davioud, which opened in 1862.

The Annexation of 1860
In 1860, the villages outside the Farmers General Wall (*Enceinte des Fermiers Généraux*) and inside the Thiers Fortifications (*Fortifications Thiers*) were annexed, more than doubling the surface area of Paris and enlarging it to its present boundary. Eleven towns were incorporated into Paris: the biggest was Belleville (population fifty-five thousand), followed by Batignolles-Monceau (forty-four thousand) and Montmartre (thirty-three thousand); the others were Auteuil, Passy, La Chapelle, La Villette, Charonne, Bercy, Vaugirard, and Grenelle—all names of familiar neighborhoods in Paris today. The city's population increased from 1.2 million to 1.6 million.

The new system of twenty arrondissements (eight more than before annexation), organized clockwise in the shape of a snail, fixed the Louvre (and no longer the Île de la Cité) as the center of the new Paris, since it was in the 1st arrondissement. As a further demonstration of the primacy of the Right Bank compared to the Left Bank, the westernmost end of the Île de la Cité, including the Palais de Justice and Place Dauphine, is in the 1st arrondissement because it is opposite the 1st arrondissement on the Right Bank, and the eastern two-thirds of the island are in the 4th arrondissement because they are opposite the 4th arrondissement on the Right Bank.

The Farmers General Wall was demolished within less than a month in January 1860 and opened up a second (after the Grands Boulevards) circular series of wide boulevards within the recently enlarged city, which exists to this day. Of the fifty-four *barrières* (entrances to the city) in the Farmers General Wall, twenty-six were replaced by *places*. Only four of the

Figure 73. The Barrière de Clichy in the Farmers General Wall, 1851, which was demolished along with the wall in 1860. PHOTOGRAPH BY GUSTAVE LE GRAY (1820–1884).

fifty-four customs pavilions remain today: at Place Denfert-Rochereau (Porte d'Enfer), Place de la Nation (formerly Place du Trône), Place Stalingrad (at the bottom of the Bassin de la Villette), and Place de la République Dominicaine (at the entrance to the Parc Monceau).

A third circular series of boulevards around the periphery of the newly expanded city, known as the *Boulevards des Maréchaux*, was created just inside the Thiers Fortifications.

Just as Louis XIV's demolition of the Charles V/Louis XIII Walls led to the expansion of the city to greenfield sites outside the old walls, the Annexation of 1860 and subsequent demolition of the Farmers General Wall led to the subdivision for residential construction of many properties in the former villages surrounding the city. Haussmann encouraged this development as a way to relieve the congestion in the historic center. It was also a partial solution to the problem of where the many people displaced by the *Grands Travaux* should go.

One of the most important developments took place in the emptiest part of the annexed land—the *Plaine Monceau*, in the new 17th arrondissement. In 1852, in conjunction with their construction of the Auteuil railroad line and the Boulevard Pereire, brothers Émile and Isaac Pereire acquired the land that would become the Quartier Monceau, bordered on the south by today's Boulevard de Courcelles, on the west by the Rue de Courcelles, on the north by the Thiers Fortifications, and on the east by the Rue de Tocqueville. At that time, the Plaine Monceau was farmland, with almost no roads north of the Rue Cardinet. The Boulevard Pereire, which was completed in 1854, was the first major road to be built on the Plaine Monceau.

In 1854, Haussmann decided to urbanize the Plaine Monceau by constructing four major roads: the extension of the Boulevard Malesherbes to the Porte d'Asnières; the Avenue de Villiers, from the Barrière de Monceau in the Farmers General Wall to the Porte Champerret; the Avenue de Wagram, from the Barrière du Roule in the Farmers General Wall to the Boulevard Malesherbes; and the Avenue Niel. Haussmann also determined to construct four squares at the intersections of these new roads: the rectangular Place Malesherbes (renamed Place du Général-Catroux in 1977), the quadrangular Place du Brésil, the pentagonal Place de Wagram, and the circular Place Pereire (renamed Place du Maréchal-Juin in 1973).

The completion of these streets and squares was followed by the construction of the greatest number of streets in any part of Paris during the Second Empire. Among others, the Rues de Prony, de Jouffroy, Ampère, and Brémontier all opened in the 1860s. Because all the streets in the neighborhood were new and wide, and because nearly all the buildings that line them were built during the last third of the nineteenth century, the Monceau Quarter (along with the Île Saint-Louis with its seventeenth-century *hôtels particuliers*) features perhaps the most homogeneous architecture in Paris. Exceptional *hôtels particuliers* and *villas* were built between 1860 and 1880, and *immeubles de rapport* in the *haussmannien* style were constructed from 1870 through the end of the century—all destined for the *grande bourgeoisie*.

It was on the Plaine Monceau, near the Parc Monceau, that four of Paris's great collectors built their residences, all now museums: Henri Cernuschi (Cernuschi Museum of Asian Arts, 7 Avenue Vélasquez), Moïse de Camondo (Camondo Museum of Decorative Arts, 63 Rue de Monceau), and Nélie Jacquemart and Édouard André (Musée Jacquemart-André, 158 Boulevard Haussmann).

❧

When Napoléon III was in exile in London, he admired its many parks and squares. Inspired by Hyde Park and St. James's Park, in particular, he laid out plans for four large parks around the edge of Paris. Outside the Thiers Fortifications, the engineer Adolphe Alphand designed the Bois de Boulogne (1852–1858; 2,100 acres/850 hectares; the Jardin d'Acclimatation was added in 1860) to the west, and the Bois de Vincennes (1857–1866; 2,500 acres/995 hectares) to the east. Within the Thiers Fortifications, Alphand created the Parc des Buttes-Chaumont* (1864–1867; 61 acres/25 hectares) to the north, and the Parc Montsouris (1867–1878; 37 acres/15 hectares) to the south.

In 1860, the Ville de Paris acquired half (20 acres/8 hectares) of the original Parc Monceau from the Orléans family. (The Orléans family had sold the other half in 1852 to the Pereire brothers, who subdivided

---

* Because nothing grew on their soil, the mounds (*buttes*) were originally nicknamed "*Chauve-mont*" ("bald mountain"), which evolved into Chaumont.

Figure 74. The Bois de Boulogne, looking north. PHOTOGRAPH FROM *PARIS VU EN BALLON ET SES ENVIRONS* (1909).

the land to create an exclusive residential quarter with streets named after artists: Vélasquez, Ruysdael, Rembrandt, Van Dyck, Alfred de Vigny, and Murillo.) Alphand redesigned the park in the English style and in 1861 it opened as the first new public park in Paris under the Second Empire.

Alphand also redesigned the Jardin du Luxembourg, but only after Haussmann trimmed land off three sides of the garden that was created when the fields of the neighboring Carthusian monastery to the south were added to the garden of the Palais de Luxembourg laid out by Marie de Médicis to reach its maximum size of approximately 100 acres/40 hectares. First, Haussmann built the Boulevard Saint-Michel down the east side of the garden in 1859. Then he cut off the northeast corner of the garden in order to build the Rue de Médicis in 1860 to connect the Quartier de l'Odéon with the Quartiers du Val de Grâce, de l'Observatoire, and de la Rue d'Enfer. The construction of the Rue de Médicis required the Fontaine de Médicis, built in 1620, to be moved to its present site, 36 yards/30 meters closer to the palace; the long basin in front of the fountain was added at the same time. Finally, Haussmann destroyed the nursery and botanical garden in the triangular area on the south side of the garden bordered by the Boulevard Saint-Michel, Rue d'Assas, and today's Rue Auguste-Comte, in order to extend and widen the Avenue de l'Observatoire north to the Rue Auguste-Comte (built in 1866 as a western extension of the short Rue l'Abbé de l'Épée on the east side of Boulevard Saint-Michel). He then sold the land on either side of the northern extension of the Avenue de l'Observatoire, for residential development on the east side and for state buildings on the west side. It was at this time that Gabriel Davioud constructed the ornamental gates and fence that surround the entire Luxembourg Garden today, and Alphand transformed what remained of the old Chartreux nursery garden at the south end of the park into an English garden with winding paths, and planted a fruit garden in the southwest corner. The large octagonal fountain behind the palace was added in 1873. Today the Jardin du Luxembourg occupies 57 acres/23 hectares.

On a smaller scale, Alphand designed twenty-four *squares*, similar to the private communal gardens that Napoléon III admired in

Figure 75. The Luxembourg Garden and Palace, looking north, with the fan-shaped Place de l'Odéon in the upper right. *PARIS VU EN BALLON ET SES ENVIRONS* (1909).

Figure 76. The Square de la Tour Saint-Jacques in 1858, with the Place du Châtelet and the Théâtre de la Ville under construction in the foreground. PHOTO-GRAPH BY CHARLES LOUIS MICHELEZ (CIRCA 1817–1883).

London—seventeen in old Paris and seven in the new arrondissements annexed in 1860. The first such *square*, which opened in 1856, was the Square de la Tour Saint-Jacques. Unlike in London, the *squares* of Paris have always been open to the public.

Second Phase: A Network of New Boulevards and Places (1859–1867)

In the first phase of his *Grands Travaux*, Haussmann constructed 6 miles/9.5 kilometers of new roads. In the second phase, which was extended to take into account the annexation of the suburbs of Paris, he created, enlarged, and extended three ring roads within Paris, and extended the *Grande Croisée* through the construction of 16 miles/26 kilometers of new wide boulevards and avenues and of scores of *places* (squares) so that the Great Cross connected all the neighborhoods in the new, greater Paris. Finally, he connected the new train stations with each other and with the city center.

Boulevards and Ring Roads

Before Haussmann, the "boulevard" was primarily a road that went around the city through relatively sparsely inhabited areas. Haussmann reinforced this function by creating or improving two circular boulevards, or ring roads (*rocades*), at the inner and outer limits of the territory annexed in 1860—known as the *Boulevards Extérieurs* and the *Boulevards des Maréchaux*, respectively—and by extending the *Grands Boulevards* (the first ring road) to connect with the second ring road (the *Boulevards Extérieurs*). He then built boulevards and avenues as structural urban thoroughfares to criss-cross the city, intersecting with the ring roads and with each other at scores of *places* (squares) around the city. In this way, he complied with Napoléon III's injunction to "unify" the city—to tie it together.

Les Grandes Places

Of all of the *Grands Travaux* undertaken by Haussmann, none so perfectly fulfilled Napoléon III's desire to *"aérer, unifier, et embellir"* Paris as did the many *grandes places* constructed across the city, which opened up densely crowded spaces, connected the city's different neighborhoods, and were often monumental in their design.

To funnel the traffic on the network of new boulevards and avenues to the ring of Grands Boulevards built by Louis XIV, rebuilt by Rambuteau, and extended by Haussmann, the *decumanus maximus* on the Right Bank (the new Rue de Rivoli) and its equivalent on the Left Bank (the Boulevard Saint-Germain), and the new railroad stations, Haussmann constructed *grandes places* at strategic locations around the city, including

THE RING ROADS OF PARIS

The three circular boulevards, or ring roads (*rocades*), inside today's Paris, starting with the newest at its outer edge and working toward the historic center because each new ring resulted in changes to the older rings, are described below.

Boulevards des Maréchaux

The Rue (or Route) Militaire was constructed inside the entire circumference of the Thiers Fortifications between 1841 and 1844. The year after the annexation of the territory between the Farmers General Wall (the former city limit) and the Thiers Fortifications (the new city limit) in 1860, the construction of a circular boulevard 130 feet/40 meters wide and 21 miles/33.7 kilometers long on the site of the Rue Militaire was declared to be "of public use" ("*d'utilité publique*"). In 1864, the boulevard was broken into nineteen sections, each named after one of the twenty-six marshals appointed during the First Empire; three other sections named after other military leaders were added in the twentieth century. The Boulevards des Maréchaux were further improved following the demolition of the Thiers Fortifications in the 1920s.

The Boulevards des Maréchaux are sometimes also called the Boulevards Extérieurs, although that term was used earlier—and is used in this book—to describe the boulevards just outside the Farmers General Wall.

Boulevards Outside the Farmers General Wall— *Boulevards Extérieurs*

From 1784 to 1791, the Farmers General Wall with its 54 customs houses (*barrières*) designed by Claude-Nicolas Ledoux was constructed around the border of Paris with a road running along its exterior and a walkway (*chemin de ronde*) along its interior. This wall was built to collect the *octroi*, a tax on goods entering the city. The principal entrance to the west was at the Barrière de Neuilly (today's Place de l'Étoile), and to the east was at the Barrière du Trône (today's Place de la Nation), both on the Right Bank. The boulevards built outside of the wall comprised, clockwise from the Place de l'Étoile, the Boulevards de Wagram, de Courcelles, des Batignolles, de Clichy, de Rochehouart, de la Chapelle, de la Villette, de Belleville, de Ménilmontant, de Charonne, de Picpus, de Reuilly, and de Bercy; across the Pont de Bercy on the Left Bank: the Boulevards Vincent Auriol, Auguste Blanqui, Saint-Jacques, Raspail, Edgar Quinet, de Vaugirard, Pasteur, Garibaldi, and de Grenelle; finally continuing on the Right Bank with the Avenue Kléber leading from the Place du Trocadéro to the Place de l'Étoile. The route of this second ring of boulevards is traced by métro lines 2 and 6 between the Place Charles de Gaulle Étoile and the Place de la Nation, on the Right and Left Banks, respectively.

The wall was demolished immediately after the annexation of 1860, and the surrounding boulevards were widened to 138 feet/42 meters or more to incorporate the space occupied by the wall itself and the walkway inside the wall.

When the Farmers General Wall constituted the city limit, the boulevards outside the wall were logically called the *Boulevards Extérieurs*. After the city limit was extended to the Thiers Fortifications by the Annexation of 1860 and the Boulevards des Maréchaux were built inside the Thiers Fortifications, some people began to call them the (new) Boulevards Extérieurs, making the old Boulevards Extérieurs the new Boulevards Intérieurs.

Grands Boulevards

The Grands Boulevards were built on the *Nouveau Cours* constructed by Pierre Bullet between 1668 and 1705 on the site of the Charles V/Louis XIII Wall that curved around the city on the Right Bank before it was demolished by Louis XIV. The Nouveau Cours was designed to link the Porte Saint-Honoré (at today's Place de la Madeleine) and the Porte Saint-Antoine (at today's Place de la Bastille), a distance of nearly 3 miles/4.4 kilometers. The Grands Boulevards were rebuilt as modern boulevards by Rambuteau in the 1830s, adding sidewalks and installing a public lighting system of gas lamps.

The Grands Boulevards comprise, from west to east, the Boulevards de la Madeleine, des Capucines, des Italiens, Montmartre, Poissonnière, de Bonne Nouvelle, Saint-Denis, Saint-Martin, du Temple, des Filles du Calvaire, and Beaumarchais.

Haussmann extended the Grands Boulevards east from the Place de la République with the construction of the Avenue de la République and the Boulevard du Prince Eugène (now Boulevard Voltaire),

Figure 77. From the top of the Arc de Triomphe de l'Étoile, the Avenue des Champs-Élysées is on the right, and the Avenue Friedland is on the left.

both connecting with the circular Boulevards Extérieurs, with the Boulevard Voltaire leading to the Place de la Nation.

Haussmann extended the Grands Boulevards west from the future Place de l'Opéra through the construction of the Boulevard Haussmann and the Avenue de Friedland leading to the Place de l'Étoile.

Boulevards du Midi

Starting in 1760, Louis XV built the Boulevards du Midi on the southern edge of the city, originally designed by Pierre Bullet to mirror on the Left Bank the Nouveau Cours (Grands Boulevards) built by Louis XIV a century earlier on the Right Bank. Whereas the neighborhoods around the Grands Boulevards were by then densely populated, the area around the Boulevards du Midi was not. Starting at the Hôtel des Invalides and heading east, they comprised the Boulevards des Invalides, du Montparnasse, the part of the Boulevard Raspail between Boulevard Montparnasse and the Place Denfert Rochereau (at the time, called Boulevard d'Enfer), and the Boulevards Saint-Jacques, Auguste-Blanqui (leading to Place d'Italie), and de l'Hôpital (ending at the Seine). At the eastern end of the Boulevards du Midi was the Pont d'Austerlitz (1854). On the Right

Bank, the Boulevard Mazas (1853, renamed Boulevard Diderot in 1879) then completed the circle at the Place de la Nation.

At the western end of the Boulevards du Midi, Haussmann added a connection to the Right Bank by constructing the Boulevard de l'Alma (1858, renamed Avenue Bosquet in 1864), leading to the Pont de l'Alma (1856) and the Place de l'Alma (1858), from which the Avenue Joséphine (1858, renamed Avenue Marceau in 1879) led to the Place de l'Étoile, completing the circle.

In 1857, Haussmann finally completed the ring road on the Left Bank by constructing the Boulevards de Port Royal and Saint-Marcel to extend the Boulevard Montparnasse east to the Pont d'Austerlitz, thereby creating another semicircular boulevard inside the Boulevards Extérieurs built on the former Farmers General Wall.

The area around the Boulevard Montparnasse developed quickly following the construction of the Gare Montparnasse in 1852 and the Rue de Rennes leading from the train station to the Boulevard Saint-Germain in 1855.

twenty-six at former *barrières* in the Farmers General Wall that was demolished in 1860.

Haussmann's greatest squares—some new, others rebuilt on a grander scale—included, roughly from west to east:

On the Right Bank:

- Place de l'Étoile, 8ᵉ, 16ᵉ, 17ᵉ.
- Place du Trocadéro, 16ᵉ.
- Place de l'Alma, 8ᵉ, 16ᵉ.
- Place de la Concorde, 1ᵉʳ.
- Place de l'Opéra, 2ᵉ, 9ᵉ.
- Place du Châtelet, 1ᵉʳ, 4ᵉ.
- Place de la Bastille, 4ᵉ, 11ᵉ, 12ᵉ.
- Place de la République, 3ᵉ, 10ᵉ, 11ᵉ.
- Place de la Nation, 11ᵉ, 12ᵉ.

On the Left Bank:

- Place Denfert-Rochereau, 14ᵉ.
- Place d'Italie, 13ᵉ.

Train Stations—The New Gates to the City

The six great railway stations of Paris are, clockwise and starting on the Right Bank, the Gares Saint-Lazare (serving Normandy), du Nord (North), de l'Est (East), de Lyon (serving the southeast), d'Austerlitz (serving the southwest), and Montparnasse (serving the west). All six *grandes gares* were first built around the periphery of the city just inside the Farmers General Wall by different private companies between 1837 and 1849. As the original train stations each only had two tracks (one for departing trains and another for arriving trains), they were all enlarged and rebuilt repeatedly as traffic increased, during the Second Empire and thereafter.

Napoléon III considered the new train stations to be the new gates (*portes*) to Paris. It was, therefore, a priority for Haussmann to connect them with each other and with the city center.

To connect the *grandes gares* with each other, and to transport troops to the Thiers Fortifications, between 1851 and 1862 the *Chemin de Fer de Petite Ceinture* (Little Belt Railway) was built just inside the defensive wall that surrounded Paris and the villages outside the Farmers General Wall.

Haussmann constructed extensive roadworks to connect the train stations with the city center. Perhaps the two best examples were both completed in 1855. On the Right Bank Haussmann built his first and longest *percée*—the straight Boulevards de Strasbourg and de Sébastopol (one leading to the other), with a combined length of 1.3 miles/2.1 kilometers and a width of 98 feet/30 meters, to connect the Gare de l'Est to the Grands Boulevards and the Place du Châtelet, which intersected with the east-west Rue de Rivoli and was the epicenter of *la Grande Croisée*. On the Left Bank he built the Rue de Rennes—another important *percée* measuring three-quarters of a mile/1.2 kilometers long and 65 feet/20 meters wide—in a straight line to connect the Gare Montparnasse with the Boulevard Saint-Germain. It was originally intended to continue the Rue de Rennes all the way to the Seine, where the Institut de France stands, but the last section was never built, which explains why the first street number is 41 Rue de Rennes.

The Historic Center and the Île de la Cité

The oldest parts of Paris—the Marais, the Quartier Latin, and the Île de la Cité, which had all been inside the city wall built by Philippe-Auguste around 1200—were also the most densely populated, impoverished, and insalubrious. Little had changed there since the Middle Ages. As instructed by Napoléon III—with the exception of the Marais, where Rambuteau had constructed two *percées* in the 1830s—Haussmann determined to open them up.

In the Latin Quarter, Haussmann successfully opened up the area around the Montagne Saint-Geneviève, where the Panthéon stands, by enlarging existing roads and building several important *percées*: To the west, he entirely rebuilt the Rue Soufflot, first constructed by Rambuteau; to the south, he built the Rue Gay-Lussac, Rue Claude Bernard, and Avenue des Gobelins; to the east, he widened part of the Rue Mouffetard, and built the Rue Monge.

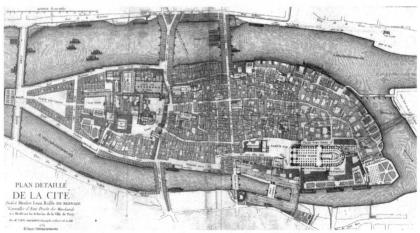

Figure 78. Detailed map of the Île de la Cité by Jean Delagrive, 1754.

Figure 79. The Tribunal de Commerce, circa 1865. PHOTOGRAPH BY CHARLES MAR-
VILLE (1813–1879).

But more than anywhere else in Paris, the *Grands Projets* transformed
the Île de la Cité, an impenetrable labyrinth of narrow, dark, and danger-
ous streets and alleys, the narrowest of which were only 1 or 2 yards/
meters wide, where the population density—and risk of disease—was
extremely high. Haussmann's solution was to demolish all of the old
streets and neighborhoods, and more than twenty churches and chapels,
located between the Conciergerie and the Cathédrale Notre-Dame de
Paris.

In the empty space Haussmann built three huge new public buildings—the Tribunal de Commerce (1860–1865, architect Antoine-Nicolas
Bailly; inspired by the city hall of Brescia in Italy, which Napoléon III
admired), the Caserne de la Cité (1862–1867, architect Victor Calliat;
now the Préfecture de Police), and the Hôtel-Dieu (1863–1878, architects
Emile-Jacques Gilbert and Arthur-Stanislas Diet). At the same time he
substantially enlarged the Palais de Justice. Haussmann built three new
streets—the Boulevard du Palais in front of the Palais de Justice, the Rue

76. PARIS — Caserne de la Cité

Figure 80. The Caserne de la Cité. POSTCARD BY UNKNOWN PHOTOGRAPHER.

de Lutèce in front of the new Préfecture de Police, and the Rue d'Arcole alongside the new Hôtel-Dieu—and he rebuilt 5 of the 9 bridges on the island: the Pont d'Arcole, Pont Notre-Dame, and Pont-au-Change leading to the Right Bank, and the Petit Pont and Pont Saint-Michel leading to the Left Bank, along with the adjoining embankments.

At the west end of the island, Haussmann saw to it that the restoration of the Sainte-Chapelle and the façade of the Conciergerie on the Quai de l'Horloge between the rectangular Tour de l'Horloge and the twin Tour César and Tour d'Argent, begun during the July Monarchy, was completed. In 1868, a floor was added to the crenellated Tour Bonbec so that it was the same height as the twin towers to the east. Finally, a new façade was built along the Quai de l'Horloge between the Tour Bonbec and the twin towers, similar in design to the façade built between the twin towers and the Tour de l'Horloge initiated by Rambuteau.

Under Haussmann, architects Louis Duc, Étienne-Théodore Dommey, and others expanded the Palais de Justice by demolishing the

Figure 81. The recently renovated Sainte-Chapelle and the Palais de Justice, circa 1854. Note that the Tour Bonbec (the tower furthest to the right) is lower than it is today, and that the new and higher building between the twin towers and the Tour Bonbec, the Tribunal de Commerce, the new Pont au Change, and the Cour de Cassation have yet to be built. PHOTOGRAPH BY ÉDOUARD BALDUS (1813–1889).

Figure 82. This photograph shows the edge of the new Tribunal de Commerce on the left, and the new, higher façade between the twin towers and the Tour Bonbec, to which a floor has been added, on the right. Beyond them is the new Cour de Cassation and the new Pont au Change with the "N" for Napoléon III in the foreground. *PARIS ET SES ENVIRONS—* COLLECTION GEORGES SIROT (PHOTOGRAPH CIRCA 1890–1900).

residential quarters (*le logis du roi*) and other historic buildings within the precincts of the Palais de la Cité and constructing new buildings in the empty space to house courtrooms.

In 1854, the east side of the triangular Place Dauphine was demolished and architect Honoré Daumet built the monumental façade on the west side of the Palais de Justice, on the Rue de Harlay, overlooking the now two-sided Place Dauphine (completed in 1869).

Between 1861 and 1892, a new courthouse for the Cour de Cassation (the highest court of appeals for civil and criminal matters) was built on the Quai de l'Horloge, just west of the Tour Bonbec, and then rebuilt to repair the damage caused by the fire set during the Commune on May 24, 1871 (architects Louis Lenormand, Louis Duc, Ernest-Georges Coquart, and Paul Blondel).

The south side of the west end of the island, facing the Left Bank, was only demolished and developed post-Haussmann, following the fire of May 24, 1871. First, the new headquarters for the *Police Judiciaire* (the criminal investigation division of the *Police nationale*) was built at 36 Quai

Figure 83. The east side of the triangular Place Dauphine backing on the Rue de Harlay, circa 1865, before it was demolished by Haussmann. PHOTOGRAPH BY CHARLES MARVILLE (1813–1879).

Figure 84. The new western façade of the Palais de Justice, circa 1870, facing the Rue de Harlay and the remaining two sides of the Place Dauphine. PHOTO-GRAPH PROBABLY BY CHARLES MARVILLE (1813–1879).

des Orfèvres between 1875 and 1880.* Then its neighbor at 14 Quai des Orfèvres, the Tribunal Correctionnel (part of the Tribunal de Grande Instance), with its faux medieval tower recalling the Tour de l'Horloge on the north side of the island and its façade pock-marked by bullets fired during the liberation of Paris in August 1944, was built between 1907 and 1914.

At the east end of the island, Haussmann cleared the buildings around Notre-Dame, including the old Hôtel-Dieu, a large building that strad-dled the Île de la Cité and the Left Bank in front of Notre-Dame, qua-drupling the size of the *parvis* (square) in front of the cathedral. At the

---

* The *PJ* is the direct successor of the *Sûreté*, which was founded in 1812 by Eugène François Vidocq as the criminal investigative bureau of the Paris police.

Figure 85. The old Hôtel-Dieu in front of Notre-Dame alongside the Seine, in 1862. Note that demolition has begun in front of the Hôtel-Dieu to clear the site for the Préfecture de Police and the new Petit Pont is under construction. The old Pont Saint-Michel is in the foreground.

Figure 86. The new Hôtel-Dieu overlooking the new square (*parvis*) in front of Notre-Dame, 1878. PHOTOGRAPH BY HENRI ÉMILE CIMAROSA GODEFROY (1837–1913).

eastern tip of the island behind Notre-Dame, he built a new city morgue to replace the old one on the Quai du Marché-Neuf that he demolished to construct the Caserne de la Cité. Today the *Mémorial des Martyrs de la Déportation* (Memorial to the Deported) stands on the former site of the morgue.

Between 1844 and 1864, Viollet-le-Duc restored the cathedral itself, replacing most of the sculptures on the western façade. Between around 1853 and 1859, he also replaced the original spire that had fallen into disrepair and was removed in 1786; the new spire was 315 feet/96 meters high, 59 feet/18 meters higher than the first spire.

Figure 87. The east end of the Île de la Cité as seen from the Tour Saint-Jacques on the Right Bank, circa 1864, before the demolition of the old Hôtel-Dieu and every other building between Notre-Dame and the Palais de Justice at the west end of the island, and the construction of the new Hôtel-Dieu, Préfecture de Police, and Tribunal de Commerce. The domed Panthéon is on the hill in the distance. PHOTOGRAPH BY CHARLES SOULIER (1840–1875).

Figure 88. View from the Tour Saint-Jacques of the construction of the new Hôtel-Dieu on the Île de la Cité. The recently completed Caserne de la Cité and Tribunal de Commerce (with the dome) are on the right. PHOTOGRAPHER UNKNOWN.

Figure 89. View from the Tour Saint-Jacques of the new Hôtel-Dieu, circa 1867. PHOTOGRAPHER UNKNOWN.

Between 1866 and 1876, the huge, new Hôtel-Dieu was built on the north side of the enlarged parvis, extending all the way to the river (architects Émile Jacques Gilbert and Arthur-Stanislas Diet). Haussmann rebuilt the Rue d'Arcole along the east side of the new Hôtel-Dieu, and replaced the Pont d'Arcole suspension pedestrian bridge (1828) with a metal bridge for vehicular traffic (1854–1856).

The *Grands Travaux* caused enormous social disruption throughout Paris, but nowhere more so than on the Île de la Cité. Following its transformation from medieval residential neighborhood to administrative center, the population of the island fell from twenty thousand before the *Grands Travaux* to five thousand by 1900; it is less than one thousand today.

Figure 90. The Île de la Cité after *les Grands Travaux*. PHOTOGRAPH FROM *PARIS VU EN BALLON ET SES ENVIRONS* (1909).

THE RULES OF HAUSSMANNIAN PARIS

Haussmann applied a rigorous esthetic when rebuilding Paris, and in the process created a new adjective to describe his style: *haussmannien*.

His avenues and boulevards were straight, wide, and flat. Haussmann tripled the average width of a street to 80 feet/24 meters. The widest (Avenue de l'Impératrice, now Avenue Foch) was nearly 400 feet/120 meters wide. If mounds (*monceaux*) were in the way of a road, he removed them, and if there were dips in the road, he filled them in, in a process known as *nivellement* (leveling).

Haussmann would go to great lengths—and expense—to achieve the desired result. Haussmann covered the Canal Saint-Martin between the Rue du Faubourg du Temple and the Place de la Bastille—nearly half its 2.86-mile/4.6-kilometer length—to build the Boulevards Richard Lenoir and Jules Ferry. When he realized that the new Avenue du Prince-Eugène (Boulevard Voltaire) had to cross the Canal Saint-Martin, rather than raising the street to go across a bridge over the canal, he had the canal lowered 20 feet/6 meters and covered.

Symmetry was all-important. The new Boulevard de Sébastopol on the Right Bank did not line up with the rebuilt Pont au Change leading to the Île de la Cité. To solve this problem, Haussmann's architect Gabriel Davioud recentered the Place du Châtelet (first built by Napoléon Ier on the site of the demolished medieval fort, the Grand Châtelet) so that it was directly opposite the bridge, and moved the Fontaine du Palmier originally installed by Napoléon Ier to an island in the center of the square, so that the new Boulevard de Sébastopol on the east side of the square was balanced by the old Rue Saint-Denis on the west side of the square. Haussmann added the two theaters on the east and west sides of the square to provide further symmetry. Similarly, on the south side of the Île de la Cité the new Boulevard Saint-Michel on the Left Bank did not line up with the rebuilt Pont Saint-Michel. Davioud used the same solution to this problem, building the Place Saint-Michel (1855–1860) with its monumental fountain directly in front of the Pont Saint-Michel, so that the new Boulevard Saint-Michel to the left of the fountain was balanced by the new Rue Danton to the right of the fountain.

Intersecting streets had to be at right angles. Haussmann demolished the Rue d'Arcole, which had only been built by Rambuteau in 1837 but was at an 80-degree angle to Notre-Dame, and rebuilt it at a perfect 90-degree angle.

Perspective was also important. Major avenues and streets were anchored by monuments. For example, the new Boulevard Henri IV has the Colonne de Juillet 1830 in the Place de la Bastille at one end, and a direct view of the Panthéon at the other end; so does the new Pont Louis-Philippe leading to the western tip of the Île Saint-Louis. The new Rue de Solférino (near the Musée d'Orsay, named after the battle won in Italy by Napoléon III) is centered on the gleaming white Sacré Coeur Basilica in the distance. Haussmann even insisted that the architect of the new Tribunal de Commerce on the Île de la Cité next to the new Pont au Change move the large dome from the center of the building nearer the new Boulevard du Palais so that it would line up with the new Boulevard de Sébastopol across the Seine.

Important buildings were set off to their best advantage by creating squares (*places* or *parvis*) in front of them or by building avenues leading to them, such as the grand but little-used Avenue Victoria leading to the Place de l'Hôtel de Ville, whose size was quadrupled by Haussmann. Haussmann added a grand new entrance on the west side of the Palais de Justice (architect Honoré Daumet) and planned to demolish the entire Place Dauphine in order to create an impressive *parvis* overlooking the Pont Neuf and the Seine. In the end, only the east side of the triangular Place Dauphine was demolished, which explains why the grand new entrance looks so out of place and out of proportion, cramped as it is by the two surviving sides of Place Dauphine and the garden in between.

One of the most dramatic examples of Haussmann's squares is his much enlarged Parvis Notre-Dame. From the beginning, the square (*parvis*) in front of Notre-Dame had been hemmed in by the Hôtel-Dieu hospital and the Rue Neuve Notre-Dame. The old Hôtel-Dieu had developed gradually since its original founding in the seventh century. It was located on the south side of the parvis, with buildings on two bridges and along both banks of the Seine. The Rue Neuve Notre-Dame (originally called Rue Neuve), which led directly to the center of Notre-Dame's façade, and the old parvis were both built by Bishop Maurice de Sully in 1163 as part of the project to construct the new cathedral. The Rue Neuve was 250 feet/76 meters long and 20 feet/6 meters wide, and was no doubt the straightest and widest road built in Paris since Roman times. The old parvis was cramped—approximately one-quarter the size of the current parvis; to see the towers of Notre-Dame one would have had to crane one's neck very high. After Haussmann created the new parvis, Parisians could admire the full size and grandeur of Notre-Dame for the very first time, from both the new parvis and the Left Bank. The outline of the old parvis and the Rue Neuve Notre-Dame that led to it is traced by light-colored stones embedded in the new parvis in 1970.

Arguably the best example of both the monumental *place* and symmetry is the magnificent Place de l'Étoile surrounding the 164-foot-/50-meter-high Arc de Triomphe, recently finished by Louis-Philippe. The Étoile went from five avenues radiating from the *place* to twelve, with matching buildings designed by Jacques-Ignace Hittorff ringing its perimeter.

The façades of all buildings had to be made of cut stone (*pierre de taille*) and of a uniform design. The Rue de Rivoli was the model.

Most new buildings along the new avenues and boulevards were *immeubles* (or *maisons*) *de rapport*, or *immeubles* (or *maisons*) *à loyer*—income-generating buildings with apartments for rent. They followed the same general style that soon became known as *haussmannien*, and still is:

- Ground floor (*rez-de-chaussée*) and basement with fronts usually parallel to the street. The ground floor was often occupied by shops or offices.

- *Mezzanine* or *entresol* intermediate level, with low ceilings; often also used by shops or offices.

- Second, *piano nobile* floor (*étage noble*, or noble floor) with a continuous wrought-iron balcony. This floor, in the days before elevators became commonplace in the 1890s, was the most desirable floor, and had the largest and best apartments, often with higher ceilings.

- Third and fourth floors in the same style as the second floor, but with less elaborate stonework around the windows, sometimes without balconies and with lower ceilings.

- Fifth floor with a single, continuous, undecorated balcony.
- Mansard roof,* angled at 45 degrees, covered in slate with garret rooms and dormer windows, originally occupied by lower-income tenants or servants of the people living on the floors below, but today increasingly converted into apartments.

During the July Monarchy, the windows of apartment buildings were bracketed by wooden shutters that lay flat against the exterior wall when open. After Haussmann, shutters folded in half on the sides of the window so they were not visible from the street.

Before Haussmann, builders could put balconies, cornices, and entablatures wherever they wanted on a building, so long as the building respected the applicable height restriction. This often resulted in a lack of "harmony" between neighboring buildings that offended Haussmann's sense of order. To address the problem, Haussmann decreed that the balconies, cornices, and roofs of all new buildings on the same street must follow the same line in order to create *"un seul ensemble architectural"* ("a single architectural whole").

Haussmann's streets were all furnished with the same, distinctive "street furniture": gas lamp posts, newspaper kiosks, advertising pillars (the cylindrical *colonnes Morris*, which were first installed in Berlin in 1855; the advertising concession for the pillars in Paris was held by Gabriel Morris), cast-iron public drinking fountains (*fontaines Wallace*, designed by Charles-Auguste Lebourg and financed by the English philanthropist Sir Richard Wallace, of the Wallace Collection in London), benches, and, of course, *urinoirs* (better known as *vespasiennes*).

Since the eight new arrondissements were developed applying Haussmann's strict zoning rules, the architecture and street furniture in even the poorest districts of Paris (the 18th and 19th arrondissements) resembles that found in the wealthiest neighborhoods of Paris.

---

* Although the "mansard roof" was first used by Pierre Lescot on the wing of the Louvre that he built around 1550, it was named after the architect François Mansart, who made it popular in the seventeenth century. The mansard roof became especially fashionable during the Second Empire.

In addition to roads and squares, Haussmann built or rebuilt 11 bridges across the Seine:

- 1853: Petit Pont (first built in Roman times).
- 1853: Pont Notre-Dame (known as the Grand Pont in Roman times; called the "Devil's Bridge" due to accidents caused by its five small spans; the three middle spans were replaced by a single metal span in 1919).
- 1853: Pont National (widened in 1944).
- 1854: Pont d'Arcole (replacing a suspension bridge for pedestrians built in 1828).
- 1854: Pont d'Austerlitz (replacing the bridge originally built in 1807).
- 1855: Pont des Invalides (built for the Exposition Universelle de 1855, replacing a suspension bridge built in 1821).
- 1856: Pont de l'Alma (replaced in 1974).
- 1857: Pont Saint-Michel (rebuilt as part of the *Grande Croisée* project).
- 1860: Pont au Change (rebuilt as part of the *Grande Croisée* project).
- 1862: Pont Louis-Philippe (replacing the suspension bridge built in 1833).
- 1876: Pont de Sully (crossing the eastern tip of the Île Saint-Louis at the beginning of the new Boulevard Henri IV).

The Pont de l'Alma was named to commemorate the French, British, and Ottoman armies' victory over the Russian army at the Battle of Alma in 1854 during the Crimean War. The original bridge had four stone sculptures in front of its piers representing different kinds of French soldiers who took part in the war. The Zouave wore the traditional uniform worn by French soldiers in North Africa. The Zouave is the only original statue that was transferred to the replacement bridge built between 1970 and 1974, and is still used as an informal measure for the level of the

Seine in Paris. The other statues were moved to three different museums around France.

—◆—

The *Grands Travaux* were designed by an evolving team of architects selected by Haussmann from the *Section Architecture de l'Académie des Beaux-Arts* and employed by the *Service d'Architecture de la Ville de Paris*. At the beginning of Haussmann's term as prefect of the Seine, each architect was assigned to particular types of monuments or buildings. After 1866, each of ten architects was given responsibility for two of the then twenty arrondissements. Haussmann would choose architects from among the *Service ordinaire d'architecture* or elsewhere for important projects according to their experience and availability. The emperor had his own architect to work on the Louvre (first Louis Visconti, and after his death in 1853, Hector Lefuel), and the commissions for certain high-profile projects were awarded to architects on the basis of a competition (*concours*), such as Charles Garnier, the architect of the opera house that now bears his name.

It was during the Second Empire that architects started to engrave their names and the date of construction on the buildings they designed.

Other notable buildings and other structures that were built during the Second Empire (and their architects) include:

- 1853: Orangerie (Louis Visconti), in the Tuileries Garden, 1er.
- 1861: Jeu de Paume (Lucien Viraut), in the Tuileries Garden, 1er.
- 1860–1869: Église Saint-Augustin (Victor Baltard), 8 Avenue César Caire, 8e.
- 1861–1867: Église de la Sainte-Trinité (Théodore Ballu), Place d'Estienne d'Orves, 9e.
- 1861–1865: New Gare du Nord (Jacques-Ignace Hittorff), 18 Rue de Dunkerque, 10e.
- 1869–1875: Hôtel (now Musée) Jacquemart-André (Henri Parent), 158 Boulevard Haussmann, 8e.

Figure 91. Elevation of the Church of Saint Augustine by its architect, Victor Baltard (1805–1874). Despite the enormous dome (259 feet/79 meters high), it was not necessary to shore up the walls with flying buttresses since the frame of the building was made of cast-iron. The church was originally intended to be the final resting place of Napoléon III and Empress Eugénie, but they died in exile in England and were interred in St. Michael's Abbey in Farnborough.

Figure 92. Plan for *les Halles centrales de Paris*, 1863. ILLUSTRATION BY VICTOR BALTARD (1805–1874).

In addition, scores of public buildings went up throughout the city, and especially in the eight new arrondissements. New town halls (*mairies*) were built for six of the twelve original arrondissements; the other six were enlarged. Separate schools for boys and girls (*écoles de garçons, écoles de filles*) were built in every arrondissement, as were fire stations (*casernes sapeurs-pompiers*). Between 1854 and 1874, Baltard built ten glass and cast-iron pavilions to serve as food halls next to the market site known as Les Halles ever since the Middle Ages, which required the demolition of three hundred buildings. Two more pavilions were added in 1935. Between 1863 and 1865, Baltard's student Jules de Mérindol built 4 pavilions of the same type for the same purpose in the Carreau du Temple, and four more in the Place du Marché Saint-Honoré. Between 1860 and 1867, Mérindol built three similar *halles* to centralize the city's slaughterhouses (*abattoirs*) near the Porte de la Villette at the northeastern edge of Paris. Baltard also restored the following medieval churches on the Left Bank:

- Église Saint-Étienne-du-Mont, 5ᵉ.
- Église Saint-Séverin, 5ᵉ.
- Église Saint-Germain des Prés, 6ᵉ

Finally, the engineer Eugène Belgrand, who was appointed director of Water and Sewers of Paris in March 1855, designed the extensive water supply networks (one for drinking water and one for water to wash the streets and water the new parks and gardens) and sewer network, which are still used today.

Water was brought to Paris from the rivers Dhuys and Vanne via aqueducts, each 80 miles/130 kilometers long, and then stored in six new reservoirs built on the city's highest elevations in Passy, Ménilmontant, Belleville, les Buttes-Chaumont, Charonne, and Montsouris; 520 miles/840 kilometers of pipes were installed in addition to the existing network of 435 miles/700 kilometers of pipes to deliver water to residents.

The existing sewer system discharged waste directly into the Seine. Belgrand designed and built a new system with 370 miles/600 kilometers of high and wide sewers under the sidewalks and streets of Paris, which led to a collection point in Asnières, on the northwestern edge of the city. The new system was so popular that tours of the sewers of Paris were organized in 1889. The Musée des Égouts de Paris, at 93 Quai d'Orsay, 7ᵉ, near the Pont de l'Alma, is still giving tours.

The Louvre

Independent of Haussmann's *Grands Travaux*, the Louvre reached its peak during the reign of Napoléon III.

Between 1852 and 1857, following the demolition of the remaining buildings between the Tuileries Palace and the Louvre, the emperor's architects Louis Visconti and Hector Lefuel built a series of wings and pavilions along the Rue de Rivoli to mirror the Grande Galerie constructed along the Seine 250 years earlier by Henri IV. They also built the two interior wings and six courtyards to create the Cour Napoléon, where I. M. Pei's pyramid now stands.

Between 1861 and 1870, Lefuel built a new façade on the western end of the Grande Galerie. Between 1865 and 1868, he added the *Grands Guichets* (large gates) between the Pavillon Lesdiguières and the Pavillon de la Trémoille, which open on the Place du Carrousel and served as the grand entrance to the New Louvre of Napoléon III.

Figure 93. The Cour Napoléon du Louvre, after the construction of the interior wings and courtyards. *PARIS ET SES ENVIRONS*—COLLECTION GEORGES SIROT (PHOTO-GRAPH CIRCA 1890–1900).

The End of the Haussmann Era

Haussmann had planned an ambitious third phase of his *Grands Travaux*, but he was not able to carry it out. During his nearly seventeen years in power, Haussmann made many enemies because of his autocratic style and huge cost overruns. Finally, on January 5, 1870, three days after Napoléon III was compelled to appoint the leader of the republican opposition as head of the government, Haussmann was removed from his position as *préfet*.

Although many works associated with the Haussmann era were started before he arrived in office (the Rue de Rivoli, Boulevard de Sébastopol, Les Halles) or were completed long after he left office (the Opéra Garnier [completed 1875], Avenue de l'Opéra [1877], Boulevard Saint-Germain [1877], Boulevard Henri IV [1879, originally named *Boulevard Saint-Germain Rive Droite*], Avenue de la République [1889], Boulevard Raspail [1907], Boulevard Haussmann from the Rue Taitbout to the Rue Drouot [1927]), his impact on the city of Paris was enormous. The improvements made between 1852 and 1870 included:

- 70 *percées* built by Haussmann, totaling 40 miles/64 kilometers in length with an average width of 80 feet/24 meters—three times the previous average.

- 736 new streets, totaling 124 miles/200 kilometers in length, mostly built by the developers of new subdivisions.

- 420 miles/676 kilometers of new sidewalks.

- 20,000 gas streetlamps installed alongside streets.

- 8,000 public benches installed along streets.

- 80,000 trees planted alongside boulevards, avenues, and quais.

- 20,000 buildings demolished.

- 40,000 private buildings constructed, primarily *immeubles de rapport*.

- Scores of public buildings constructed (*mairies, écoles, églises, hopitaux, casernes sapeurs-pompiers*).

- 24 *squares* built (small gardens similar to the private communal gardens that Napoléon III admired in London).

- 370 miles/600 kilometers of new sewers.

It should also be noted that 117,553 families (350,000 people) were displaced by the *Grands Travaux*, representing 20 percent of the population of Paris.

THE FRANCO-PRUSSIAN WAR (1870–1871)

France's dominant position in continental Europe was challenged by Prussia's decisive victory over the Austrian Empire in the Austro-Prussian War (or Seven Weeks' War) during the summer of 1866. On July 19, 1870, the Prussian prime minister Otto von Bismarck provoked Napoléon III into declaring war on Prussia. The Prussian army quickly defeated the French army led by Napoléon III at Sedan, in northeastern France near the Belgian border, and Napoléon III surrendered on September 2 and was taken prisoner with 104,000 of his soldiers.

THE END OF THE SECOND EMPIRE

On September 4, Napoléon III was deposed by the Chambre des Deputés, ending the Second Empire and beginning the Third Republic. Empress Eugénie fled to England.

In 1871, Napoléon III was released by the Prussians and joined his wife in England, where he died in 1873. Eugénie remained in England until her death in 1920.

Émile Zola wrote a series of twenty novels known as *Les Rougon-Macquart* about the history of a family between 1851 and 1871 that gives a panoramic account of the Second Empire. *Les Fleurs du Mal* by Charles Baudelaire and *Madame Bovary* by Gustave Flaubert were both published in 1857, at the height of the reign of Napoléon III.

Ironically for a man who built so many, no street in Paris is named after Napoléon III and the only square to bear his name is the undistinguished Place Napoléon III in front of the Gare du Nord, which was only named after France's second emperor in 1987.

CHAPTER 9

The Third Republic (1870–1940)

The Third Republic governed France from 1870 to 1940, when it was replaced by the Vichy government following France's defeat by Nazi Germany. (Vichy was replaced by the Fourth Republic in 1946.) The seventy years of the Third Republic started and finished with wars with Germany and included the fifth bloody revolution within eighty years, but they were also marked by periods of economic prosperity and cultural development.

THE SIEGE OF PARIS (1870–1871)

After deposing Napoléon III, the Chambre des Deputés established the first provisional government of the Third Republic, which decided to continue the war despite the French army's defeat at the Battle of Sedan. As the Prussian army then marched unopposed on Paris, the French government moved to Bordeaux and wealthy Parisians fled the city, leaving mainly workers to defend it. Since Paris was surrounded by the formidable Thiers Fortifications, the Prussians laid siege to the city on September 25, 1870, establishing their headquarters in the Château de Versailles. On October 13, an errant shell fell on the Château de Saint-Cloud and the resulting fire burned out the interior of the building. The ruins were demolished in 1892.

On January 18, 1871, Wilhelm I, king of Prussia, was proclaimed emperor (*Kaiser*) of a unified German Empire (*Deutsches Reich*) in the Hall of Mirrors at the Château de Versailles.

On January 28, after an exceptionally cold autumn and winter and having run out of food, Paris finally surrendered. Thirty thousand Parisians died of starvation or illness during the four months of the siege.

On February 26, a preliminary peace accord was signed by the recently elected head of the provisional national government, Adolphe Thiers (the same man who as prime minister built the fortifications around Paris in the 1840s), which was ratified by the Treaty of Frankfurt on May 10. Under its terms, France ceded Alsace (which had been under French control since 1648) and Lorraine (a French province since 1766) to Germany and agreed to pay a war indemnity of five billion francs.

On March 1, thirty thousand Prussian troops marched down the Champs-Élysées in a victory parade. After camping in the Tuileries for two days, they left Paris to occupy temporary encampments to the east of the city, where they remained until France paid the agreed indemnity in full.

The Franco-Prussian War marked the beginning of Germany's rise as a great power, and the end of France's dominance in continental Europe.

THE COMMUNE (1871)

Republican Parisians, believing that the new national government would restore the monarchy, resolved to set up their own government.

On March 10, 1871, Thiers moved the National Assembly from Bordeaux to Versailles instead of Paris, to avoid demonstrations.

On March 18, in an attempt to disarm the increasingly radical Parisians, the national government sent soldiers from Versailles to remove two hundred cannons from Montmartre. They were attacked by a citizens' militia known as the National Guard and forced to withdraw.

On March 28, the central committee of the National Guard occupied the Hôtel de Ville and established a rival government called the Paris Commune (named after the city's governing body during the Revolution). The subsequent confrontation between the army and the outnumbered *Communards*, or *Fédérés* (Federates), culminated in "*la semaine sanglante*" ("the Bloody Week") between May 21 and 28, 1871.

On May 24, Communards set fire to the center of Paris, burning down or badly damaging many buildings connected with the government, including, roughly from west to east:

- Palais des Tuileries.
- Palais du Louvre.

Figure 94. On May 11, 1871, the painter Gustave Courbet and other Communards pulled down the Vendôme Column with the statue of Napoléon Ier on top, in the center of the Place Vendôme. PHOTOGRAPH BY FRANÇOIS "FRANCK" GONET DE VILLECHOLLES (1816–1906).

- Ministère des Finances (on the Rue de Rivoli).
- Palais-Royal.
- Palais d'Orsay (on the site of the future Gare/Musée d'Orsay).
- Musée de la Légion d'Honneur.
- Palais de Justice.
- Hôtel de Ville.

On May 28, the army stormed the Père Lachaise Cemetery, where the Communards made their last stand. After ferocious fighting, 147 Communards, many of them wounded, surrendered. All were lined up and shot against a wall of the cemetery thereafter known as the "*Mur des Fédérés*" ("Wall of the Communards").

Figure 95. The ruins of the western façade of the Palais des Tuileries as seen from across the Rue de Rivoli, looking toward the Seine, 1871. PHOTOGRAPH BY ALPHONSE LIÉBERT (1827–1914).

Figure 96. The ruins of the Ministry of Finance on the Rue de Rivoli. PHOTOGRAPH BY ALPHONSE J. LIÉBERT (1827–1914).

Figure 97. Destruction caused by the fire on the Rue de Rivoli, 1871.
PHOTOGRAPH BY BRUNO AUGUSTE BRAQUEHAIS (1823–1875).

Figure 98. The Hôtel de Ville in 1871, after the fire. PHOTOGRAPH BY
CHARLES MARVILLE (1813–1879).

By the end of the insurrection, between six thousand and twenty thousand Parisians had been killed and forty-three thousand arrested.

PARIS AFTER THE COMMUNE

At the end of 1871, the national government returned to Paris and the Ministère des Finances moved into the new wing of the Louvre along the Rue de Rivoli.

Paris quickly bounced back from the Franco-Prussian War and the Commune. By 1873 France had already made the last of three payments of its indemnity to Germany, which in total were equivalent to 25 percent of France's annual gross domestic product, and rebuilding got underway.

Figure 99. The Conciergerie and the Cour de Cassation under repair after the fires of the Bloody Week. Note that one of the twin towers and the Tour Bonbec on the right have lost their conical roofs. PHOTOGRAPH BY HIPPOLYTE BLANCARD (1843–1924).

Figure 100. The new Hôtel de Ville behind the Pont d'Arcole. PHOTOGRAPH BY
GUSTAVE LE GRAY (1820–1884).

Following the destruction caused by the fires set by the Commune,
the Palais-Royal, the Ministère des Finances, and the Palais de Justice
were repaired. The Hôtel de Ville was entirely rebuilt (1873–1883, architects Théodore Ballu and Édouard Deperthes), as were the Museum of
the Legion of Honor and the Colonne Vendôme (1873–1875). The ruins
of the Tuileries Palace, however, were demolished (1882), as were the
ruins of the Palais d'Orsay (1898).

In 1872, building began on the Basilique du Sacré-Coeur in pure-
white travertine (a type of limestone) on Montmartre (architect Paul
Abadie). Its construction was originally intended to "expiate the crimes
of the Commune." The basilica was finally completed in 1914 and consecrated in 1919.

In 1880, at the same time as the 14 Juillet was designated a national holiday, the government granted a general amnesty for the events of the Commune.

On July 29, 1881, the Parliament passed a law on the freedom of the press in France. Among its many provisions, it forbade the posting of unofficial bills on public buildings, where only official notices were permitted to be posted. The law was soon followed by the appearance of the notice

Figure 101. Reconstruction of the Vendôme Column, 1873. PHOTO-GRAPH BY CHARLES MARVILLE (1813–1879) OR AUGUSTE HIPPOLYTE COLLARD (1812–1893).

Figure 102. "Post No Bills Law of 29 July 1881."

"Défense d'afficher—Loi du 29 juillet 1881" ("Post no bills—Law of July 29, 1881"), which is still seen stenciled on buildings throughout Paris.

The day after Victor Hugo died on May 22, 1885, the French government officially—and finally—returned the Panthéon to its status as "The Temple of Great Men." On June 1, 1885, more than two million people joined the funeral procession from the Arc de Triomphe de l'Étoile, where Victor Hugo's coffin had laid in state overnight, to the Panthéon, where his remains were laid to rest in the crypt. Victor Hugo was the first person to be buried in the Panthéon in over fifty years. The first woman to be buried in the Panthéon for her own accomplishments was Nobel Prize winner Marie Curie, whose remains were transferred in 1995.

In 1888, the Poste Centrale du Louvre (architect Julien Guadet)—the biggest mail distribution center in France—was inaugurated on the corner of the newly constructed Rue du Louvre (1853) and Rue Étienne-Marcel (1858–1880), both in the 1st arrondissement. Construction began in 1880, as soon as the Rue Étienne-Marcel was completed. Louis XV had originally purchased the Hôtel d'Armenonville on this site in 1757 to be used as the Hôtel des Postes. It was demolished to make way for the new central post office. After more than 125 years, the Poste Centrale du Louvre closed in 2015. The building is being renovated by architect Dominique Perrault for mixed use, to include a hotel, offices, shops, and social housing units.

LA BELLE ÉPOQUE

The period between 1889 and 1914—the heart of the *Belle Époque*, which is generally considered to have begun after the Commune—brought peace, prosperity, and innovation to France and especially to Paris, where the arts thrived. Brothers Auguste and Louis Lumière patented their *cinéamatographe* in 1895 and promptly screened their first moving picture at a *cinéma* near the Opéra Garnier on the Boulevard des Capucines. Armand Peugeot produced his first automobile in 1889, soon followed by René Panhard and Émile Levassor in 1891, while Louis Renault sold his first car in 1898. (André Citroën did not found his company until 1919.) France soon became the world's largest automobile manufacturer until it was finally surpassed by Great Britain in 1933. France was also a leader in aviation, boosted by Louis Blériot's winning in 1909 the prize of one thousand pounds sterling offered by the *Daily Mail* to the first person to fly an airplane across the English Channel. Blériot's flight to Dover took thirty-six minutes and thirty seconds. His plane is on display at the Musée des Arts et Métiers.

Society was reordered in republican France. The *haute bourgeoisie* and the *bourgeoisie "tout court"* (the upper middle class and the middle class in general) continued to climb the social ladder to become the dominant class. *Financiers*, property developers, industrialists, merchants, and traders with France's new colonies made their fortunes. Aristocrats who had fallen on hard times married their daughters, and the daughters of other *"nouveaux riches"* from abroad, trading their titles for money. Some of the new wealth was spent on the last of the grand *hôtels particuliers*, which were built in the latest chic district of Paris, the 16th arrondissement, bordered by the Seine to the east and the Bois de Boulogne to the west. Between 1896 and 1902, the Palais Rose, perhaps the grandest and most famous *hôtel particulier* in the 16th arrondissement, at 40 Avenue Foch, was built by Comte Boniface de Castellane after he married the daughter of the American railroad magnate Jay Gould; it was demolished in 1969. Perhaps the best surviving *hôtel particulier* in the 16th arrondissement is the Hôtel de Polignac (1904), at 43 Avenue Georges-Mandel, which was built by the widow of Prince Edmond de Polignac, who was heiress to the Singer Sewing Machine fortune; it now houses the Singer-Polignac Foundation.

On the cultural front, the Impressionists held their first salon in 1874. Auguste Rodin (1840–1917), considered by many to be the founder of modern sculpture, made his mark. The Musée Rodin, in the Hôtel Biron at 79 Rue de Varenne, 7ᵉ, with its sculpture garden, is one of the jewels of Paris. The museum first opened in 1919 and reopened after three years of restoration work on November 12, 2015—Rodin's 175th birthday. Montmartre was the artistic and literary center of Paris. The artists van Dongen, Braque, Brancusi, Juan Gris, Modigliani, and Max Jacob all lived and worked in the *Bateau-Lavoir* (the "Washhouse Boat," so dubbed by Max Jacob), a former ballroom and piano factory that was divided into twenty small workshops in 1889. Picasso joined them in 1902. All but the façade of the Bateau-Lavoir burned down in 1970, but the structure was entirely rebuilt in 1978.

The Belle Époque introduced *Art Nouveau* (1890–1914) and cabarets like the Moulin Rouge in Pigalle and Le Chat Noir and Le Lapin Agile on Montmartre, as depicted in the paintings and posters of Henri de Toulouse-Lautrec (1864–1901). Famous authors like Émile Zola (1840–1902), whose open letter *J'accuse* in 1898 provoked public outrage at the government's handling of the Dreyfus affair, Guy de Maupassant (1850–1893), and Jules Verne (1828–1905) published their best-selling books. Edmond Rostand (1868–1918) wrote the play *Cyrano de Bergerac* in 1897. English chic had arrived with the opening of Old England men's store on the Boulevard des Capucines, next to the Grand Hôtel, in 1866, to be followed by the opening of Maxim's on the Rue Royale in 1893 and Fouquet's on the Avenue des Champs-Élysées in 1899. "Maxim's" and "Fouquet's" were written and pronounced in the English manner.

Paris attracted artists from other countries, too, including Russia. Between 1909 and 1929, Serge Diaghilev's avant-garde Ballets Russes dance troupe, whose dancers included Vaslav Nijinsky and George Balanchine, was based in Paris. In 1913, Igor Stravinsky's *Le Sacre de Printemps* (The Rite of Spring) premiered at the newly opened Théâtre des Champs-Élysées, performed by the Ballets Russes and choreographed by Nijinsky.

In 1904, France and England signed the *Entente Cordiale*, a series of agreements that finally resolved the historic conflicts between these longtime enemies, anticipating the alliance between the two countries during the Great War.

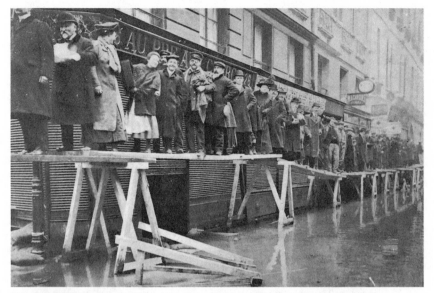

Figure 103. The Rue du Bac, 7ᵉ, during the Great Flood of January 1910.

In January 1910, the Seine overflowed its embankments and flooded the center of Paris. On many buildings near the Seine can be found plaques that indicate the high level mark of the *Crue Janvier 1910* (28.28 feet/8.62 meters).

The Belle Époque ended abruptly in 1914, with the beginning of World War I.

Building Works

Much of the first twenty years after the Commune, when Haussmann's right-hand man Adolphe Alphand served as *Directeur des Travaux de Paris* until his death in 1891, was spent completing projects initiated by Napoléon III and Haussmann, including the Opéra Garnier (started 1862, completed 1875), followed by the Avenue de l'Opéra (1864–1877), Boulevard Saint-Germain (1855–1877),* Boulevard Henri IV (1866–1879),

---

* The Boulevard Saint-Germain was built in three phases: The eastern section, in the relatively poor 5th arrondissement, opened in 1855; the western section, in the aristocratic 7th arrondissement, opened in 1865; and these two sections were connected when the middle section in the 6th arrondissement opened in 1877.

Figure 104. The Avenue de l'Opéra leading to the Opéra Garnier. Photograph by Neurdein. *PARIS ET SES ENVIRONS*—COLLECTION GEORGES SIROT (PHOTOGRAPH CIRCA 1890–1900).

Avenue de la République (1868–1889), Rue Dante (1877–1897), Rue du Louvre (1880–1915), and later Rue Danton (1888–1895), Rue Réaumur (1890–1907), Boulevard Raspail (1890–1907), and Boulevard Haussmann (1923–1927). After the decree of public use authorized the expropriation of the land and the construction of the street, it might be many years before works finally began, and construction would often be interrupted for many more. Paris was truly a construction site for the entire second half of the nineteenth century.

Haussmann believed that major monuments and even squares should form part of an *ensemble architectural*. When he built the *Grande Croisée*, he completed the Avenue de Rivoli started by Napoléon Ier and entirely rebuilt the Place du Châtelet first constructed by Napoléon Ier, flanked by two theaters with Napoléon Ier's Fontaine du Palmier in the center.

When he built the Place de l'Étoile—arguably the most magnificent of his *grandes places*—he added seven avenues to the circular square to make a twelve-pointed star and built identical *hôtels particuliers* around its perimeter, but the Arc de Triomphe was already there. Of all of the *Grands Travaux* undertaken by Haussmann (albeit finished by Alphand), none was more ambitious than the Opéra Garnier, which is the centerpiece of an architectural ensemble entirely carved out of the congested center of Paris over an eighteen-year period that also includes the Avenue de l'Opéra (a half-mile/689 meters long and 98 feet/30 meters wide), originally intended to be named Avenue Napoléon, lined from top to bottom with *immeubles haussmanniens* and anchored at one end by the Place de l'Opéra in front of the opera house and at the other end by the Place du Théâtre Français (now named the Place André Malraux) in front of the Comédie Française and leading to the Louvre. The opera house itself stands alone on an "island" surrounded by four streets forming the shape of a diamond: the Rues Auber, Scribe, Gluck, and Halévy, named after one French playwright (Auber) and three French composers—all built by Haussmann to allow Garnier's masterpiece to be admired from all angles. Normally, an *avenue* would have been lined with trees, but at Garnier's insistence none line the Avenue de l'Opéra in order not to impede the view of his magnificent opera house.

In 1881–1882, the so-called Jules Ferry laws (named after the president of the Council and minister of public instruction) provided for free secular education for all, and resulted in the construction of many schools for boys and girls throughout Paris and France.

Between 1885 and 1889, the circular Halle au Blé was rebuilt in its present form to become the Bourse de Commerce (architect Henri Blondel), located next to Les Halles and the Église Saint-Eustache in the 1st arrondissement.

Between 1883 and 1901, the enlarged "new Sorbonne" ("*la Nouvelle Sorbonne*") was built on a huge *îlot*—a rectangular block along the Rue Saint-Jacques between the Rue des Écoles and the Rue Cujas in the 5th arrondissement. The north wing along the Rue des Écoles houses the impressive Palais de l'Académie de Paris.

Figure 105. The Nouvelle Sorbonne. POSTCARD BY ND PHOT.

Between 1886 and 1889, the Galerie de Zoologie (architect Louis-Jules André) was built at the back of the Jardin des Plantes in the 5th arrondissement. After its closure in 1965 due to its dilapidated condition, it was beautifully remodeled between 1987 and 1994, when it reopened as the Grande Galerie de l'Évolution.

In 1889, the Musée Guimet (architect Charles Terrier) opened at 6 Place d'Iéna, 16ᵉ, to display the Asian art collected by Émile Guimet (1836–1918), an industrialist from Lyon.

In 1889, Paris hosted another World Exposition, featuring Gustave Eiffel's tower, rising 1,063 feet/324 meters above the Champ de Mars. It took two years and two months to erect the tower.

In 1893, the Olympia music hall opened at 28 Boulevard des Capucines, 9ᵉ.

Art Nouveau had an impact on the architecture of Paris. The rigid rules of the *haussmannien* esthetic—exemplified by the strict *alignement* of uniform façades along the Rue de Rivoli—were relaxed starting around 1890.

Arguably, the change in policy started with the construction of the commercial buildings at the west end of the Rue Réaumur, 2ᵉ and 3ᵉ, between 1894 and 1897 (the east end was built by Haussmann between 1854 and 1858), when the Ville de Paris conducted a *concours des façades* to recognize the most beautiful façade on the street. The first winner, in 1897, was the building at 116 Rue Réaumur, which featured sculpted figures supporting the balcony. The competition was expanded to all of Paris the following year, and continued until 1938. The next two winners were the Castel Béranger (architect Hector Guimard) at 14 Rue La Fontaine, 16ᵉ (1898), and the *hôtel particulier* of French architect Richard Bouwens Van der Boijen at 8 Rue de Lota, 16ᵉ (1899). It was also during the Belle Époque that corner buildings with cupolas appeared throughout the city, such as the Hôtel Astoria on the Champs-Élysées (which burned down in 1971) and many of the new *grands magasins* (department stores).

Figure 106. View down the Avenue des Champs-Élysées from the Arc de Triomphe de l'Étoile toward the Louvre. *PARIS ET SES ENVIRONS*—COLLECTION GEORGES SIROT (PHOTOGRAPH CIRCA 1890–1900).

With the passage of a new urban regulation on August 13, 1902, the strict uniformity of *haussmannisme* was officially superseded by a "picturesque" ("*pittoresque*") style of architecture: Buildings were no longer required to match their neighbors. They were permitted to be more individualistic (*autonome*), with distinctive façades including bow windows (*fênetres en saillie*), loggias, sculptures, and other ornamentation. As a result, many streets featured an eclectic variety of buildings. This trend is particularly noticeable on the Avenue des Champs-Élysées, the Grands Boulevards, and the Boulevard Raspail.

During the 1890s, metal, glass, and reinforced concrete replaced stone as the preferred construction materials. The new process was called "*le système Hennebique*" after its inventor François Hennebique, who in 1893 built the first concrete building in Paris in the Art Nouveau style as his company headquarters (architect Édouard Arnaud, ceramicist Alexandre Bigot) at 1 Rue Danton, 6ᵉ.

Also during the 1890s, the elevator—invented by the American Elisha Otis in 1861 and refined by the French engineer Félix Léon Eydoux in 1867—was integrated into the design of apartment buildings, immediately making apartments at the top of buildings the most desirable.

At the turn of the twentieth century, Paris was the scientfic and cultural capital of the world. To let its light shine, in 1900 Paris hosted the largest ever World's Fair, which was certainly the pinnacle of the Belle Époque.

The age of industrialization saw a series of world's fairs in London, Paris, and the United States—but between 1855 and 1900 Paris held five world's fairs, as many as all the others combined. Few things changed the urban landscape of Paris more than the *Expositions Universelles* of 1889, 1900, and 1937.

EXPOSITIONS UNIVERSELLES/WORLD'S FAIRS

The first world's fair was the Great Exhibition of the Works of Industry of All Nations at the Crystal Palace in London in 1851. It was followed by the world's fair in New York City in 1853. Napoléon III decided to host his own *Exposition Universelle* in 1855, featuring the *Palais de l'Industrie* in the Jardin des Champs-Élysées. To facilitate access to the exhibition, he instructed Haussmann to extend the Rue de Rivoli from the Tuileries Palace to the Rue Saint-Antoine, and to build the Hôtel du Louvre to accommodate imperial guests. The fair was attended by 4.5 million visitors.

London held its second International Exhibition in 1862. Paris responded in 1867, holding its second *Exposition Universelle* on the Champ de Mars, in front of the École Militaire. Most exhibits were

Figure 107. The Palais du Trocadéro, built in 1878 and demolished in 1936 to make way for the Palais de Chaillot. *PARIS ET SES ENVIRONS*—COLLECTION GEORGES SIROT (PHOTOGRAPH CIRCA 1890–1900).

located in the temporary, oval Palais du Champ de Mars. *Bateaux Mouches* (named after the *la Mouche* neighborhood in Lyon where the boats were manufactured) were first employed to permit tourists to view the pavilions from the river.* The fair was attended by nine million visitors.

Philadelphia hosted a world's fair in 1876, marking the centennial of the signing of the Declaration of Independence.

Paris's third *Exposition Universelle* was held in 1878—only seven years after the Commune—and featured the new Palais du Trocadéro in a distinctive Moorish style, that served as a concert and conference hall after the fair. A vast exhibition hall covered the Champ de Mars. Sixteen million visitors attended the fair.

While no major buildings remain from the first three *Expositions Universelles*, the interior of the Théâtre de la Gaîté Montparnasse was made out of materials recovered from the Théâtre de l'Exposition Universelle de 1867; the residential enclave Villa Beauséjour (7 Boulevard de Beauséjour, 16ᵉ) includes three Russian *isbas* (log huts) taken from the Russian Pavilion of the Universal Exhibition of 1867; and la Cité Fleurie (61-64 Boulevard Arago, 13ᵉ), a collection of artists' studios, was constructed between 1878 and 1888 from façades and structures taken from the *Pavillon de l'Alimentation* (Food Pavilion) of the Exposition Universelle de 1878.

The next three *Expositions Universelles* provided Paris with some of its most important monuments.

In 1889, one hundred years after the fall of the Bastille, Paris held another, even grander *Exposition Universelle* on the Champ de Mars and the Trocadéro, and commissioned engineer Gustave Eiffel to build his famous wrought-iron tower—*la dame de fer* (the iron lady)—for the occasion. At 1,063 feet/324 meters—nearly twice as high as the next tallest structure in the world at the time, the Washington Monument (completed in 1888)—it was a remarkable demonstration of French engineering skill.** The enormous glass and

---

* The Bateaux Mouches open excursion boats began service at the Port de la Conférence, 8ᵉ, in 1953.

** The Eiffel Tower was finally surpassed as the world's tallest structure by the Chrysler Building (1,046 feet/319 meters) in 1929, which was in turn surpassed by the Empire State Building (1,250 feet/381 meters) in 1931.

Figure 108. Aerial view of Paris from a balloon, showing the river Seine, the Eiffel Tower, and buildings of the Universal Exposition of 1889 covering the Champ de Mars. PHOTOGRAPH BY ALPHONSE J. LIÉBERT (1827–1914).

metal Galerie des Machines was constructed in front of the École Militaire to display sixteen thousand machines;* it was demolished in 1911. The fair was attended by thirty-two million visitors.

In 1893, Chicago hosted the Columbian Exposition, twenty-two years after the Chicago Fire razed the city.

Paris started the new century with its most spectacular fair ever—the *Exposition Universelle de 1900*—that attracted more than fifty million visitors from France and abroad. Paris also hosted the second Summer Olympics of the modern era in 1900 as part of the World's Fair. The principal venue of the exposition stretched from the Jardin des Champs-Élysées across the Seine to the Esplanade

---

* By far the most popular exhibit was the Edison Company's, which featured Thomas Edison's many inventions, including his latest—the phonograph. Outside the fairgrounds, Buffalo Bill's Wild West Show—with its star Annie Oakley, cowboys, one hundred Indians, two hundred horses, and twenty buffaloes—was the talk of the town.

Figure 109. The Grand and Petit Palais, with the Avenue des Champs-Élysées on the right. PHOTOGRAPH FROM *PARIS VU EN BALLON ET SES ENVIRONS* (1909).

des Invalides, and down the river to the Pont de l'Alma. The glass-topped Grand Palais (architects Henri Deglane, Albert Thomas, Albert Louvet, and Charles Girault) and the Petit Palais (architect Charles Girault) were constructed as exhibition halls. They were connected to the Left Bank and the exhibitions on the Esplanade des Invalides by the Alexandre III Bridge, the widest in Paris (131 feet/40 meters), a gift from the Russian czar that was modeled on a similar but much longer bridge in Saint Petersburg. The esplanade and bridge created an impressive new "axis" stretching in a straight line nearly 1 mile/1.6 kilometers from the Hôtel des Invalides to the Champs-Élysées.

Figure 110. The new Gare d'Orsay, which opened in 1900. POSTCARD BY L.D.

Figure 111. The Palais de Chaillot was built for the Universal Exposition of 1937; after the Exposition the Nazi and Soviet pavilions were taken down. POSTCARD FROM THE LATE 1930S BY GREFF.

The *Quai des Nations*, featuring dozens of picturesque national pavilions, was constructed along the Left Bank of the Seine between the Pont Alexandre III and the Pont de l'Alma.

To transport tourists to the exposition, three new train stations were built on the Left Bank: the Gare d'Orsay and the Gare des Invalides, both next to the Seine in the center of Paris, and the Gare Montparnasse to the south.

Finally, to connect the main venue of the exhibition to the annex in the Bois de Vincennes, at the eastern end of the city, Paris built its first subway, Métro line 1, on the Right Bank between the Porte Maillot on its western edge to the Porte de Vincennes on its eastern edge.* When excavating the Métro, part of a tower of the Bastille fortress was discovered and moved to the Square Henri-Galli at the beginning of Boulevard Henri IV, next to the Seine. The Métro's iconic Art Nouveau entrances were designed by Hector Guimard.

In the early twentieth century, the United States held World Expositions in Buffalo (1901), St. Louis (1904), San Francisco (1915), and Chicago (1933–1934).

Paris held its last Universal Exposition in 1937, for which it built the new Palais de Chaillot on the Place du Trocadéro (replacing the Palais du Trocadéro built for the 1878 fair, it now houses the Musée National de la Marine [Maritime Museum], the Musée de l'Homme [Museum of Man], and the Cité de l'Architecture et du Patrimoine [Museum of Architecture and Heritage]) and the Palais de Tokyo (which now houses the Musée de l'Art Moderne de la Ville de Paris).** Facing each other on the Right Bank on opposite sides of the Pont d'Iéna, in front of the Eiffel Tower, were the pavilions built by Nazi Germany and the Soviet Union; they were demolished after the Exposition. Thirty million visitors attended the fair.

---

* London's first underground train opened in 1863; New York's in 1872. The Paris Métro (short for *chemin de fer Métropolitain*) now has sixteen lines (the last line, the Météor, was inaugurated in 1998) and 303 stations, and is 133 miles/214 kilometers long. It is the second busiest metro in Europe, after Moscow. Châtelet-Les Halles is the world's largest subway station.

** The Palais de Tokyo was so named because of its location on the Avenue de Tokio [sic], which was renamed the Avenue de New-York in 1945.

Between 1909 and 1913, four of Paris's most famous *grands magasins* (department stores)—what Émile Zola called "*les temples de la consommation*" ("temples of consumption")—were built on the Right Bank, all using *le système Hennebique*.

THE EVOLUTION OF SHOPPING IN PARIS

The *Belle Époque* marked a high point in French fashion, and also in how and where the French shopped, which had gone through many changes over the centuries.

Before the arrival of sidewalks in the mid-nineteenth century, *la boue de Paris* (the Paris mud) made walking in the streets a dirty business. The rich traveled by carriage. Indoor shopping was an instant hit.

Galerie du Palais

In the sixteenth century, the Galerie du Palais was Paris's first shopping arcade, with shops set up in wooden galleries on either side of the Grande Salle (Great Hall) of the Palais de Justice (Law Courts).

After the Palais de Justice burned down on March 25, 1618, Queen Marie de Médicis's official architect, Salomon de Brosse, rebuilt the Great Hall, which now included a gallery with even more shops and was the place to see and be seen in the seventennth century.

The Gallery was so popular that it was enlarged several times. By 1700, it accommodated 180 merchants.

Palais-Royal

Between 1781 and 1786, the Duc de Chartres (future Duc d'Orléans and later Philippe-Égalité) rebuilt the Palais-Royal. He constructed shopping arcades, with rental apartments above, on three sides around the central garden (architect Victor Louis). On the south side, he built *les galeries de bois* (wooden galleries) for additional shops. From 1786 until 1830 (when it was surpassed by the Grands Boulevards), the Palais-Royal was the most popular place for Parisians to promenade, including Napoléon Bonaparte when he first arrived in Paris as an eighteen-year-old artillery lieutenant in 1787.

The success of the arcades inspired the Rue des Colonnes (1792) and the Rue de Rivoli (built with arcades from the Place de la

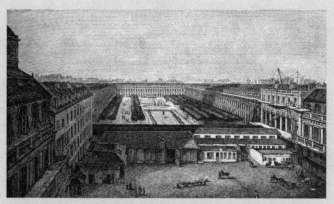

Figure 112. The Galeries de Bois in front of the Garden of the Palais-Royal in 1828. RECONSTITUTION BY T. J. H. HOFFBAUER.

Concorde to the Louvre between 1802 and 1835, and extended with arcades to the Rue du Louvre and without arcades to the Rue Saint-Antoine between 1849 and 1856). All the arcades were lined with shops. The wooden galleries of the Palais-Royal may also have inspired the covered *passages* of the first half of the nineteenth century.

Passages

More than forty covered shopping passages or galeries (covered galleries) were built on the Right Bank, mainly near the Grands Boulevards, between 1820 and 1850. Twenty passages were built in the 1820s alone; another nine were built between 1839 and 1847.

Haussmann's boulevards (all equipped with sidewalks and "street furniture") and the arrival of the grands magasins (department stores) led to the disappearance of most of the passages. Seventeen passages still survive.

Grands Magasins

In 1838, Aristide Boucicault founded Le Bon Marché, which became Paris's first department store (*grand magasin*) and one of the first in the world. The flagship store on the Rue de Sèvres, 7ᵉ, was built in 1869, and was the model for subsequent department stores.* The

---

* Émile Zola's novel *Au Bonheur des Dames* (*The Ladies' Paradise*, 1883) is set in a department store inspired by Le Bon Marché.

Figure 113. Au Printemps department store on Boulevard Haussmann, 9ᵉ.
PHOTOGRAPH BY LÉON AND LÉVY.

large store of Au Printemps on the Boulevard Haussmann, 9ᵉ, behind the Opéra Garnier, opened in 1909. Its neighbor, Galeries Lafayette, opened its grand store in 1912. La Samaritaine opened its Art Nouveau emporium on the Right Bank across from the Pont Neuf in 1910 (architect Frantz Jourdain); its Art Déco façade was added between 1926 and 1928 (architect Henri Sauvage). The Bazar de l'Hôtel de Ville on the Rue de Rivoli, with its famous rotunda, opened in 1913.

In 1912, the project to cover the Bièvre (Beaver) river in Paris, which Belgrand had begun in 1877, was finally completed. The river originally flowed into the Seine near the Austerlitz train station but had become polluted by tanneries and other industries. The bucolic Square des Peupliers, in the village-like Butte aux Cailles neighborhood, 13ᵉ, was built over the covered river in 1926.

Figure 114. Tanneries on the Bièvre river, 1904. PHOTOGRAPH BY LOUIS VERT (1865–1924).

In 1913, after two years of construction, the Théâtre des Champs-Élysées (architect Henry van de Velde) opened at 15 Avenue Montaigne, 8ᵉ. It was the first example of Art Déco architecture in Paris.

Also in 1913, the first law on the protection of national monuments was passed.

In 1914, the new brick and stone Galerie des Gobelins (architect Jean-Camille Formigé) was constructed at 42 Avenue des Gobelins, 13ᵉ. It is now part of the *Administration Générale du Mobilier National* (National Furniture Administration), which originally was responsible for the administration of all furniture and objects in the royal residences and now administers the furniture and furnishings of the French state.

WORLD WAR I

The Great War started in August 1914, pitting France, Russia, and Great Britain against Austria-Hungary and Germany. Most of the conflict was fought in northern France, but during the first week of September 1914 German troops advanced to within 30 miles/50 kilometers of Paris before being pushed back by the French and British armies in the First Battle of the Marne. One and a half million French soldiers were killed in the trench warfare that dragged on for four long years, with hostilities finally ending on November 11, 1918, the anniversary of which has ever since been celebrated as a national holiday in France (Armistice Day), the United Kingdom (Remembrance Day), and the United States (Veterans Day).

Near the end of the war, the Germans developed a special long-range siege gun, known as the "Paris Gun" and nicknamed "Big Bertha," to bombard Paris. It was the largest artillery gun of the war, with a total barrel length of 112 feet/34 meters (the barrel was so long that it needed to be supported by a cable), and was able to shell Paris from a distance of 75 miles/120 kilometers. Between March and August 1918, the gun fired a total of around 350 shells, at a maximum rate of around twenty per day. The shells killed 250 people, wounded 620, and caused considerable property damage. The worst incident occurred on March 29, 1918, when a single shell hit the roof of the Saint-Gervais-Saint-Protais Church behind the Hôtel de Ville, causing it to collapse on the congregation below who were attending a Good Friday service, killing ninety-one people and injuring sixty-eight.

World War I formally concluded with the signing of the Treaty of Versailles on June 28, 1919. The treaty, which ended the German Empire, was signed in the same Hall of Mirrors of the Château de Versailles where the German Empire was proclaimed in 1871. Many commentators believe that the severe terms imposed on Germany by the Allies sowed the seeds for World War II.

ENTRE-DEUX-GUERRES AND LES ANNÉES FOLLES

During the twenty-year period between the two wars, France had forty-two governments, but Paris was the intellectual and cultural capital of the world.

In 1921, the population of Paris peaked at 2,906,472. It then decreased through the rest of the century as people moved to the suburbs.

Between 1913 and 1927, the seven volumes of Marcel Proust's masterpiece *À la Recherche du Temps Perdu* (*In Search of Lost Time*) were published. Most of the books were written when Proust (1871–1922) lived at 102 Boulevard Haussmann, 8ᵉ, from 1907 to 1919.

During *les Années Folles* (the Crazy Years) of the 1920s, Art Déco replaced Art Nouveau. Artists and writers from around the world gravitated to Paris and particularly to Montparnasse. Picasso and other artists moved their studios there from Montmartre. Hemingway (as recounted in his 1964 memoir *A Moveable Feast*), Scott and Zelda Fitzgerald, and other American expatriate writers from the Lost Generation congregated at Le Dôme, La Rotonde, La Coupole, Le Select, or La Closerie des Lilas, which are all still in business on the Boulevard Montparnasse.

Between 1914 and 1930, the Avenue des Champs-Élysées was the place to go for luxury shopping and entertainment, with the boutiques of fashion designers Louis Vuitton, Jeanne Lanvin, and Madeleine Vionnet, and showrooms for carmakers Renault and Panhard et Levassor, as well as the famous cinemas Le Normandie and Le Colisée along with many cafés and restaurants. Offices began to take over the avenue in the 1930s.

Between 1931 and 1940, Paris suffered from the Great Depression that had started in the United States in 1929.

Building Works Between the Wars
With the arrival of the twentieth century, Paris entered the age of city planning (*urbanisme*)—and no city has been subject to more planning than Paris. Kings and emperors no longer decided what to build. The city government, with its commissions and their urban planning studies, took over.

With outbreaks of tuberculosis aggravated by a growing population living in inadequate accommodations, providing sanitary housing was a priority. So was public transport, especially the construction of Paris's subway system. By 1914, ten Métro lines had been completed. Other lines would be built in the 1930s.

While many urban planning studies were carried out and projects presented in the first half of the twentieth century, the combination of two world wars and the Great Depression prevented most of them from

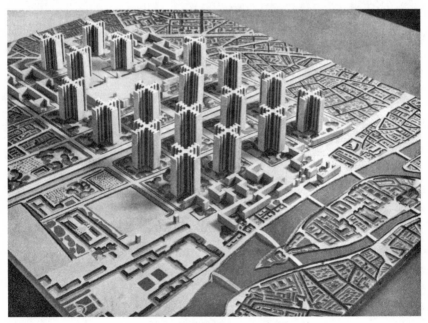

Figure 115. Model of Le Corbusier's Plan Voisin, 1925.

actually being carried out. Some of the projects proposed would have changed Paris's historic center forever—such as the *Plan Voisin* designed by the Swiss-French architect Le Corbusier (1887–1965) in 1925, which would have razed the Marais and built skyscrapers in its place. By the time major building works began in the 1960s, it had finally become official policy to preserve the historic center of Paris. In the area outside the historic center, however, renovation projects proliferated.

The biggest project undertaken during the period *entre-deux-guerres* (1919–1939) was certainly the demolition of the *Fortifications Thiers*, when Paris once again became an "open city." Originally, the area around this last city wall was intended to become a *ceinture verte* (green belt) around Paris. In the end, a wide range of projects constructed over many decades, both before and after World War II, filled this vast empty space.

Chronology

After the Great War, the *Fortifications Thiers* were demolished between 1919 and 1929, creating an enormous construction site 22 miles/35 kilometers long and a quarter-mile/400 meters wide on which were built the Parc des Expositions at the Porte de Versailles (starting in 1923), the Cité Universitaire (a university campus with residential buildings, 1927), several stadiums, gymnasiums, and schools, but mostly *habitations à bon marché* (later called *habitations à loyer modéré*—low/moderate cost housing projects). Paris's ring road, the Boulevard Périphérique, was constructed on the outside section of the same space between 1958 and 1973.

Between 1904 and 1926, Jean Claude Nicolas Forestier laid out the gardens and promenades of the Champ de Mars, where part of the Exposition Universelle of 1900 had been held. Between 1906 and the 1920s, two stretches of land 100 yards/90 meters wide bordering either side of the Champ de Mars were platted for the construction of grand *hôtels particuliers* and apartment buildings.

In 1919, the Basilica of Sacré-Coeur was finally consecrated, and Paris's first airport, Le Bourget, started commercial operations 7 miles/11 kilometers northeast of the city.*

---

* Charles Lindbergh landed his airplane *The Spirit of St. Louis* at Le Bourget on May 21, 1927, after the first nonstop solo flight across the Atlantic Ocean.

Figure 116. The Basilica of the Sacred Heart on Montmartre, looking north. PHO-
TOGRAPH FROM *PARIS VU EN BALLON* (1909).

Between 1922 and 1926, the Mosquée de Paris was built in the 5th arrondissement, behind the Jardin des Plantes, in memory of the Muslim soldiers from the colonies who fought for France and died in World War I.

Between 1894 and 1905, 138,766 Parisians died of tuberculosis, with 40 percent of them living in 6.5 percent of the buildings in Paris. Seventeen "*îlots insalubres*" ("unhealthy zones") were designated based on their mortality rate from tuberculosis. The overcrowded and impoverished Beaubourg area to the east of Les Halles was deemed to be the area of Paris most susceptible to the outbreaks. Between 1923 and 1934, *Îlot insalubre numéro 1* was demolished, clearing the *Plateau Beaubourg*, which remained vacant until the Centre Pompidou was built there in 1977.

In 1924, the Summer Olympic Games were held in Paris.

Between 1924 and 1927, the Salle Pleyel music hall was built at 252 Rue du Faubourg Saint-Honoré, 8ᵉ.

Between 1924 and 1931, the Gare de l'Est was doubled in size.

In 1925, the morgue, which had been constructed in 1868 at the east end of the Île de la Cité, was demolished and a garden (*le Square de l'Île-de-France*) was put in its place.

In 1926, the Square Viviani was created next to the Église Saint-Julien-le-Pauvre, 5ᵉ.

Between 1926 and 1928, the Art Déco building of La Samaritaine department store was constructed on the Right Bank opposite the Pont Neuf (architect Henri Sauvage).

In 1927, the Musée de l'Orangerie opened to exhibit eight murals of water lilies (*nymphéas*) by Claude Monet.

In 1928, the French-Polish sculptor Paul Landowski created the statue of Sainte-Geneviève on the Pont de la Tournelle.[*]

Between 1930 and 1932, the width of the Pont de la Concorde was doubled.

In 1931, Paris hosted the Exposition Coloniale in the Bois de Vincennes, for which was built the Palais de la Porte Dorée at 293 Avenue Daumesnil, 12ᵉ. Since 2007, the building houses the *Cité nationale de l'histoire de l'immigration* (Museum of Immigration).

Also in 1931, the massive brick Institut d'Art et de l'Archéologie, with its *façade exotique*, was inaugurated at 6 Avenue de l'Observatoire, 6ᵉ (architect Paul Bigot).

In 1931–1932, the Grand Rex cinema was built in the Art Déco style at 1 Boulevard Poissonnière, 2ᵉ. With a capacity of twenty-eight hundred spectators, it is still the largest cinema in Europe.

In 1932, the striking ensemble of three residential buildings on the Carrefour Curie (named after Pierre Curie, husband of Marie) was inaugurated on the Left Bank at the junction of the Rue Dauphine, the Rue de Nevers, and the Quai de Conti, opposite the Pont Neuf. The architect Joseph Marrast (1881–1971) chose to face the buildings in brick to recall the two surviving original buildings at the western end of the Place Dauphine that were constructed during the reign of Henri IV. The scale of the ensemble is roughly comparable to that of the new Art Déco building of La Samaritaine department store at the other end of the Pont Neuf.

---

[*] Landowski is the same sculptor who in 1931 created the huge Christ the Redeemer sculpture atop Corcovado in Rio de Janeiro.

In 1932, Paris's second airport, Orly, opened 8 miles/13 kilometers south of Paris.

In 1934, the Parc Zoologique de Paris opened in the Bois de Vincennes.

In 1935, construction of the Église Sainte-Odile (architect Jacques Barge) in the Neo-Byzantine style got underway at 2 Avenue Stéphane-Mallarmé, 17ᵉ, just inside the Boulevard Périphérique near the Porte de Champerret. The project was only completed in 1946. It was part of the *Chantiers du Cardinal* program begun in 1931 to promote the construction and maintenance of Catholic churches in and around Paris. The concrete bell tower, which is 235 feet/72 meters tall and stands out on the Paris skyline, is the highest in the city. The church is also 72 meters long, another reference to the 72 disciples of Jesus Christ.

In 1937, Paris hosted its last International Exposition, for which it built the Palais de Chaillot on the Place du Trocadéro, 16ᵉ (replacing the Palais du Trocadéro built for the 1878 fair), and the Palais de Tokyo on Avenue du Président-Wilson, 16ᵉ (now the Musée d'Art Moderne de la Ville de Paris).

CHAPTER 10

1940–Present

WORLD WAR II

Seven weeks after invading France, the German army occupied Paris on June 14, 1940. In the early morning of June 23, 1940, Hitler made his first and only visit to Paris, when he was photographed on the terrace of the Palais du Trocadéro, with the Eiffel Tower in the background. His favorite building was the Opéra Garnier.

On July 10, 1940, the pro-Axis Vichy government, led by the World War I hero Marshal Philippe Pétain, replaced the Third Republic.

During the four-year-long occupation, the German High Command was headquartered at the Hôtel Crillon on the Place de la Concorde,* and the *Abwehr* (German intelligence service) at the Hôtel Lutétia on Boulevard Raspail on the Left Bank.**

On August 24, 1944, Free French troops led by General Philippe Leclerc entered Paris, soon followed by Allied troops. On August 25, the German commander, General Dietrich von Cholitz, surrendered to the Free French at the Hôtel Meurice. Fortunately, he disobeyed Hitler's order to destroy Paris before the Allied troops arrived. That same day, General Charles de Gaulle and his entourage walked from the Arc de Triomphe down the Avenue des Champs-Élysées to the Place de la Concorde, braving sniper fire.

---

* The Hôtel Crillon reopened in 2017 after extensive renovations.

** The Hôtel Lutétia reopened in 2018 after extensive renovations.

Almost no building works took place in Paris between 1940 and 1946. However, many old buildings were demolished, especially in the Marais.

Beginning in 1941, *l'îlot insalubre numéro 16*, roughly located between the Quai de l'Hôtel de Ville and the Quai des Célestins to the south, and the Rue François-Miron and Rue Saint-Antoine to the north, was in large part demolished. Fortunately, the Église Saint-Gervais, as well as the Hôtel de Sens (now housing the Forney art library), the Hôtel d'Aumont (now the Tribunal Administratif de Paris, at 7 Rue de Jouy), and their gardens, were spared.

After the war, the demolition of the west side of the Rue des Jardins Saint-Paul behind the Saint-Paul-Saint-Louis Church in 1946 uncovered a 260-foot-/80-meter-long remnant of the Philippe-Auguste Wall. On the east side of the street is the Village Saint-Paul, a square block of buildings that were renovated in 1979 and now includes eighty mainly antiques shops located around newly constructed inner courtyards.

At the western end of the *îlot insalubre numéro 16*, behind the Saint-Gervais-Saint-Protais Church, the area around the Rue des Barres, which dates back to the Middle Ages, was rehabilitated by the architect Albert Laprade between 1945 and 1971 and turned into a picturesque pedestrian zone.

In the middle of the *îlot*, the Cité Internationale des Arts (with residential and studio space for artists) was finally built in 1965, set back from the quai at 18 Rue de l'Hôtel de Ville, just west of the Pont Marie.

LES TRENTE GLORIEUSES (1946–1975)

"Les Trente Glorieuses" ("The Glorious Thirty") refers to the thirty years of rapid economic growth in France following the end of World War II. The name comes from French demographer Jean Fourastié's 1979 book *Les Trente Glorieuses, ou la révolution invisible de 1946 à 1975* (*The Glorious Thirty, or the Invisible Revolution from 1946 to 1975*). The title is derived from *Les Trois Glorieuses* (The Glorious Three), referring to the three days of the July Revolution in France, which took place from July 27 to July 29, 1830. Alongside the economic boom, the cultural life of Paris once again flourished. Writers

and artists moved from Montparnasse to Saint-Germain-des-Prés, where they met at the Brasserie Lipp (opened in 1877 by Alsatian Léonard Lipp) and Café de Flore (opened around 1890). The philosopher Jean-Paul Sartre and writer Simone de Beauvoir held court at the Café Les Deux Magots (opened 1891), where brass plaques engraved with their names are affixed to the wall above their usual tables in the corner.

Marked by the horrors of the war, the avant-garde "Theater of the Absurd" emerged in Paris, with the playwrights Eugène Ionesco, Samuel Beckett, and Jean Genet. Actors Jean-Louis Barrault and his wife Madeleine Renaud were at the height of their art.

Pablo Picasso and Marc Chagall left Paris for the south of France, where they ended their long artistic careers.

Photographers Henri Cartier-Bresson (who founded Magnum Photos in 1947), Willy Ronis, Robert Doisneau, and Marc Riboud recorded iconic images of Paris.

Singers Edith Piaf, Yves Montand, Léo Ferré, Georges Brassens, Jacques Brel, Barbara, Serge Reggiani, Georges Moustaki (who wrote "Milord" for Piaf), and Jean Ferrat topped the hit parade.

At the end of the 1950s, the New Wave of French cinema arrived, led by directors François Truffaut, Jean-Luc Godard, Claude Chabrol, Eric Rohmer, and Jacques Rivette.

THE FOURTH (1946–1958) AND FIFTH (1958–PRESENT) REPUBLICS

General Charles de Gaulle (1890–1969), leader of the Free French Forces during the German occupation, was the first head of the government under the Fourth Republic, but resigned in 1946 when the new constitution failed to provide for the presidential system of government that he wanted.

The twenty-one governments of the Fourth Republic (the longest lasted thirteen months) first focused on rebuilding France's infrastructure after the war, and then on fighting France's colonial wars in Indochina between 1946 and 1954 and in Algeria between 1954 and 1962. As a result, they postponed modernizing Paris.

In 1958, Charles de Gaulle returned to politics to deal with the Algerian crisis, which the unstable Fourth Republic had proved unable to resolve. At his instigation, a new constitution was adopted, creating the Fifth Republic with increased power for the president. De Gaulle was elected president in 1959 and served for ten years.

In 1959, de Gaulle appointed the writer André Malraux (who wrote the novel *La Condition Humaine* in 1933) as the first minister of cultural affairs (1959–1969).

In 1962, the Loi Malraux was passed, extending the protection of France's *patrimoine* from individual historic monuments to include entire historic neighborhoods designated as *secteurs sauvegardés*. The 310 acres/126 hectares of the Marais and 420 acres/171 hectares of the faubourg Saint-Germain were designated "safeguarded sectors" under the law in 1964 and 1972, respectively. (They are still the only *secteurs sauvegardés* in Paris, governed by respective *Plans de sauvegarde et de Mise en valeur*.) The government undertook a long-term program to restore the *hôtels particuliers* in both sectors, which today house ministries (especially in the 7th arrondissement), state and municipal agencies (especially in the 4th arrondissement), and museums.

During the 1960s Malraux also initiated a program to clean the soot-covered stone monuments and buildings of Paris, turning Notre-Dame, the Arc de Triomphe, and the Louvre from black to white. The program took nearly two decades to complete, and then it was necessary to start again. At the same time, owners of private buildings in Paris were required to clean and repair the exteriors of their buildings at least once every ten years in a process known as "*ravalement*."

In 1968, the *département de la Seine* was divided into four *départements*: Paris (75), Hauts-de-Seine (92), Seine-Saint-Denis (93), and Val-de-Marne (94). The three departments surrounding Paris are known as "*la petite couronne*" ("the little crown"). The *département de la Seine-et-Oise* was divided into three *départements*: Essonne (91), Yvelines (78), and Val-d'Oise (95). In 1976, these seven *départements* were named the *Région de l'Île de France*.

In May 1968, students in the Latin Quarter rebelled against the establishment, nearly bringing down the government. Miraculously, no one died.

In 1969, Charles de Gaulle resigned as president; he died in 1970, at age seventy-nine.

In 1970, the University of Paris was divided into thirteen autonomous universities, identified as Université de Paris I–Sorbonne Panthéon, Université de Paris II–Panthéon Assas, etc.

Georges Pompidou (1911–1974), de Gaulle's prime minister between 1962 and 1968, succeeded him as president in 1969 and continued the modernization campaign that he had started as prime minister, including the following projects that are most closely associated with him:

- Introduction of high-rise buildings in Paris, and especially the Tour Montparnasse.

- Opening Paris to the automobile through the construction of the Boulevard Péripherique (the ring road around the city) and the *voies sur berges* (the express highways in the city alongside the Seine).

- Demolition of the Baltard Pavilions and redevelopment of Les Halles.

- Construction of the Centre Pompidou modern art museum (1971–1977).

The economic downturn brought on by the oil crisis of late 1973 marked the end of the *Trente Glorieuses*.

The elections of subsequent presidents of France and mayors of Paris are included in the section below on building works carried out since World War II.

Building Works Since World War II

During the twentieth century, more square feet/meters of space were built in Paris than in all previous centuries combined. Most of the construction took place in the second half of the century for residential purposes in response to the surge in population and the need to upgrade dilapidated housing, and almost all of it in the double-digit arrondissements outside the historic center.

THE EVOLUTION OF THE POPULATION OF PARIS AND ITS ARRONDISSEMENTS

59 BC	25,000	At the beginning of the Roman conquest of Gaul
150 AD	80,000	Peak of the Roman era
510	30,000	Drop due to the barbarian invasions of the third and fourth centuries
700s	20–30,000	
1000	20,000	Lowest point after the Viking invasions of the ninth century
1200	110,000	Recovery of the High Middle Ages
1250	160,000	
1300	228,000	
1328	250,000	Golden Age of Saint Louis
1340	300,000	
1400	280,000	
1500	200,000	Drop due to the Black Plague and the Hundred Years War
1550	275,000	Renaissance recovery
1594	210,000	Drop due to the Wars of Religion
1634	420,000	Dramatic recovery under Henri IV and Louis XIII
1700	515,000	
1750	565,000	
1789	630,000	Peak of the eighteenth century, on the eve of the Revolution
1801	546,856	Drop due to the Revolution and the Revolutionary Wars
1811	622,636	
1817	718,966	
1831	785,862	

1836	899,313	
1841	935,261	
1846	1,053,897	
1851	1,053,262	
1856	1,174,346	
1861	1,696,141	New city limits doubled the surface area of Paris
1866	1,825,274	
1872	1,851,792	Temporary stagnation due to the Siege of Paris and the Commune
1876	1,988,806	
1881	2,269,023	
1886	2,344,550	
1891	2,477,957	
1896	2,536,834	
1901	2,714,068	
1906	2,763,393	
1911	2,888,110	
1921	2,906,472	Historic peak in population despite World War I
1926	2,871,429	
1931	2,891,020	
1936	2,829,753	
1946	2,725,374	Drop due to World War II
1954	2,850,189	
1962	2,790,091	Dramatic migration to the suburbs between 1962 and 1975
1968	2,590,771	
1975	2,299,830	Population stabilizes
1982	2,176,243	
1990	2,152,423	

1999	2,125,851
2010	2,243,833
2014	2,241,346

N.B. These numbers reflect Paris *intra muros*. The population of the urban area around Paris—the *banlieue**—has steadily increased from one million in 1835, to two million in 1863, to three million in 1885, to four million in 1904, to 10,516,110 in 2011. In 2019, the population of the Île-de-France region, including Paris and its *banlieue*, was estimated to be 12,213,364.

Since the annexation of the surrounding villages in 1860, which created the current city limits and twenty arrondissements of Paris, there have been major population shifts among the arrondissements. The 1st through 11th arrondissements in the center of Paris have declined in population, while the 12th through 20th arrondissements on the periphery have grown in population:

Arrondissement	1872	2016
1st	74,286	16,252
2nd	73,578	20,260
3rd	89,687	34,788
4th	95,003	27,487
5th	96,689	59,108
6th	90,288	40,916
7th	78,553	52,512
8th	75,553	36,453
9th	103,767	59,629
10th	135,392	91,932
11th	167,393	147,017
12th	87,678	141,494

---

* *La banlieue* originally referred to the area outside a city that was under the city's authority (*ban*), which extended the distance a man could walk in one hour (a *lieue*—later estimated to be around 2.5 miles/4 kilometers).

13th	69,431	181,552
14th	69,611	137,105
15th	75,449	233,484
16th	43,332	165,446
17th	101,804	167,835
18th	138,109	195,060
19th	93,174	186,393
20th	92,772	195,604
TOTAL	1,851,792	2,190,327

Credit: Institut National de la Statistique et des Études Économiques

In 1954, the population of Paris finally returned to its 1936 level of 2.8 million, boosted by 135,000 postwar immigrants, mostly from Algeria, Morocco, Italy, and Spain. With the exodus of middle-class Parisians to the suburbs, the population of the city declined during the 1960s and 1970s before finally stabilizing around 2.2 million in the 1980s.

Postwar housing in Paris was old and run-down. In 1954, 35 percent of Paris apartment buildings had been built before 1871, 81 percent of Paris apartments did not have their own bathroom, and 55 percent did not have their own toilet. Largely to deal with this housing crisis, the postwar years saw a dramatic increase in *urbanisme* (city planning) intended to renovate and modernize the city, and the introduction of the PUD (*plan d'urbanisme directeur*), the POS (*plan d'occupation des sols*), the PLU (*plan local d'urbanisme*), the ZUP (*zone à urbaniser en priorité*), and the ZAC (*zone d'aménagement concerté*), along with many other acronyms.

Paris's industries were principally located in the 13th, 15th, and 19th arrondissements, and in *la banlieue* (suburbs). To make room for development, the government "deindustrialized" Paris after World War II, using tax incentives and zoning changes to force factories and warehouses to relocate outside the city. The closures included the Peugeot factory on the Île Séguin in Boulogne-Billancourt and the Citroën factory beside the

Figure 117. The industrial area alongside the Seine in the 15th arrondissement, now occupied by the Front de Seine/Beaugrenelle development. PHOTOGRAPH FROM *PARIS VU EN BALLON* (1909).

Seine in the west of the city; les Abattoirs (slaughterhouses) de la Villette in the north; and the Bercy wine warehouses (*entrepôts*), les Grands Moulins de Paris, and the Panhard et Levassor automobile factory in the east. Most of the urban renovation projects undertaken in Paris during the Fifth Republic focused on these deindustrialized areas.

In 1955, the government began a new large-scale project to construct apartment blocks for low-income Parisians, called HLMs (*habitations à loyer modéré*), usually on the edges of the city or in the suburbs.[*]

In 1956, the government encouraged high-rise construction by eliminating the old building height restriction of 102 feet/31 meters—the seven-story structures of Haussmann's Paris.

In the 1960s and 1970s, scores of high-rise office and apartment buildings were built, mostly on the periphery of the city. Most office buildings were to the west, whereas the towers to the east were nearly all residential. The only two towers built in the center of Paris were the administrative center of the Préfecture of Paris (1957–1964, 17 floors) on the Boulevard Morland, 4ᵉ, and the Zamansky (or Jussieu) Tower (1970, 295 feet/90 meters high, 27 floors) in the center of the Jussieu campus of the University of Paris in the 5th arrondissement. Outside the city center, on the Left Bank there was the huge *Italie 13* project to renovate the former working class neighborhood of the 13th arrondissement and build residential high-rises (1955–1975); the Front de Seine (or Beaugrenelle) mixed-use development, consisting of 20 towers alongside the Seine in the deindustrialized 15th arrondissement (1962–1990); and the construction of office buildings around the Montparnasse train station in the Quartier de la Gaïeté, including the 886-foot-/207-meter-high Tour Montparnasse (1972)—the only skyscraper in Paris. Finally, in 1958 construction began in La Défense, Europe's largest purpose-built business district, located on 400 acres/162 hectares to the west of Paris.

Georges Pompidou, who famously said, "*Il faut adapter la ville à l'automobile*" ("The city must adapt to the automobile"), built two enormous roadworks projects to bring the automobile into Paris:

---

[*] Today, approximately ten million people in France (15 percent of the population) live in HLMs.

- The 22-mile-/35-kilometer-long Boulevard Périphérique ring road built between 1960 and 1973 on the outer edge of the former no-man's-land surrounding the Thiers Fortifications.

- The riverside express highways known as the *voies sur berges*, built between 1964 and 1967 on the Right Bank and a shorter stretch on the Left Bank.

Pompidou was primarily responsible for the modernization of Paris, both when he was prime minister under President Charles de Gaulle between 1962 and 1968, and when he was president from 1969 until his unexpected death in 1974. It was Pompidou who approved the construction of the Tour Montparnasse and the destruction of Les Halles. These two projects made clear the risk to Paris's urban landscape posed by unrestricted development and provoked the opposition to more skyscrapers in Paris and the support for the preservation and conversion of historic buildings such as the Gare d'Orsay.

Pompidou also started the presidential tradition of sponsoring a cultural monument as part of his legacy—in his case, the modern art museum named the Pompidou Center in his honor, near Les Halles.

With the election of Valéry Giscard d'Estaing as president in 1974 and the election of Jacques Chirac as the first mayor of Paris since the Revolution in 1977,[*] Pompidou's modernizing programs came to an abrupt halt. In particular, the construction of skyscrapers stopped when, at the instigation of President Giscard d'Estaing, the Ville de Paris approved the *Plan d'Occupation des Sols* in 1977 that imposed a maximum height of 121 feet/37 meters on all buildings in Paris and promoted instead the renovation and rehabilitation of old buildings.

As his cultural legacy, Giscard d'Estaing initiated the conversion of the Gare d'Orsay into the Musée d'Orsay.

The election of François Mitterrand as president in 1981 marked the beginning of *Grands Projets* not seen since the Second Empire, as well as, starting in 1983, a vast program for the development of the east side of

---

[*] The office of the mayor was briefly reestablished after the February Revolution of 1848 and again after the fall of the Second Empire in 1870, but did not last long in either case.

HIGH-RISES AND GRATTE-CIELS/SKYSCRAPERS

Ever since Louis XV there have been restrictions on the height of buildings in Paris. Starting in 1784, the authorized height varied depending on the width of the street. The rules changed regularly, with the construction of ever-wider avenues and boulevards. Finally, in 1956, the then 102-foot/31-meter restriction on the height of buildings in Paris was eliminated.

Between 1960 and 1975, nearly 160 high-rise buildings more than 164 feet/50 meters high were constructed in Paris; 130 more were built just outside Paris. More than half the high-rises in Paris— formally known as *immeubles de grande hauteur* (IGH) and many of them massive apartment blocks appropriately known as *immeubles-barres* (bar buildings, high-rise buildings that are longer than they are high)—were built in the 13th and 15th arrondissements. A particularly massive example of the *immeuble-barre* is the giant HLM designed by Jean Dubuisson and built between 1960 and 1964 alongside the tracks of Gare Montparnasse at 8-26 Rue du Commandant René-Mouchotte, 14e.

The first residential IGH to be built in Paris was the Tour Croulebarbe (architect Édouard Albert, 200 feet/61 meters high, 22 floors) in the 13th arrondissement. It was built between 1957 and 1961.

The huge *Italie 13* project followed in the 1960s and 1970s in the former working class neighborhood of 215 acres/87 hectares in the 13th arrondissement. Development included the area around the Place d'Italie, the district now known as *Les Olympiades*, and the Masséna district along the Boulevards des Maréchaux. *Les Olympiades* district comprises 8 residential towers, each 341 feet/109 meters tall with 36 floors and named after a city that hosted the Olympics, built on a raised pedestrian plaza (*dalle*, or slab) with parking underneath, following the principles espoused by the architect Le Corbusier in his *Plan Voisin* of 1925.

Between 1962 and 1990, the development of the 30-acre/12-hectare district now known as the *Front de Seine* or *Beaugrenelle* took place alongside the river in the 15th arrondissement, with 20 towers, all 394 feet/120 meters high, for mixed residential and commercial use, also built on an elevated pedestrian plaza.

By far the highest building in Paris, at 689 feet/210 meters and 59 floors—and the only skyscraper (defined as a building with a roof height of at least 492 feet/150 meters)—is the controversial Tour Montparnasse in the northeastern corner of the 15th arrondissement, in front of the Gare Montparnasse. It was built between 1969 and 1973 as part of the development of the 20-acre/8-hectare site around the Maine-Montparnasse neighborhood. The Tour Montparnasse was also the tallest building in France until 2011, when it was surpassed by the Tour First (758 feet/231 meters high) in La Défense.

There are only two high-rise buildings in the center of Paris: the administrative center of the Préfecture de Paris (1957–1964, 17 floors) on Boulevard Morland, 4e, and, on the other side of the Seine, the Zamansky Tower (1970, renovated 2004–2009, 280 feet/85 meters high, 29 floors) on the Jussieu campus of the University of Paris, 5e. To this list might also be added the Centre Pompidou, 4e, which is nearly 150 feet/45 meters high, with 7 floors.

Most of the high-rise buildings in Paris are in the urban renovation zones in the outer arrondissements:

- 12e—especially around Bercy.
- 13e—by far the largest number of high-rises of any arrondissement.
- 14e—the Tour Montparnasse and other buildings nearby.
- 15e—the 20 towers of the Front de Seine/Beaugrenelle.
- 18e—especially around the Porte de la Chapelle.
- 19e—La Cité Curial-Cambrai (1966, architect André Coquet) alone has 16 towers.
- 20e—especially on the Hauts de Belleville and the Rue des Orteaux.

The first office towers to be built at La Défense, to the west of Paris, were the Esso Tower (1966, demolished 1993) and the Nobel Tower (1966, now named the Tour Initiale). Like its contemporaries the Olympiades and the Front de Seine in Paris, the towers at La Défense were built on a pedestrian plaza. A second generation of 9 towers followed between 1970 and 1974, when the new president Valéry Giscard d'Estaing expressed his disapproval of the Tour Gan (now named the Tour CB21), which could be seen from the center of Paris. It qualified as the first "*gratte-ciel*" (literally, "skyscraper") in La Défense since it was 587 feet/179 meters tall, with 44 floors.

Construction of skyscrapers gradually resumed at La Défense, but came to an abrupt halt in Paris itself when in 1977 Giscard d'Estaing imposed a maximum height of 121 feet/37 meters on buildings in the city.

As of 2019, there are nineteen skyscrapers in La Défense—and one in Paris: the Tour Montparnasse. La Défense is now the largest purpose-built business district in Europe with 36 million square feet/3.35 million square meters of office space.

In 2010, the City of Paris Council voted to relax its previous height restriction of 121 feet/37 meters to allow building heights of up to 164 feet/50 meters for residential buildings and 590 feet/180 meters for commercial buildings.

The first residential building at the new maximum height (2 metal-clad towers featuring stepped forms and angular balconies) went up in 2015 at 46-56 Avenue de France, the main artery in the modern Tolbiac district of the 13th arrondissment, next to the Bibliothèque Nationale de France.

In the summer of 2015 the City of Paris approved plans to build a triangular skyscraper built of glass and steel known as the *Tour Triangle*, designed by the Swiss firm Herzog & de Meuron, at the Porte de Versailles. At 590 feet/180 meters high (42 floors)—the maximum allowed under the new law—it will be the first skyscraper to be built in Paris since the Tour Montparnasse in 1973. Construction was held up by litigation for nearly five years but is expected to begin in 2020 and to finish in time for the 2024 Paris Olympics.

Les Tours Duo, with one tower 410 feet/125 meters high (29 floors) and the other tower the maximum 590 feet/180 meters high (39 floors), designed by Jean Nouvel, broke ground in 2017 in the Masséna-Bruneseau sector of the ZAC Paris Rive Gauche in the 13th arrondissement. Completion is scheduled for 2021.

In 2018, the new Palais de Justice, begun in 2012 and designed by Renzo Piano, opened in the ZAC Clichy-Batignolles in the 17th arrondissement, just inside the Boulevard Périphérique. The centerpiece is a 525-foot-/160-meter-high tower, with 38 floors.

The Eiffel Tower, at 1,063 feet/324 meters, however, remains the tallest structure in Paris.

Figure 118. The Quartier Tolbiac with the Grands Moulins de Paris and the Halle aux Farines (now the campus of Université de Paris VII–Denis Diderot) in the center, and the train tracks leading to the Gare d'Austerlitz on the right.

Paris, especially the formerly industrial areas around Bercy on the Right Bank and Tolbiac on the Left Bank.

During Mitterrand's fourteen years as president (he was reelected for a second seven-year term in 1988), the following major buildings were started or finished:

- Pyramide du Louvre (1983–1989, architect I. M. Pei), part of the ambitious Grand Louvre project to renovate and expand the Louvre Museum (1981–1993).
- Institut du Monde Arabe (1983–1987, Jean Nouvel, Pierre Soria, Gilbert Lézénès, and Architecture Studio), on the Seine next to the Pont de Sully, 5e.

- Grande Arche de la Défense (1983–1989, Johann Otto von Spreckelsen), in La Défense.
- Opéra de la Bastille (1983–1989, Carlos Ott), on the Place de la Bastille, 12ᵉ.
- Cité des Sciences et de l'Industrie and la Géode (1980–1986, Adrien Fainsilbert), in the Parc de la Villette, 19ᵉ.
- Cité de la Musique (1984–1995, Christian de Portzamparc), in the Parc de la Villette, 19ᵉ.
- Ministère de l'Economie et des Finances (1982–1988, Paul Chemetov and Borja Huidobro), at Bercy, 12ᵉ.
- Bibliothèque Nationale de France (1989–1995, Dominique Perrault), at Tolbiac, 13ᵉ.

In addition, two new urban passageways were created to open up the city to pedestrians: one north-south with the redesign of the banks of the Bassin de la Villette, the Canal Saint-Martin, and the Port de l'Arsenal; the other east-west with the creation of the *Coulée Verte René-Dumont* (1988–1993, formerly known as the *Promenade plantée*) on the 3-mile/4.5-kilometer stretch from the Place de la Bastille alongside the Avenue Daumesnil to the Bois de Vincennes, built mostly on the abandoned tracks of the Bastille–La Varenne railroad, much of it elevated on a viaduct.

Finally, in the 1990s three large new parks were built on the edges of Paris:

- Parc de la Villette (85 acres/35 hectares), 19ᵉ.
- Parc de Bercy (33 acres/13.5 hectares), 12ᵉ.
- Parc André Citroën (35 acres/14 hectares), 15ᵉ.

A fourth park opened in 2007: Parc Martin Luther King, 17ᵉ (part of the ZAC Clichy-Batignolles). It is still under construction and is expected to be finished by the end of 2020, when it will reach its full size of 25 acres/10 hectares.

In 1995, Jacques Chirac was elected president. He was reelected for a second term (shortened from seven to five years) in 2002. His cultural legacy was the Musée du Quai Branly (designed by Jean Nouvel), displaying indigenous art from around the world and located next to the Eiffel Tower.

Jacques Chirac was succeeded as mayor of Paris by Jean Tiberi (1995–2001), Bertrand Delanoë (2001–2014), and Anne Hidalgo (2014–present).

In 2007, Nicolas Sarkozy was elected president. His proposal to install a new Maison de l'Histoire de France in the building next to the Hôtel de Soubise occupied by the Archives Nationales in the Marais was abandoned after he lost his bid for a second term.

In 2012, François Hollande was elected president. He did not run for a second term and left no legacy project in Paris.

In 2017, Emmanuel Macron was elected president. His cultural legacy will no doubt be the repair of Notre Dame Cathedral after its roof and spire were destroyed by fire on April 15, 2019.

A chronology of the principal building works and restoration projects carried out in Paris since World War II follows.

Chronology

Between 1953 and 1958, the modern Y-shaped UNESCO headquarters was built on Place de Fontenoy, 7ᵉ, in front of the École Militaire. The architects were Bernard Zehrfuss of France, Marcel Breuer of the United States, and Pier Luigi Nervi of Italy.

Between 1953 and 1962, the moving Mémorial des Martyrs de la Déportation/Memorial to the Deported (architect Georges-Henri Pingusson), in memory of the two hundred thousand French Jews who were deported during the Second World War, was built on the Square de l'Île de France at the eastern tip of the Île de la Cité.

Between 1954 and 1963, the huge, circular (550 yards/500 meters in circumference) Maison de la Radio et de la Télévision (architect Henry Bernard) was built in the 16th arrondissement, next to the Pont de Grenelle. It was renovated between 2005 and 2014.

Between 1955 and 1959, the V-shaped NATO headquarters (architects Marcel Breuer and Bernard Zehrfuss) was built on Boulevard Lannes, 16ᵉ. (It now houses the Université de Paris IX–Dauphine.)

Between 1956 and 1964, the 17-story *cité administrative* of the Préfecture de Paris was built at 17 Boulevard Morland, 4ᵉ, across the river from the Jussieu campus.

In 1958, the development of La Défense got underway. The CNIT (*Centre national de l'industrie et des techniques*/Center of New Industries and Technologies) was the first building constructed; it primarily serves as a convention center. La Défense is now Europe's largest purpose-built business district with 36 million square feet/3.35 million square meters of office space, located on 400 acres outside Paris. As of 2019, there were nineteen skyscrapers with a roof height of at least 492 feet/150 meters in La Défense (and one in Paris—the Tour Montparnasse). La Défense is named after the iconic statue *La Défense de Paris*, which was erected in 1883 to commemorate the soldiers who had defended Paris during the Franco-Prussian War. The district is located at the westernmost end of the 6-mile-/10-kilometer-long Historical Axis of Paris, which starts at the Louvre in central Paris, goes up the Champs-Élysées, past the Arc de Triomphe, through the suburb of Neuilly-sur-Seine, before finally reaching La Défense.

Between 1958 and 1972, the huge, modern Jussieu campus of the University of Paris (architect Édouard Albert) was built in the 5th arrondissement alongside the Seine on the former site of the *Halle aux vins* (wine market) built by Napoléon Bonaparte, and until the Revolution the site of the Abbaye Saint-Victor.

In stages between 1958 and 1973, the Boulevard Périphérique (ring road) was built on the no-man's-land surrounding the old Thiers Fortifications, which had been demolished in the 1920s.

In 1959, the Kinopanorama cinema (850 seats) opened at 60 Avenue de la Motte-Piquet, 15ᵉ, in the Quartier Grenelle. It closed in 2002.

In 1960, the North Atlantic Treaty Organizaton (NATO) moved into new purpose-built headquarters at the Porte Dauphine, 16ᵉ. After France withdrew from NATO in 1966, NATO moved to Brussels. The Université de Paris–Dauphine was founded in 1968 and took over the former NATO headquarters.

Starting in 1960 and continuing through the 1970s, multi-level underground parking garages were constructed to keep unsightly above-ground garages from marring the cityscape. (Thirty-five *parkings* were constructed during Pompidou's brief presidency alone.) Many excavations have revealed ancient ruins, such as the remains of the Gallo-Roman city found beneath the Parvis de Notre-Dame, where the Archaeological Crypt is now located. The discovery of these ruins delayed the end of construction of the underground parking garage, which began in 1963, until 1971.

In 1961, the Musée d'Art Moderne de la Ville de Paris was inaugurated. It is located in the eastern wing of the Palais de Tokyo constructed for the International Exhibition of Arts and Technology of 1937, and is located at 11 Avenue du Président Wilson, 16ᵉ.

Between 1962 and 1990, the development of the Front de Seine/ Beaugrenelle took place along the Seine in the 15th arrondissement, with its 20 towers, all 394 feet/120 meters high, for mixed residential and commercial use.

In 1964, the dry moat, which was originally in front of the Perrault Colonnade of the Louvre but had been filled in, was re-excavated.

Between 1964 and 1967, the *voies sur berges* (express highways at river level along portions of both the Right and Left Banks of the Seine) were built. They were inaugurated by Prime Minister Georges Pompidou, after whom the *voie express de la Rive Droite* was named. The plan to build an express highway on the Left Bank opposite the Île Saint-Louis was abandoned after Pompidou's sudden death in 1974. The area intended for the expressway between the Pont de Sully and the Pont d'Austerlitz was made into a riverside promenade named the Square Tino Rossi.

Between 1967 and 1974, the futuristic Aérogare/Terminal 1 of Paris Charles de Gaulle Airport (architect Paul Andreu) was built in farmland near Roissy, 14 miles/22 kilometers northeast of Paris. Because of its round shape, the terminal was soon dubbed "le Camembert."* It has recently been renovated. Terminal 2 has seven sub-terminals 2A to 2G that opened between 1982 and 2008, and has also been upgraded.

---

* In 1976, the first commercial flight of the Concorde supersonic jet took off from CDG bound for Rio de Janeiro via Dakar.

Terminal 3, which hosts charters and low-cost airlines, opened in 1990. The construction of Terminal 4 is planned for 2024, in time for the Summer Olympic Games, which Paris will host. A new CDG Express train between CDG and the Gare de l'Est in Paris is planned for 2023.

Between 1968 and 1975, *Les Olympiades* (architects Michel Holley and André Martinat), a district of residential towers in the 13th arrondissement, was built as part of the *Italie 13* project on land vacated by the Panhard automobile factory. It comprises 8 towers built on a raised pedestrian plaza with parking underneath. Each tower is 341 feet/109 meters tall with 36 floors and is named after a different city that hosted the Olympics.

Between 1969 and 1973, the 689-foot-/210-meter-high, 59-story Montparnasse Tower (architects Beaudoin, Cassan, Hoym de Marien, and Saubot) was constructed. It is the only skyscraper in Paris today.

In March 1969, the central food market located at Les Halles for eight hundred years was transferred to Rungis, near Orly Airport, south of Paris.

In 1971, eleven of the twelve Baltard Pavilions at Les Halles dating from the Second Empire were demolished. One was moved to Nogent-sur-Marne, just east of the Bois de Vincennes.

Between 1972 and 1979, the new underground shopping center, the Forum des Halles (architects Claude Vasconi and Georges Pencreac'h), was built, along with Europe's biggest subway station, with gardens above. In their design of the exterior of the buildings, reminiscent of umbrellas, the architects endeavored to echo Napoléon III's admonition to Haussmann with respect to the design of Les Halles that "*Ce sont de vastes 'parapluies' qu'il me faut; rien de plus*" ("I need vast umbrellas, nothing more"), in reference to the iron pillars used to support the glass roofs of the train stations of the era. The above-ground area formerly occupied by Les Halles was redeveloped starting in 2011. The centerpiece of the new project is a huge undulating glass canopy (*la canopée*) above a large terrace, which was completed in 2016. The adjoining Nelson Mandela Garden was completed in 2018.

Also between 1972 and 1979, the three lines of the RER (*Réseau Express Régional*), a suburban train network, were put into service, linking Paris with its suburbs and airports.

In 1972, the Parc des Princes sports stadium opened in the 16th arrondissement.

In 1974, the Palais des Congrès (architect Guillaume Gillet) and the Hôtel Concorde Lafayette (now named the Hyatt Regency Paris Étoile) opened at the Porte Maillot; the Hôtel Sheraton opened at Montparnasse; and the Mercuriales towers opened at the Porte de Bagnolet.

In 1977, after six years of construction, the Centre National d'Art et de Culture Georges-Pompidou (architects Renzo Piano and Richard Rogers)—commonly known as the Centre Pompidou or Beaubourg—was inaugurated in memory of the late president. It is located on the former *Plateau Beaubourg*, which had remained vacant since the demolition of *îlot insalubre numéro 1* in 1934 and from which it gets its nickname. Another nickname is *la raffinerie* (the refinery) because of its industrial appearance and in particular the fact that all its utility pipes (color-coded for function) are visible on the east side of the building along the Rue du Renard. As part of the redevelopment of the Quartier Les Halles neighborhood, in addition to the demolition of *îlot insalubre numéro 1* and the Baltard Pavilions, 132 houses were demolished between the Centre Pompidou and the Forum des Halles and replaced with modern commercial and residential buildings.

During the 1970s, the restoration of the Place des Vosges, which had become derelict, and the gentrification of the Marais, got underway. It would take two decades to complete.

Between 1980 and 1986, the Cité des Sciences et de l'Industrie and La Géode (architect Adrien Fainsilbert) were built on the north section of the site of the old *abattoirs* (slaughterhouses) in the 19th arrondissement at the northeastern edge of Paris. Between 1983 and 1989, the Parc de la Villette (the third largest park in Paris), with its bright red architectural follies, was built on the southern section. The transformation of the old Abattoirs de la Villette had been initiated by President Giscard d'Estaing.

In 1981, the high-speed train (*train à grande vitesse*, or TGV) line between Paris and Lyon was inaugurated. The trip took two hours and forty minutes.

In 1982, the Parc Georges-Brassens (1921–1981), named after the singer-poet who lived nearby, opened at 38 Rue des Morillons, 15ᵉ.

In 1983, the development of the industrial east of Paris began.

In 1984, the Palais Omnisports de Paris-Bercy (POPB), an indoor sports and concert venue, opened on the east side of Paris. It was renovated and renamed the AccorHotels Arena in 2015.

Also in 1984, the Zénith concert hall opened on the edge of the Parc de la Villette, 19ᵉ.

In 1985, the Bassin de la Villette was redesigned.

In 1986, the transformation of the Gare d'Orsay (built for *the Exposition Universelle de 1900*) into the Musée d'Orsay, initiated by President Giscard d'Estaing and focusing on art during the period between 1848 and 1914, was completed. The Impressionist collection was moved from the Musée du Jeu de Paume in the Tuileries Garden to the Musée d'Orsay; the Musée du Jeu de Paume was substantially redesigned by architect Antoine Stinco and reopened in 1991 as the Galerie Nationale du Jeu de Paume, specializing in contemporary art. The Musée d'Orsay was renovated between 2009 and 2011.

Also in 1986, the restored Cour Carrée was inaugurated by President Mitterrand as part of his *Grand Louvre* project.

In 1987, the glass and steel Institut du Monde Arabe (Institute of the Arab World, architects Jean Nouvel, Pierre Soria, Gilbert Lézénès, Architecture Studio; begun in 1983), next to Jussieu, was inaugurated. Its south façade featured 242 glass panes covered by lens-like mechanisms that (used to) open and close depending on the light.

In 1989, Paris and France celebrated the Bicentennial of the Revolution. To mark the event, the following monuments, all begun in 1983, were inaugurated:

- Louvre Pyramid (architect I. M. Pei).
- Opéra de la Bastille (Carlos Ott).
- Grande Arche de la Défense (Johann Otto von Spreckelsen).

Both the Dôme Église and the Pont Alexandre III were regilded for the occasion.

Also in 1989, the sidewalks were removed from the Place Vendôme. In their place, eight hundred stainless steel *clous* (low cylindrical columns called "nails" or "studs") mark the edge of the road.

Between 1990 and 1995, the Avenue des Champs-Élysées was redesigned. Parking was put underground, side alleys were eliminated, sidewalks were widened to 70 feet/21.5 meters, and a second row of trees (which had been eliminated in the 1870s) was replanted.

During the 1990s until 2002, the front façade and the 2 towers of Notre Dame Cathedral were restored (but not the sides or back).

During the 1990s, grass was planted on the Esplanade des Invalides. The esplanade was previously covered with packed sand since it was frequently used for world's fairs and other temporary expositions. At first the new esplanade was equipped with the traditional signs warning "*interdiction de marcher sur la pelouse*" ("forbidden to walk on the grass"), but they were later removed when the large rectangular green spaces proved to be popular for pickup soccer games.

In 1990, the Ministère de l'Economie et des Finances and its six thousand employees moved from the Richelieu Wing of the Louvre (built by Napoléon III between 1852 and 1857, and occupied by the Ministry of Finance since 1871) and other buildings to its massive new building (architects Paul Chemetov and Borja Huidobro; begun in 1982) in Bercy, 12ᵉ. The new building is 405 yards/370 meters long and follows the trace of the former Farmers General Wall, starting literally with its feet in the Seine.

In 1993, following the departure of the Ministry of Finance, the reconstructed Richelieu Wing (*aile Richelieu*) of the Louvre reopened, its three inner courtyards (Marly, Puget, and Khorsabad) now covered with glass roofs, significantly increasing the exhibition space of the museum. The Grand Louvre project—worthy of Napoléon III himself—was finally completed.

In 1991, the transformation of the old Musée du Jeu de Paume in the Jardin des Tuileries into the new Galerie Nationale du Jeu de Paume was completed.

Also in 1991, the ZAC (*zone d'aménagement concerté*)* Paris Rive Gauche (PRG) was created, covering an area along the Left Bank east of the Gare d'Austerlitz of 320 acres/130 hectares, including 64 acres/26 hectares built over the tracks leading to the Austerlitz train station. It consists of three sectors: from west to east, Austerlitz, around the renovated Gare d'Austerlitz train station; Tolbiac, around the Bibliothèque Nationale de France; and Masséna Nord, around the Grands Moulins. It is the largest city planning project undertaken since the *Grands Travaux* of Haussmann during the nineteenth century. Development will continue through the 2020s.

Between 1991 and 1995, the glass and steel building for the Fondation Cartier (architect Jean Nouvel) was built on the former site of the American Center, at 261 Boulevard Raspail, 14ᵉ.

In 1992:

- The Parc André Citroën with its two monumental *serres* (greenhouses) opened next to the Seine in the 15th arrondissement on the site of a former Citroën automobile manufacturing plant, which closed in 1974.
- Euro Disney (now known as Disneyland Paris) opened in Marne-la-Vallée, a new town located 20 miles/32 kilometers east of Paris.

Between 1992 and 1995, the Bibliothèque Nationale de France (architect Dominique Perrault), with its four glass towers resembling four open books on a raised platform, was built along the Seine in the 13th arrondissement. It is the centerpiece of the Tolbiac sector of the Paris Rive Gauche project.

In 1993, the *Petite Ceinture* (Little Belt) railway just inside the Boulevard Périphérique was abandoned.

---

* Created in 1967 and modified since, ZACs are public initiatives intended to actively redevelop large urban areas through a combination of public and private investment. The City of Paris appoints a single architect to prepare an overall design for the new neighborhood. Other architects then design individual buidings in keeping with the lead architect's specifications. There are currently fifteen ZACs in Paris. By far the largest are the ZAC Paris Rive Gauche and the ZAC Clichy-Batignolles.

In 1994:

- The Musée National d'Histoire Naturelle in the Jardin des Plantes reopened after seven years of renovation work.
- Charléty Stadium, just inside the Boulevard Périphérique in the 13th arrondissement, originally built in 1939, was renovated.
- The Eurotunnel was inaugurated and Eurostar service between Paris Gare du Nord and London Waterloo Station began.
- The new American Center (architect Frank Gehry) was built in the Parc de Bercy. After the closure of the American Center in 1996, the building was acquired by the City of Paris in 1998 to become the site of the Cinémathèque, which has one of the world's largest film archives.

Between 1994 and 1997, as part of the ZAC Bercy (covering 50 hectares/124 acres), the Parc de Bercy (30 acres/12 hectares) was constructed on the Seine in the 12th arrondissement on the site of a former wine depot. Apartment buildings were built alongside the new park.

Between 1994 and 2007, the Pont Neuf was restored.

In 1995, the Cité de la Musique (City of Music, architect Christian de Portzamparc, begun in 1984) opened in the Parc de la Villette, 19ᵉ. It was renamed Philharmonie 2 in 2015.

In 1996, the 1-mile-/1.6-kilometer-long Viaduc des Arts (with its sixty-four vaults), along Avenue Daumesnil, 12ᵉ, opened; it forms part of the 2.9-mile-/4.7-kilometer-long *Promenade Plantée* (now called the *Coulée Verte René-Dumont*) leading from the Place de la Bastille to the Porte de Vincennes, and was the inspiration for the High Line in New York City.

In 1998:

- A gold-leafed pyramid cap was added to the top of the obelisk in Place de la Concorde.
- The Stade de France stadium, with a capacity of eighty thousand spectators, opened in the northern suburb of Saint-Denis in time

to host the FIFA World Cup soccer tournament (which France won).

- The driverless Métro line 14—the *Météor*, an acronym of *Métro Est-Ouest Rapide*—opened, with its eastern terminus in the newly developed Tolbiac quarter of the 13th arrondissement.

In 1999, the Léopold-Sédar-Senghor Footbridge (architect Marc Mimram) opened, connecting the Rue de Solférino (next to the Musée d'Orsay) and the Jardin des Tuileries.

In 2000, the fountains and the statues in and around the Place de la Concorde were restored.

Between 2000 and 2009, the Tour Saint-Jacques was restored. In 2012, it opened to the public for the first time.

In 2002, Paris organized the first *Paris Plage*, transforming the *voie express Georges Pompidou* on the Right Bank of the Seine into a beach complete with sand and parasols for a month in the summer.

In 2003, the city of Boulogne-Billancourt (bordering the southern edge of the 16th arrondissement, the second largest city in the Île de France after Paris) created the ZAC Île Seguin-Rives de Seine. It comprises three sectors: Île Seguin (28 acres/11.5 hectares) and the new Quartier Trapèze (93 acres/37.5 acres)—occupied by Renault factories throughout the twentieth century until they were closed in 1992—and the Quartier Pont de Sèvres (62 acres/25 hectares), which had been developed during the 1960s and was in need of renovation. While not in Paris proper, the ZAC Île Seguin-Rives de Seine (covering a total of 183 acres/74 hectares—10 percent of the surface area of Boulogne-Billancourt) is second in size only to the enormous ZAC Paris Rive Gauche (321 acres/130 hectares) in neighboring Paris.

In 2005, both the Grand Palais (with the largest glass roof in Europe) and the Petit Palais reopened after renovation.

In 2006:

- The Musée du Quai Branly (architect Jean Nouvel)—President Jacques Chirac's legacy cultural project—opened near the Eiffel Tower.

- Both the Musée de l'Orangerie (originally adapted to display the Water Lilies/*Nymphéas* by Claude Monet in 1927) in the Tuileries Garden and the medieval Donjon du Château de Vincennes in the Bois de Vincennes reopened after restoration.
- The Passerelle (footbridge) Simone-de-Beauvoir (architect Dietmar Feichtinger) opened, connecting the Bibliothèque Nationale de France and the Parc de Bercy.
- The first section of new *Tramway* opened on the southern stretch of the Boulevards des Maréchaux. Extensions were opened in 2012 and 2018, continuing counter-clockwise as far as the Porte d'Asnières, 17ᵉ.

In 2007, the ZAC Clichy-Batignolles was created on 133 acres/54 hectares in the 17th arrondissement in the northwest of Paris. The development was to be built around two key projects: the construction of Parc Martin-Luther-King (25 acres/10 hectares) and the construction of a new Palais de Justice.

Also in 2007, the renovation and restructuring of the Bibliothèque Nationale de France—site Richelieu on the Rue Vivienne, 2ᵉ, began. It is scheduled for completion in 2020.

Between 2008 and 2014, the façade of the Sainte-Chapelle was restored.

In 2010, the Cité de la Mode et du Design (City of Fashion and Design) opened in a converted warehouse on the Quai d'Austerlitz in the 13th arrondissement. It is easily recognizable by its green-sheaved exterior staircase on the Seine side of the building, once described by President Sarkozy as "*le truc vert*" ("the green thing").

In 2012, the façades of the Conciergerie and the Tour de l'Horloge were restored.

Between 2012 and 2015, the façade of the Ministère des Affaires Étrangères on the Quai d'Orsay, 7ᵉ, was restored.

In 2012, 1.4 miles/2.2 kilometers of the *voie express* on the Left Bank between the Musée d'Orsay and the Pont de l'Alma were closed to automobiles and converted to pedestrian use. The 2 miles/3.3 kilometers of the *voie express Georges Pompidou* on the Right Bank were permanently closed to traffic in October 2016.

In 2013, Notre Dame Cathedral celebrated the 850th anniversary of the laying of the first stone by Bishop Sully. To mark the event, four of the ten bells that had been installed in 1856 were removed from the towers of Notre-Dame and put on display behind the church on the Rue du Cloître Notre-Dame, and nine new bells were installed. The biggest and oldest (1686) bell, named *Emmanuel* and weighing thirteen tons, remains in the South Tower.

In 2013, the façade of the Préfecture de Police across the square from Notre-Dame was restored.

Between 2013 and 2015, the dome of the Panthéon was restored.

In September 2014, the Fondation Jérôme Seydoux-Pathé (73 Avenue des Gobelins, 13ᵉ) opened after seven years' work. It was designed by Renzo Piano (who designed the Pompidou Center together with Richard Rogers), and has been aptly nicknamed "the Armadillo."

In October 2014, the Musée Picasso (5 Rue de Thorigny, 3ᵉ) reopened after five years of renovation and enlargement, and the Fondation Louis Vuitton, designed by Frank Gehry and located in the Bois de Boulogne, was inaugurated. Its shape is reminiscent of a ship with twelve giant glass sails.

In 2014, the façades of the Palais-Royal and the Hôtel de Sully were restored.

In January 2015, the new Paris Philharmonic (Philharmonie de Paris, or Philharmonie 1) concert hall, designed by Jean Nouvel and featuring "terraced vineyard" seating for twenty-four hundred around a central stage, opened in the Parc de la Villette, next to the Cité de la Musique, which was renamed Philharmonie 2. Construction began in 2006.

In June 2015, Mayor Anne Hidalgo announced plans to "reinvent" seven of Paris's squares (Bastille, Nation, Gambetta, Panthéon, Madeleine, Italie, Fêtes) to make them more accessible to pedestrians. Work began in 2018 and is scheduled for completion in 2020.

On November 12, 2015 (Rodin's 175th birthday), the Musée Rodin in the Hôtel Biron at 79 Rue de Varenne, 7ᵉ, reopened after three years of restoration work.

In January 2016, Paris and 130 communes within a ring of inner suburbs were joined to create the *Métropole du Grand Paris* (Metropolis of Greater Paris), or *Paris Métropole*, where four new lines of high-speed trains linking suburban business hubs, known as *Le Grand Paris Express*, will be built between 2015 and 2030. The new region covers 294 square miles/762 square kilometers and includes seven million people, more than triple the population now living in the central city.

In April 2016, *la Canopée des Halles* (92 feet/28 meters high) was inaugurated after five years of work.

In October 2016, the new Russian Orthodox cathedral, officially named Sainte-Trinité, with its five gilded onion domes, opened next to the Seine at the Place de la Résistance, 7ᵉ, next to the Pont de l'Alma. It was built on the site of the former headquarters of the French meteorological office, and was entirely funded by the Russian government.

In April 2017, *la Seine Musicale*, a performing arts center designed by Japanese architect Shigeru Ban and French architect Jean de Gastines in the shape of an ocean liner, with a distinctive "sail" made of solar panels shading the egg-shaped auditorium, opened on the Île Seguin in Boulogne-Billancourt. The performance complex is the centerpiece of a plan conceived by Jean Nouvel for the ZAC Île Seguin-Rives de Seine to make a culture hub of the island.

On September 30, 2017, the Monnaie de Paris (the Mint), located at 11 Quai Conti, 6ᵉ, reopened after six years of renovation work, rebranded "11 Conti-Monnaie de Paris."

In October 2017, work began on the restoration of the July Column in the Place de la Bastille. It is scheduled to reopen to the public in 2020 for the first time in thirty years.

In 2018, the development of the Quartier Trapèze, part of the ZAC Île Seguin-Rives de Seine located on 28 acres/11.5 hectares formerly occupied by Renault factories in Boulogne-Billancourt (but not on the island), was completed after twelve years of construction. It comprises private and social housing, offices, and green space, including a 17-acre/7-hectare park.

In April 2018, the new Palais de Justice, begun in 2012, opened in the ZAC Clichy-Batignolles in the 17th arrondissement, just inside the

Boulevard Périphérique. The centerpiece of the new court complex, which was designed by Renzo Piano (who, along with Richard Rogers, designed the Pompidou Center), is a 525-foot-/160-meter-high, 38-story tower.

In July 2018, a new entrance opened to the Gallo-Roman baths, known as "*les Thermes du Nord*" or "*les Thermes de Julien*," and the Musée National du Moyen Âge (National Museum of the Middle Ages) in the Hôtel de Cluny on the newly pedestrianized Rue du Sommerard, 5ᵉ (architect Bernard Desmoulin). The renovation of the museum itself will continue until the end of 2021.

In 2018, the Fondation Cartier announced its intention to open a second exhibition space for contemporary art in the building currently occupied by the Louvre des Antiquaires, across the Rue de Rivoli from the Louvre Museum. The new space will be designed by Jean Nouvel and is expected to open in 2024.

In 2018, the Conseil de Paris voted to start the ZAC Bercy-Charenton on one of the last large spaces still available for development: 170 acres/70 hectares in the southern part of the 12th arrondissement between the Parc de Bercy and the Bois de Vincennes, much of it covered by railroad tracks and related infrastructure.

On April 15, 2019, the original wooden attic and lead-covered roof of Notre Dame Cathedral, along with its 150-year-old spire (*flèche*), whose tip reached 315 feet/96 meters above the ground, were destroyed by fire. The following day President Macron vowed to rebuild the cathedral within five years. During the summer of 2020, the government confirmed that the spire built by Viollet-le-Duc would be rebuilt as it was, and that the frame supporting the roof (*la charpente*) would be rebuilt in wood.

In October 2019, the Musée d'Art Moderne de la Ville de Paris reopened after three years of restoration and redesign work by h2o Architectes.

In 2020, new pedestrianized versions of the Places de la Bastille, de la Nation, Gambetta, du Panthéon, de la Madeleine, d'Italie, et des Fêtes are scheduled to reopen, and the July Column in the center of the redesigned Place de la Bastille will reopen to the public after three years of restoration work for the first time in thirty years.

In 2021, the following major projects are scheduled for completion, some postponed from 2020 because of the COVID-19 pandemic:

- The Bibliothèque Nationale de France—site Richelieu on the Rue Vivienne, 2ᵉ, will reopen after fourteen years of renovation and restructuring.
- The Musée Carnavalet, dedicated to the history of the city of Paris, will reopen in the Marais after five years of restoration work.
- The Fondation Pinault will open a new museum of contemporary art in the Bourse de Commerce next to Les Halles after six years of restoration and adaptation by Japanese architect Tadao Ando.
- La Samaritaine department store, extensively restructured, will reopen next to the Pont Neuf sixteen years after it closed.
- Construction of *Les Tours Duo*, with one tower 410 feet/125 meters high (29 floors) and the other tower the maximum-allowable 590 feet/180 meters high (39 floors), designed by Jean Nouvel, in the Masséna-Bruneseau sector of the ZAC Paris Rive Gauche, will be completed. It will be the third highest structure in Paris after the Eiffel Tower and the Tour Montparnasse.

In 2024, Paris will host the Summer Olympics. Only Paris (1900, 1924, 2024) and London (1908, 1948 and 2012) will have hosted three Olympic Games. To accommodate events both in Paris and in its surrounding suburbs, dozens of infrastructure projects are planned, including the construction of an Olympic Village in the northern suburb of Saint-Ouen and an Aquatics Center near the Stade de France in the neighboring suburb of Saint-Denis. In addition, Paris Charles de Gaulle Airport plans to build a new Terminal 4 in time for the Olympics. Several important projects are also planned within Paris to be ready to welcome visitors to the 2024 Olympics:

- The Grand Palais will be renovated, closing in January 2021.
- In May 2019, the City of Paris announced plans to build a new park stretching 1 mile/1.6 kilometers from the Palais de Chaillot

on the Right Bank, across the Pont d'Iéna (which will become a pedestrian-only passage), past the Eiffel Tower on the Left Bank, and down the Champ de Mars to the École Militaire. At over 100 acres/40 hectares, it will be the city's largest public green space.

- In July 2020, the renovation and expansion of the Gare du Nord, Europe's busiest train station was announced. The station accommodates about seven hundred thousand passengers each day, serving as the terminus for the Eurostar from London and the Thalys from Belgium, Germany, and the Netherlands, and as a stop for four suburban train lines and two Métro lines. The 155-year-old station will more than triple in size from about 377,000 to 1,335,000 square feet/35,000 to 124,000 square meters.

Conclusion

Paris has been a work in progress for over two thousand years. Like a venerable old tree with growth rings that record its age, at first it grew within a series of seven concentric walls—from the first wall built around the Île de la Cité by the Romans in the fourth century to the last "wall"—the Boulevard Périphérique—built between 1958 and 1973 outside the former Thiers Fortifications erected in the nineteenth century. But because Paris was confined within this series of walls, over time new building works were undertaken in old neighborhoods—the fields of monasteries and later the gardens of important *hôtels particuliers* in the historic center of Paris and in its outskirts that had been subdivided and developed— so that new construction now coexists side by side with older buildings. Nineteenth-century *immeubles de rapport* stand next to seventeenth-century *hôtels particuliers*. Haussmann's *grands boulevards* run parallel to medieval streets like the Rue Saint-Honoré, Rue Saint-Denis, and Rue Saint-Martin. Even individual buildings can straddle different centuries and styles. Construction of the Église Saint-Gervais-Saint-Protais began in 1494 in the Gothic style, but was delayed by the Wars of Religion and lack of funds. Its façade (the last part of any church to be built) was finally constructed between 1615 and 1621 in the new baroque style. Even seemingly unremarkable buildings have evolved over centuries. The modest Maison de la Colombe (4 Rue de la Colombe, 4ᵉ) on the Île de la Cité was originally built as a two-story house in 1297 or 1298; three floors were added at the beginning of the sixteenth century; and another floor and an attic were added in 1769. In 1962, André Malraux issued a decree that saved the nearly seven-hundred-year-old building from demolition.

While, like a tree, Paris has grown organically over its long life, periodically its branches were trimmed or pruned or shaped by its great builders—Henri IV, Louis XIV, and especially Napoléon III—ensuring its healthy growth and development over the centuries.

Paris's great city builders have always ensured that important buildings and monuments form part of an *"ensemble architectural"* so that they are in harmony with their surroundings. Sometimes the ensemble is created at the same time—for example, when Haussmann built his *grandes places* like the Place du Châtelet, the Place de l'Étoile, and the Place de l'Opéra, where the squares were from the beginning surrounded by complementary buildings to create a harmonious whole. Other ensembles, however, like the buildings of which they are composed, take shape over decades and even centuries when generations of architects add new and complementary elements to a composition. The best example is certainly the evolution of the Palais du Louvre and the Palais des Tuileries into the Nouveau Louvre of Napoléon III, as first envisioned by the Grand Dessein of Henri IV.

It is the multiple layers and architectural harmony of its building works that make the city of Paris such an ongoing work of art.

The French are justifiably proud of their *patrimoine* (heritage) and for the past 180 years, ever since Viollet-le-Duc started work on the Sainte-Chapelle and Notre-Dame, they have devoted considerable resources to restore their monuments to their former glory. The 1913 law to protect the historic monuments of France was one of the first such laws in the world and has served as a model for many other countries' laws to protect their cultural heritage.

When restoring a monument, the policy is to replace worn stones and statues with new ones, whenever possible using stone from the original quarries, as was done when restoring the western façade of Notre-Dame in the 1990s, where the new blocks are noticeably whiter than the old ones, and will be done again when repairing the damage caused by the fire in April 2019.

Restoration and renovation projects do not happen overnight. It can take years—or decades—for the responsible authorities to decide what to do, for private parties to express their opinions, and for the inevitable disputes to be resolved, and then still more years to carry out the final decision. Examples abound of just how long and circuitous the road to redevelopment can be.

In 1971, all but one of the twelve iconic Baltard pavilions in Les Halles were demolished. In their place, the construction of a giant underground transportation hub (the biggest in Europe) was completed in 1977, the construction of an underground shopping center (the Forum des Halles) was completed in 1979, a garden was laid out at ground level in 1986, and many of the surrounding streets were pedestrianized. The redevelopment was generally considered to be a failure. The mirrored glass buildings of the Forum des Halles were ugly and had aged badly and the garden was, in architect Jean Nouvel's words, "disorderly." So after only twenty-five years the Ville de Paris undertook to redevelop the site. Between 2010 and 2018, a giant "cloud" canopy (*la Canopée*, inaugurated in 2016)—also controversial—was constructed above the Forum des Halles in place of the mirrored glass buildings and a new garden (inaugurated in 2018) was laid out, at a total cost of around one billion dollars/916 million euros.

After the new Société Nationale des Chemins de fer Français (SNCF, French National Railway Company), upon its creation in 1938, decided to transfer all the major train lines from the Gare d'Orsay to the Gare d'Austerlitz in 1939, the Gare d'Orsay fell into decline. In 1961, a competition held to determine how best to use the site was won by a project to build a modern hotel. In 1970, authorization was granted to demolish the Gare d'Orsay, but opposition as a result of the recent construction of the new Gare de Montparnasse and the destruction of the Baltard pavilions caused the construction permit to be denied. Following his election as president in 1974, Valéry Giscard d'Estaing decided to preserve the building to house a museum of the nineteenth century. The Musée d'Orsay opened in 1986. The galleries were renovated between 2009 and 2011.

In 1992, the Renault factory located on the Île Seguin in Boulogne-Billancourt, just southwest of Paris, closed; it had opened in 1929. In 2000, François Pinault announced a plan to build a museum for his contemporary art collection on the island. Frustrated by administrative delays, Pinault gave up after five years and built his museum in Venice instead.

In 2003, the city of Boulogne-Billancourt created the ZAC Île Seguin-Rives de Seine, which included the island and two sectors on the banks of the Seine. In 2004–2005, the factory was razed. In 2007, the American University of Paris and New York University announced plans to build a joint campus on the island, but the plans were soon abandoned. In 2009, architect Jean Nouvel's plan to develop the island as a center of art and culture was selected. In 2012, the Hauts-de-Seine department acquired the downstream one-third of the island to build a performance art center. In 2017, la Seine Musicale opened after five years of construction. Contemporary art and cultural centers and a concept hotel are planned for the upstream two-thirds of the island.

The fate of the Hôtel-Dieu hospital next to Notre-Dame has been the subject of debate—and strikes by hospital staff—for over a decade with no definitive resolution. A proposal to lease one-third of the space to a private developer for eighty years is pending.

Purely private projects also require patience. In 2005, La Samaritaine department store next to the Pont Neuf closed for safety reasons. After ten years of consultations with interested parties and countless orders and appeals, a redevelopment plan was finally approved in 2015 that includes the construction of a five-star hotel, a gourmet restaurant, shops, offices, one hundred social housing units, and a community *crèche* (nursery school). A grand reopening is expected in 2021.

While the pace of these projects seems glacial, it is worth noting that many of the most outstanding churches and other edifices in Paris took decades, and even centuries, to complete. Prominent examples of churches that took over one hundred years to complete include Notre-Dame (182 years), Saint-Gervais-Saint-Protais (127 years), Saint-Eustache (108 years), and Saint-Sulpice (101 years). The original Hôtel de Ville took ninety-six years to build. The Place de l'Étoile took two hundred years to reach its final form. The modern Louvre Palace took 324 years to complete, from the time François Ier began the construction of the new Renaissance palace in 1546 to its apex under Napoléon III in 1870—and the improvements did not stop there.

~~~

The restoration work never stops, but Paris is not content to rest on its laurels. It keeps adding to its heritage and improving its infrastructure.

Between 2011 and 2014, the Ville de Paris substantially redesigned the Place de la République to make it more pedestrian- and cyclist-friendly. In 2015, Anne Hidalgo, the new mayor of Paris, announced plans to replicate the redesign of the Place de la République and "reinvent" seven other *grandes places parisiennes*—Bastille (4e, 11e, 12e), Panthéon (5e), Madeleine (8e), Nation (11e, 12e), Italie (13e), Fêtes (19e), and Gambetta (20e)—to provide more space for gardens and to make them more accessible to pedestrians (and less accessible to cars). Work began in 2018 and is scheduled for completion in 2020.

With the imminent transfer of many courts on the Île de la Cité to the new Palais de Justice at Clichy-Batignolles and the closure of most of the Hôtel-Dieu hospital, in 2015 the French government instructed architect Dominique Perrault to reflect on how—between 2015 and 2040!—to make the *île-monument* that is the heart of Paris beat again. Dominique Perrault delivered his provocative and ambitious report, entitled *Mission Île de la Cité—Le coeur du Coeur* (Mission Île de la Cité—The Heart of the Heart) to President Hollande in December 2016.

In addition to projects initiated by the national and city governments, private foundations have made significant contributions to the architectural landscape of Paris, including the Fondation Cartier (1994) and more recently:

- Fondation Jérôme Seydoux-Pathé, opened September 2014.
- Fondation Louis Vuitton, opened October 2014.
- Fondation Pinault, scheduled to open in 2021.
- Fondation Cartier (Louvre des Antiquitaires), expected to open in 2024.

The picturesque is important, too. Even if their architecture is not exceptional, the municipal council has identified five historic villages within the city for preservation:

- Montorgueil Saint-Denis, 2ᵉ.
- Mouffetard, 5ᵉ.
- Faubourg Saint-Antoine, 11ᵉ and 12ᵉ.
- La Butte aux Cailles, 13ᵉ.
- Montmartre, 18ᵉ.

ART IN THE STREET

Paris is the capital of a country that has long set the standard for culture and refinement, and Paris has *panache*. Art is not only in its museums and galleries, it is in the street. There are many permanent installations, ranging from the 106 sculptures in the Luxembourg Garden, including 20 white marble sculptures of the queens and other illustrious women of France arrayed behind the balustrades overlooking the large octagonal fountain behind the palace that were commissioned by Louis-Philippe between 1830 and 1848, and the 20 nude sculptures by Aristide Maillol (1861–1944) radiating from the Arc de Triomphe du Carrousel in the Carrousel Garden, to the Colonnes de Buren in the Palais-Royal (1985–1986). There is the striking sculpture of Dreyfus saluting with his broken sword (1988) at the corner of Boulevard Raspail and Rue du Cherche-Midi, 6ᵉ, and the hand-painted mural of Arthur Rimbaud's poem *Le Bateau Ivre* on the Rue Férou, 6ᵉ (2012).

There have also been numerous temporary open-air exhibitions, including:

- The Bulgarian artist Christo's wrapping of the Pont Neuf in 1985.
- The exhibition of 50 voluptuous sculptures by Fernando Botero of Colombia along the Champs-Élysées in 1992–1993.

- The monumental metal sculptures by the American Mark di Suvero installed along the Esplanade des Invalides and throughout the city in 1996.
- Covering the Champs-Élysées with plants to promote ecology in 2010.
- The street artist JR's giant photographic portraits of seventy women from Africa, Asia, and South America, covering the sides of the Pont Louis-Philippe and the walls of the quais of the Île Saint-Louis in 2009.
- The canvas curtain at the base of the cupola of the Panthéon and the floor of the gallery that JR covered with photos of four thousand people from around the world in his "Inside Out" project between 2014 and 2015.
- Daniel Buren's colored panels on the twelve glass "sails" of the Fondation Louis Vuitton, that was on display between May 2016 and May 2017.
- The immense trompe-l'oeil photographic collage that JR installed around I. M. Pei's Pyramide du Louvre that made it appear to surge out of the ground, in March 2019 to celebrate the thirtieth anniversary of its inauguration.
- The display of photographic portraits of 500 healthcare givers on the façade of the Opéra de la Bastille in July 2020 in tribute to their service during the COVID-19 pandemic.

ARCHITECTURE AS ART

As the Romanian sculptor Constantin Brancusi (1876–1957) once said, "Architecture is inhabited sculpture." While cathedrals and palaces have always been designed to instill awe in the masses, as Notre-Dame and the Louvre still do, since the 1950s—and especially since the Mitterrand era—Paris has embraced modern architecture to a degree unique for a city with such a long and distinguished architectural heritage. To add to this heritage, it has sought out architects from around the world, both celebrated and little known. A selection of some of their most iconic works that now form part of Paris's architectural *patrimoine*, includes:

- 1958: UNESCO Headquarters, designed by Hungarian-American Marcel Breuer and Frenchman Bernard Zehrfuss.
- 1963: Maison de la Radio et de la Télévision, by Frenchman Henry Bernard.
- 1977: Centre National d'Art et de Culture Georges-Pompidou, by Italian Renzo Piano and Englishman Richard Rogers.
- 1987: Institut du Monde Arabe, by Frenchman Jean Nouvel.
- 1989: Opéra de la Bastille, by Uruguayan Carlos Ott.
- 1989: Pyramide du Louvre, by Chinese-American I. M. Pei.
- 1989: Grande Arche de la Défense, by Dane Johann Otto von Spreckelsen.
- 1990: Ministère de l'Économie et des Finances, by Frenchman Paul Chemetov and Chilean Borja Huidobro.
- 1993: Cinémathèque française, by American Frank Gehry.
- 1994: Fondation Cartier, by Frenchman Jean Nouvel.
- 1995: Cité de la Musique by Frenchman Christian de Portzamparc.
- 1995: Bibliothèque Nationale de France, by Frenchman Dominique Perrault.
- 2006: Musée du Quai Branly, by Frenchman Jean Nouvel.
- 2014: Fondation Jérôme Seydoux-Pathé, by Italian Renzo Piano.
- 2014: Fondation Louis Vuitton, by American Frank Gehry.
- 2015: Philharmonie de Paris, by Frenchman Jean Nouvel.
- 2017: La Seine Musicale, by Japanese Shigeru Ban and Frenchman Jean de Gastines.
- 2018: Palais de Justice, by Italian Renzo Piano.
- 2021: Fondation Pinault/Bourse de Commerce, by Japanese Tadao Ando.

MOST ICONIC MONUMENT

Which Parisian monument is the most iconic? Candidates must include:

- Notre-Dame (1163–1345), the epicenter of medieval Paris and the heart of the city.
- Arc de Triomphe (1806–1814, 1833–1836), the largest triumphal arch in Europe.
- Eiffel Tower (1887–1889), 1,063 feet/324 meters high, towering over the city.
- The Louvre (1200–Present), the world's largest art museum.

While each candidate is worthy, the Louvre stands out since it represents more than eight hundred years of evolution, spanning the history of modern Paris from the construction of the medieval fortress by Philippe-Auguste in 1200 to the opening of the spectacular Department of Islamic Arts designed by Mario Bellini and Rudy Ricciotti in 2012. It is also the largest edifice in Paris, covering 86 acres/35 hectares between the Seine and the Rue de Rivoli. As the world's most visited museum, with nearly ten million visitors each year, the Louvre is the physical manifestation of France's "mission to civilize" the world through the *rayonnement* (spreading/shining) *de la civilisation française*.

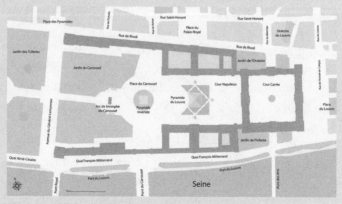

Figure 119. Plan of the Louvre Museum. AUTHOR PARIS 16.

GRAND SCALE

Paris has always operated on a grand scale. There were the city walls of Philippe-Auguste and Charles V, Henri IV's *Grand Dessein du Louvre*, Louis XIV's audacious transformation of Paris into an "open city" (not to mention Versailles), Napoléon Ier's canal networks, Napoléon III's *Grands Travaux*, and François Mitterrand's *Grands Projets*. Even when considering individual structures, Jules Hardouin-Mansart's enormous baroque, gilded dome atop the Dome Church (*l'Église du Dôme des Invalides*), where Napoléon Ier's tomb resides, may be massive, but it is in perfect harmony with the chapel it sits atop. And the monumental Fountain of the Four Bishops (Bossuet, Fénelon, Massillon, Fléchier) in the Place Saint-Sulpice, which at first may seem to be too big for the square, after reflection is just the right size.

Another striking example of big-thinking—and long-term planning— is the "Historic Axis" (*axe historique*), which was first envisioned by landscape architect André Le Nôtre in 1663 when he designed the Avenue des Tuileries (now the Avenue des Champs-Élysées), leading from the Tuileries Garden through the Champs-Élysées to the top of the Butte Chaillot, where he laid out the Étoile (now the Place de l'Étoile). In 1836 (173 years later), the Historic Axis extended like an arrow from the Palais des Tuileries through the Jardin des Tuileries to the Obelisk in the Place de la Concorde, up the Champs-Élysées to the Arc de Triomphe in the Place de l'Étoile. After the demolition of the Palais des Tuileries in 1882 following its burning during the Commune, the beginning of the Historic Axis fortuitously lined up with the Arc de Triomphe du Carrousel, which Napoléon Ier had built on the east side of the palace. Not content with a 2-mile-/3.5-kilometer-long axis, in 1989—in yet another commemoration of the two hundredth anniversary of the Revolution—Mitterrand constructed the Grande Arche de la Défense, which extended the *axe historique* a further 3 miles/5 kilometers to the west.

And the big-thinking continues, but the future of Paris is now focused on its place within the region of the Île-de-France. On January 1, 2016, Paris and the three departments surrounding the city known as *la petite couronne* (the little crown) were joined (but not merged) to create a new *Métropole du Grand Paris* (Metropolis of Greater Paris), or

Figure 120. The eastern façade of the Tuileries Palace with the Arc de Triomphe du Carrousel in front of it, circa 1860. The original *axe historique* (Historic Axis) was centered on the central pavilion of the Palais des Tuileries built by Catherine de Médicis in the sixteenth century and proceeded in a straight line through the Jardin des Tuileries, past the Luxor obelisk in the Place de la Concorde and up the Avenue des Champs-Élysées to the Arc de Triomphe de l'Étoile in the distance.

Paris Métropole. Four lines of high-speed trains known as the *Grand Paris Express*, to be built between 2015 and 2030, will link suburban business hubs with the city and with each other. The new region covers 294 square miles/762 square kilometers (about half the size of Greater London) and includes nearly seven million people, more than triple the population now living in the city *intra muros.** (The population of Greater London was estimated to be 8.8 million in 2016.)

To give impetus to the *Paris Métropole* project, Paris will host the Summer Olympics in 2024—one hundred years after the city last held the games.

---

* The *Métropole du Grand Paris* is directed by a *Conseil de la Métropole* that comprises 206 delegates representing the municipal councils in the new region in proportion to their population. No existing governmental structures were eliminated.

SMALL DETAILS

Paris pays attention to the small details, too. Examples include the esthetics of the "street furniture" ("*les meubles urbains*") of the city: the lamp posts, park benches, bus stops, *colonnes Morris, fontaines Wallace*, even the trash receptacles; the chic uniforms of the *flics* (cops), *pervenches* (meter maids), and *balayeurs* (street sweepers, who collect the garbage 365 days a year); and the (expensive) decision to illuminate the monuments of Paris—including all thirty-seven bridges—and to have twenty thousand lights on the Eiffel Tower sparkle for the first five minutes of every hour after dark until 1:00 a.m. in the winter and 2:00 a.m. in the summer.

Another example of attention to detail relates to the Historic Axis that goes from the Louvre to the Grande Arche de la Défense, and the lead copy of the marble equestrian statue of Louis XIV by Bernini that seems to be randomly placed a little in front and to the right of the Pyramide du Louvre. When I. M. Pei built his pyramid, he centered it on the Cour Napoléon, which was a few degrees off the Historic Axis, which

Figure 121. The equestrian statue of Louis XIV in the Cour Napoléon.

Figure 122. The *axe historique* as seen through the Arc de Triomphe du Carrousel, with the obelisk and the Arc de Triomphe de l'Étoile in the distance. Photograph taken in front of the equestrian statue of Louis XIV.

was originally centered on the western entrance to the now demolished Palais des Tuileries. While both the west wing of the Old Louvre and the Palais des Tuileries are perpendicular to the Seine, they were originally separated by the Charles V Wall and are not exactly parallel. (After the western end of the wall was pulled down in the 1640s, the Arc de Triomphe du Carrousel built by Napoléon Ier in 1808 was similarly centered on the eastern entrance to the Palais des Tuileries.) To acknowledge that deviation and pay homage to the *axe historique*, Pei installed the statue of Louis XIV. Stand in front of it with your back to the statue, and you will see the Arc de Triomphe du Carrousel, the Obelisk, the Arc de Triomphe de l'Étoile, and the Grande Arche de la Défense lined up like the sight on a rifle.

The Historic Axis is impressive, but in the view of many the defining feature of Paris is the Seine. Henri IV understood this when he constructed the Pont Neuf without buildings on it so that people could admire the river, the Louvre, and other structures along its banks.

In 1991, the banks of the Seine between the Pont de Sully on the eastern tip of the Île Saint-Louis and the Pont d'Iéna in front of the Eiffel Tower, as well as the Île de la Cité and the Île Saint-Louis, were declared a UNESCO World Heritage Site as an outstanding example of an architectural ensemble that influenced town-planning the world over. As UNESCO pointed out, the evolution of Paris and its history can be seen from the Seine.

Fluctuat nec Mergitur

The coat of arms of the city of Paris, which dates back to 1358, shows a sailing vessel, the symbol of the powerful guild the *Marchands de l'eau* (Watermen's Guild), in recognition of the importance of the river to the city. Since 1853, the motto of Paris has been *Fluctuat nec mergitur* (She is tossed by the waves, but does not sink).

Like the Seine, the long history of Paris has been marked by a series of highs and lows:

HIGH	LOW
Gallo-Roman period 52 BC–AD 486	Four Viking invasions 845–885
Cité-Ville-Université late Middle Ages	Hundred Years War 1337–1453
	Plagues 1348–1349, 1498, 1562
	Wars of Religion 1562–1598
Henri IV/Louis XIV 17th century	Revolution 1789–1795
First Empire 1804–1814	July Revolution 1830
	June Rebellion 1832
	June Days 1848
Second Empire 1852–1870	Siege of Paris 1870–1871/ Commune 1871
Belle Époque 1871–1914	World War I 1914–1918

Années Folles 1920s   German Occupation 1940–1945
Trente Glorieuses 1946–1975

Arguably, the Exposition Universelle of 1900 marked the peak of Paris's claim to be the capital of the world. France ruled a vast colonial empire, and Paris, with a population of 2.7 million people, was the cultural center of the world. While London and New York City had larger populations and were more important business centers, no other city offered the same combination of political and economic power, history, and culture that made Paris—in the words of the poet Paul Valéry—"the most complete city in the world."

After 1900, two world wars and the Great Depression held Paris back for much of the first half of the twentieth century. After World War II, France lost its colonies and its status as a great power, and London and New York—and since the reunification of Germany in 1990, Berlin— have challenged Paris's long-standing position as the hub of the civilized world, but Paris remains a "complete city," at no risk of becoming just a *ville-musée.*

Paris has long been the world's most popular tourist destination and, in the view of many, the world's most beautiful city—the product of one thousand years of continuous improvement and refinement of its *patrimoine.* While it will take time, there is no doubt that Notre Dame Cathedral will be rebuilt and restored to its original splendor in the very heart of Paris, for the French not only excel at *l'art de vivre,* their capital sets the standard for *l'art de la ville.*

Selected Bibliography

Ageorges, Sylvain. *Sur les traces des Expositions Universelles—Paris 1855–1937—à la recherche des pavillons et des monuments oubliés.* Parigramme, 2006.

All the Louvre—The Masterpieces / The History of the Palace / The Architecture. Louvre éditions/Beaux Arts éditions, 2012.

Atlas Historique de Paris. www.paris-atlas-historique.fr.

Ballon, Hilary. *The Paris of Henry IV—Architecture and Urbanism.* Architectural History Foundation, 1991.

Bournon, Fernand. *Paris-Atlas.* Librairie Larousse (circa 1900).

Bresc-Bautier, Geneviève. *The Louvre—Tale of a Palace.* Musée du Louvre Éditions / Somogy, 2008.

Casevecchie, Janine, and Jacques Lebar. *Paris Mediéval.* Éditions du Chêne, 2010.

Chadych, Danielle. *Le Marais—Évolution d'un paysage urbain.* Éditions Parigramme, 2005.

Chadych, Danielle, ed. *Le Guide du Promeneur de Paris.* Éditions Parigramme, 2007.

Chadych, Danielle, and Dominique Leborgne. *Atlas de Paris—Évolution d'un paysage urbain.* Éditions Parigramme, 2007.

Chadych, Danielle, and Dominique Leborgne. *Paris—The Story of a Great City.* André Deutsch, 2014.

Chadych, Danielle, and Dominique Leborgne. *Paris pour les Nuls.* Éditions First, 2016.

Conlin, Jonathan. *Tales of Two Cities—Paris, London and the Birth of the Modern City.* Atlantic Books, 2014.

Darin, Michaël. *Paris La Forme d'une Ville—Précis d'anatomie urbaine du Moyen Âge à nos jours.* Parigramme, 2016.

DeJean, Joan. *How Paris Became Paris—The Invention of the Modern City.* Bloomsbury USA, 2014.

Fenby, Jonathan. *The History of Modern France—From the Revolution to the Present Day.* Simon & Schuster, 2015.

Gagneux, Renaud, and Denis Prouvost. *Sur Les Traces des Enceintes de Paris.* Éditions Parigramme, 2004.

Haussmann, Georges Eugène. *Mémoires du Baron Haussmann.* Paris: Victor-Havard, ed., 1893; reproduced by BiblioLife.

Hibbert, Christopher. *The French Revolution*. Penguin Books, 1982.

Hoffbauer, Théodore Joseph Hubert. *Paris à travers les âges*. Paris: Firmin-Didot et Cie, 1882; reprinted Éditions Tchou, 1982.

Horne, Alistair. *Seven Ages of Paris*. Alfred A. Knopf, 2002.

Johnson, Diane. *Into a Paris Quartier*. National Geographic Society, 2005.

Jonnes, Jill. *Eiffel's Tower*. Penguin Books, 2009.

Kirkland, Stéphane. *Paris Reborn—Napoleon III, Baron Haussmann, and the Quest to Build a Modern City*. St. Martin's Press, 2013.

Krief, Philippe. *Paris Rive Droite / Paris Rive Gauche—Petites Histoires et Grands Secrets*. Éditions Massin, 2005.

Lambert, Guy. *Paris et ses passage couverts*. Éditions du Patrimoine, Centre des Monuments Nationaux.

Lambert, Guy, Dominique Massounie, and Jean-Christophe Ballot. *The Palais-Royal*. Éditions du Patrimoine, Centre des Monuments Nationaux.

Lambert, Guy, and Cécile Septet. *Paris sur Seine*. Éditions du Patrimoine, Centre des Monuments Nationaux, 2019.

Leborgne, Dominique. *Saint-Germain des Prés et son Faubourg—Évolution d'un paysage urbain*. Éditions Parigramme, 2005.

Loiseau, Laurent, and Brice Agnelli. *Paris d'Henri IV*. Éditions du Chêne, 2010.

Madranges, Etienne. *Regards sur le Palais dans la Cité ou Les 4 Dimensions*. Burlet Graphics, 2002.

Mairie de Paris, Direction des Affaires Culturelles, Sous-Direction du Patrimoine et de l'Histoire. Département Histoire de l'Architecture et Archéologie de Paris. *Études historiques des grandes places parisiennes*.

McCullough, David. *The Greater Journey—Americans in Paris*. Simon & Schuster, 2011.

Mignot, Claude. *Grammaire des Immeubles Parisiens—six siècles de façades du Moyen Âge à nos jours*. Éditions Parigramme, 2004 (*édition revue et augmentée*, 2015).

de Moncan, Patrice. *Le Paris d'Haussmann*. Les Éditions du Mécène, 2012.

Newman, Karen. *Cultural Capitals—Early Modern London and Paris*. Princeton University Press, 2007.

Pinon, Pierre. *Atlas du Paris haussmannien—La ville en heritage du Second Empire à nos jours*. Parigramme, 2002.

Pinon, Pierre. *Atlas Historique des Rues de Paris—Chemins de faubourg, Voies de lotissements, Grandes percées: La formation des Rues de l'Antiquité à nos jours*. Parigramme, 2016.

Pinon, Pierre. *Paris Détruit—Du vandalisme architectural aux grandes opérations d'urbanisme*. Parigramme, 2011.

Rearick, Charles. *Paris Dreams, Paris Memories—The City and Its Mystique*. Stanford University Press, 2011.

Rule, Christopher. *Paris—The Bridges*. Selia Limited, 2008.

Simon, Philippe. *Paris Visite Guidée—Architecture, urbanisme, histoire et actualités*. Éditions A.&J. Picard, 2007.

Texier, Simon. *Paris—Grammaire de l'architecture XXe–XXIe siècles*. Éditions Parigramme, 2009.

Texier, Simon. *Paris Contemporain—de Haussmann à nos jours, une capitale, à l'ère des Métropoles*. Éditions Parigramme, 2010.

Texier, Simon. *Paris–Panorama de l'architecture de l'Antiquité à nos jours*. Éditions Parigramme, 2012.

van Uffelen, Chris, and Markus Golser. *Paris—The Architecture Guide*. Braun Publishing AG, 2009.

Varejka, Pascal. *Paris—Promenades dans le Centre Historique*. Éditions Parigramme, 2010.

Image Credits

INTRODUCTION

Figure 1: Licensed under Creative Commons Attribution-ShareAlike 3.0 Unported license (CC BY-SA 3.0): https://creativecommons.org/licenses/by-sa/3.0/deed.en.

Figure 2: Licensed under the Creative Commons Attribution 4.0 International license (CC BY 4.0): https://creativecommons.org/licenses/by/4.0/legalcode.

Figure 3: Licensed under Creative Commons Attribution-ShareAlike 4.0 International license (CC BY-SA 4.0): https://creativecommons.org/licenses/by-sa/4.0/deed.en.

Figure 4: Licensed under Creative Commons Attribution-ShareAlike 4.0 International license (CC BY-SA 4.0): https://creativecommons.org/licenses/by-sa/4.0/legalcode.

PART I

Figure 5: David Rumsey Historical Map Collection/Wikimedia Commons.

CHAPTER 1

Figure 6: Paris Musées: http://parismuseescollections.paris.fr. CCØ Creative Commons License.

CHAPTER 2

Figure 7: Der Spiegel Geschichte (6/2010): Die Wikinger/Wikimedia Commons/Public domain.

PART II

CHAPTER 3

Figure 8: ResearchGate/Public domain.
Figure 9: Théodore Joseph Hubert Hoffbauer. *Paris à travers les âges.* Paris: Firmin-Didot et Cie, 1882.
Figure 10: Théodore Joseph Hubert Hoffbauer. *Paris à travers les âges.* Paris: Firmin-Didot et Cie, 1882.
Figure 11: Wikimedia Commons/Public domain.
Figure 12: Théodore Joseph Hubert Hoffbauer. *Paris à travers les âges.* Paris: Firmin-Didot et Cie, 1882.
Figure 13: Théodore Joseph Hubert Hoffbauer. *Paris à travers les âges.* Paris: Firmin-Didot et Cie, 1882.
Figure 14: David Rumsey Historical Map Collection/Wikimedia Commons.
Figure 15: Théodore Joseph Hubert Hoffbauer. *Paris à travers les âges.* Paris: Firmin-Didot et Cie, 1882.

CHAPTER 4

Figure 16: Wikimedia Commons/Public domain.
Figure 17: Théodore Joseph Hubert Hoffbauer. *Paris à travers les âges.* Paris: Firmin-Didot et Cie, 1882.
Figure 18: Théodore Joseph Hubert Hoffbauer. *Paris à travers les âges.* Paris: Firmin-Didot et Cie, 1882.
Figure 19: Théodore Joseph Hubert Hoffbauer. *Paris à travers les âges.* Paris: Firmin-Didot et Cie, 1882.
Figure 20: Map reproduction courtesy of the Norman B. Leventhal Map & Education Center at the Boston Public Library.
Figure 21: Wikimedia Commons/Public domain.
Figure 22: Paris Musées: http://parismuseescollections.paris.fr. CCØ Creative Commons License.

CHAPTER 5

Figure 23: Wikimedia Commons/Public domain.

Figure 24: Wikimedia Commons/Public domain.

Figure 25: Théodore Joseph Hubert Hoffbauer. *Paris à travers les âges.* Paris: Firmin-Didot et Cie, 1882.

Figure 26: Théodore Joseph Hubert Hoffbauer. *Paris à travers les âges.* Paris: Firmin-Didot et Cie, 1882.

Figure 27: Paris Musées: http://parismuseescollections.paris.fr. CCØ Creative Commons License.

Figure 28: Paris Musées: http://parismuseescollections.paris.fr. CCØ Creative Commons Zero License.

Figure 29: Paris Musées: http://parismuseescollections.paris.fr. CCØ Creative Commons Zero License.

Figure 30: Paris Musées: http://parismuseescollections.paris.fr. CCØ Creative Commons Zero License.

Figure 31: Paris Musées: http://parismuseescollections.paris.fr. CCØ Creative Commons Zero License.

Figure 32: Paris Musées: http://parismuseescollections.paris.fr. CCØ Creative Commons Zero License.

Figure 33: Architekturmuseum TU Berlin, Inv. Nr.: B 0277.

Figure 34: Kyoto University Library/Wikimedia Commons/Public domain.

Figure 35: Paris Musées: http://parismuseescollections.paris.fr. CCØ Creative Commons License.

Figure 36: Kyoto University Library/Public domain.

Figure 37: Paris Musées: http://parismuseescollections.paris.fr. CCØ Creative Commons License.

Figure 38: Paris Musées: http://parismuseescollections.paris.fr. CCØ Creative Commons License.

Figure 39: Paris Musées: http://parismuseescollections.paris.fr. CCØ Creative Commons Zero License.

Figure 40: Paris Musées: http://parismuseescollections.paris.fr. CCØ Creative Commons License.

Figure 41: Paris Musées: http://parismuseescollections.paris.fr. CCØ Creative Commons License.

Figure 42: Map reproduction courtesy of the Norman B. Leventhal Map & Education Center at the Boston Public Library.

Figure 43: Wikimedia Commons/Public domain.

Figure 44: Paris Musées: http://parismuseescollections.paris.fr. CCØ Creative Commons License.

Figure 45: Petit Atlas Pittoresque des 48 Quartiers de la Ville de Paris (1834)/BHVP.

Figure 46: Paris Musées: http://parismuseescollections.paris.fr. CCØ Creative Commons License.

Figure 47: Paris Musées: http://parismuseescollections.paris.fr. CCØ Creative Commons License.

Figure 48: Laurent Gloaguen, *Vergue.com.*

Figure 49: Harris Brisbane Dick Fund, 1946/Metropolitan Museum of Art. Creative Commons CC0 1.09 Universal Public Domain Dedication.

CHAPTER 6

Figure 50: Théodore Joseph Hubert Hoffbauer. *Paris à travers les âges.* Paris: Firmin-Didot et Cie, 1882.

Figure 51: Bibliothèque nationale de France (BnF), département Estampes et photographie, PETFOL-VE-1356 via Gallica.

Figure 52: Paris Musées: http://parismuseescollections.paris.fr. CCØ Creative Commons License.

Figure 53: Kyoto University Library/Wikimedia Commons/Public domain.

Figure 54: Bibliothèque nationale de France (BnF), département Estampes et photographie, PETFOL-VE-1356 via Gallica.

Figure 55: Paris Musées: http://parismuseescollections.paris.fr. CCØ Creative Commons License.

Figure 56: Théodore Joseph Hubert Hoffbauer. *Paris à travers les âges.* Paris: Firmin-Didot et Cie, 1882.

Figure 57: photo © Musée d'Orsay, Dist. RMN-Grand Palais / Patrice Schmidt.

Figure 58: Paris Musées: http://parismuseescollections.paris.fr. CCØ Creative Commons License.

Figure 59: Bibliothèque nationale de France (BnF), département Estampes et photographie, PETFOL-VE-1356 via Gallica.

CHAPTER 7

Figure 60: Paris Musées: http://parismuseescollections.paris.fr. CCØ Creative Commons License.
Figure 61: Detroit Institute of Art.
Figure 62: Paris Musées: http://parismuseescollections.paris.fr. CCØ Creative Commons License.
Figure 63: Bibliothèque nationale de France (BnF), département Estampes et photographie, PETFOL-VE-1356 via Gallica.
Figure 64: Rijksmuseum/Europeana Collections/Public domain.
Figure 65: Laurent Gloaguen, *Vergue.com*.
Figure 66: Bibliothèque nationale de France (BnF), département Estampes et photographie, PETFOL-VE-1356 via Gallica.
Figure 67: Laurent Gloaguen, *Vergue.com*.
Figure 68: Gift of P.L. Barter/Detroit Institute of Arts.

CHAPTER 8

Figure 69: Bibliothèque nationale de France (BnF), département Estampes et photographie, PETFOL-VE-1356 via Gallica.
Figure 70: Laurent Gloaguen, *Vergue.com*.
Figure 71: Laurent Gloaguen, *Vergue.com*.
Figure 72: Gift of France (1880)/State Library of Victoria/Wikimedia Commons.
Figure 73: The Metropolitan Museum of Art.
Figure 74: Schelcher, André, and Albert Omer-Decugis. *Paris vu en ballon et ses environs*. Paris: Hachette & Cie [1909]. Ville de Paris/BHVP.
Figure 75: Schelcher, André, and Albert Omer-Decugis. *Paris vu en ballon et ses environs*. Paris: Hachette & Cie [1909]. Ville de Paris/BHVP.
Figure 76: Paris Musées: http://parismuseescollections.paris.fr. CCØ Creative Commons License.
Figure 77: A & D/University of Michigan Library Collections.
Figure 78: *Atlas Historique de Paris*. www.paris-atlas-historique.fr.

Figure 70: Laurent Gloaguen, *Vergue.com.*

Figure 80: Public domain.

Figure 81: Laurent Gloaguen, *Vergue.com.*

Figure 82: Bibliothèque nationale de France (BnF), département Estampes et photographie, PETFOL-VE-1356 via Gallica.

Figure 83: Laurent Gloaguen, *Vergue.com.*

Figure 84: State Library of Victoria (gift from the Government of France [1880])/Wikimedia Commons.

Figure 85: Laurent Gloaguen, *Vergue.com.*

Figure 86: Paris Musées: http://parismuseescollections.paris.fr. CCØ Creative Commons License.

Figure 87: Library of Congress item 04753. Laurent Gloaguen, *Vergue .com.*

Figure 88: Paris Musées: http://parismuseescollections.paris.fr. CCØ Creative Commons License.

Figure 89: Paris Musées: http://parismuseescollections.paris.fr. CCØ Creative Commons License.

Figure 90: Schelcher, André, and Albert Omer-Decugis. *Paris vu en ballon et ses environs.* Paris: Hachette & Cie [1909]. Ville de Paris/BHVP.

Figure 91: Musée d'Orsay/Wikimedia Commons/Public domain.

Figure 92: Library of Congress's Prints and Photographs division under digital ID http://loc.gov/pictures/resource/ppmsca.12833/Wikimedia Commons.

Figure 93: Bibliothèque nationale de France (BnF), département Estampes et photographie, PETFOL-VE-1356 via Gallica.

CHAPTER 9

Figure 94: Laurent Gloaguen, *Vergue.com.*

Figure 95: Laurent Gloaguen, *Vergue.com.*

Figure 96: Metropolitan Museum of Art.

Figure 97: Laurent Gloaguen, *Vergue.com.*

Figure 98: Laurent Gloaguen, *Vergue.com.*

Figure 99: Paris Musées: http://parismuseescollections.paris.fr. CCØ Creative Commons License.

Figure 100: Laurent Gloaguen, *Vergue.com.*

Figure 101: Galerie Bassenge/Wikimedia Commons/Public domain.

Figure 102: Photograph by Russell Kelley.

Figure 103: Ryst-Dupeyron.

Figure 104: Bibliothèque nationale de France (BnF), département Estampes et photographie, PETFOL-VE-1356 via Gallica.

Figure 105: College of Architecture/University of Michigan Library Collections.

Figure 106: Bibliothèque nationale de France (BnF), département Estampes et photographie, PETFOL-VE-1356 via Gallica.

Figure 107: Bibliothèque nationale de France (BnF), département Estampes et photographie, PETFOL-VE-1356 via Gallica.

Figure 108: Library of Congress item 92514593.

Figure 109: Schelcher, André, and Albert Omer-Decugis. *Paris vu en ballon et ses environs*. Paris: Hachette & Cie. [1909]. Ville de Paris/BHVP.

Figure 110: Scanned by Claude Shoshany. Wikimedia Commons/Public domain.

Figure 111: Public domain.

Figure 112: Théodore Joseph Hubert Hoffbauer. *Paris à travers les âges*. Paris: Firmin-Didot et Cie (1882).

Figure 113: Laurent Gloaguen, *Vergue.com*.

Figure 114: Paris Musées: http://parismuseescollections.paris.fr. CCØ Creative Commons License.

Figure 115: A & D/University of Michigan Library Collections.

Figure 116: Schelcher, André, and Albert Omer-Decugis. *Paris vu en ballon et ses environs*. Paris: Hachette & Cie [1909]. Ville de Paris/BHVP.

CHAPTER 10

Figure 117: Schelcher, André, and Albert Omer-Decugis. *Paris vu en ballon et ses environs*. Paris: Hachette & Cie [1909]. Ville de Paris/BHVP.

Figure 118: Les Frigos.

CONCLUSION

Figure 119: Licensed under Creative Commons Attribution-ShareAlike 4.0 International license (CC): https://creativecommons.org/licenses/by-sa/4.0/legalcode.

Figure 120: Paris des Utopies (Yvan Christ)/Wikimedia Commons/Public domain.

Figure 121: Photograph by Russell Kelley.

Figure 122: Photograph by Russell Kelley.

VILLE DE
PARIS

IMAGES FROM THE BIBLIOTHÈQUES SPÉCIALISÉES ET PATRIMONIALES DE LA VILLE DE PARIS

Paris vu en ballon et ses environs **by André Schelcher and Albert Omer-Decugis [1909].**

Credit: Schelcher, André, and Albert Omer-Decugis. *Paris vu en ballon et ses environs*. Paris: Hachette & Cie. [1909]. Ville de Paris/BHVP

Rights: Public domain. In accordance with French law n°78-753 of July 17, 1978, non-commercial reuse is free in accordance with the legislation in force and the maintenance of the mention of Credit.

Link to book in catalog of Bibliothèques Spécialisées et patrimoniales de la Ville de Paris: https://bibliotheques-specialisees.paris.fr/ark:/73873/pf0000231716

Paris et ses environs—Collection de Georges Sirot **(1890–1900)**

An album of fifty-eight photographs of Paris and its surroundings taken between 1890 and 1900 and compiled by collector Georges Sirot (1898–1977).

Credit: Bibliothèque nationale de France (BnF), département Estampes et photographie, PETFOL-VE-1356 via Gallica

Rights: Public domain. In accordance with French law n°78-753 of July 17, 1978, non-commercial reuse is free in accordance with the legislation in force and the maintenance of the mention of Credit.

Link to album in catalog of BnF/Gallica: https://gallica.bnf.fr/ark:/12148/btv1b84470040

INDEX